The Flight from Reality in the Human Sciences

The Flight from Reality
in the Human Sciences

◆

Ian Shapiro

PRINCETON UNIVERSITY PRESS · PRINCETON AND OXFORD

Copyright © 2005 by Princeton University Press
Published by Princeton University Press, 41 William Street,
Princeton, New Jersey 08540
In the United Kingdom: Princeton University Press,
3 Market Place, Woodstock, Oxfordshire OX20 1SY

All Rights Reserved

Library of Congress Cataloging-in-Publication Data

Shapiro, Ian.
The flight from reality in the human sciences / Ian Shapiro.
p. cm.
Includes bibliographical references and index.
ISBN 0-691-12057-9 (cloth : alk. paper)
1. Social sciences—Methodology. I. Title.
H61.S5139 2005
300′—dc22   2004062829

British Library Cataloging-in-Publication Data is available.

This book has been composed in Minion with Gill Sans Display

Printed on acid-free paper. ∞

www.pup.princeton.edu

Printed in the United States of America

1   3   5   7   9   10   8   6   4   2

For all my fellow metics

CONTENTS

ACKNOWLEDGMENTS

IN REVISING the essays for this collection, I have made some links among them explicit, updated references and some of the commentary in the footnotes, and made other minor modifications. I have not, however, altered beyond this, even though I would write some of them differently were I starting afresh today.

An earlier version of chapter 1, written with Alexander Wendt, was first published as "The difference that realism makes: Social science and the politics of consent" in *Politics and Society*, Vol. 20, No. 2 (June 1992), pp. 197–224. An earlier version of chapter 4 was first published as "Gross concepts in political argument" in *Political Theory*, Vol. 17, No. 1 (February 1989), pp. 51–76. An earlier version of chapter 5 was first published as "Problems, methods, and theories in the study of politics, or: What's wrong with Political Science and what to do about it" in *Political Theory*, Vol. 30, No. 4 (August 2002) pp. 588–611. They are copyright © by Sage Publications, Inc. 1992, 1989, and 2002, respectively, and reproduced with permission from Sage Publications, Inc. An earlier version of chapter 2, written with Donald Green, was first published as "Pathologies revisited: Reflections on our critics" in *Critical Review*, Vol. 9, Nos. 1–2 (Winter/Spring 1995), pp. 235–76. It is copyright © by the Critical Review Foundation, and reproduced here with permission. An earlier version of chapter 3 was first published as "Richard Posner's Praxis" in the *Ohio State Law Journal*, Vol. 48, No. 4 (December 1987), pp. 999–1047. It is copyright © by the Ohio State Law Journal and reproduced with permission. The original essay contained a quantitative analysis of Posner's labor law and antitrust opinions as an appellate court judge on the Seventh Circuit between 1982 and 1987, which is now deleted because I lacked the time or the resources to bring it up to date. An earlier version of chapter 6 was first published as "Intellectual diversity in political science: A comment on David Laitin," in Edward D. Mansfield and Richard Sisson, eds., *The Evolution of Political Knowledge: Theory and Inquiry in American Politics* (Columbus: Ohio State University Press, 2004), pp. 47–53. It is copyright © by Ohio State University Press, 2004, and reproduced with permission.

In various incarnations the chapters comprising this book have been discussed at a great many conferences, seminars, and workshops, and they have been improved by comments from colleagues too numerous to list. You know who you are. It would, however, be remiss of me not to single out Alex Wendt and Don Green, my respective coauthors of chapters 1 and 2. I have learned enormously from both collaborations, and I greatly value the collegial spirit that gave rise to them. It goes without saying that neither collaborator bears responsibility for arguments made elsewhere in the volume, with which they might disagree. I should also mention two readers for Princeton University Press, whose enthusiasm for the volume was appreciated almost as much as the list of suggestions they made to enhance it, and Ian Malcolm—both for his incisive substantive suggestions and for shepherding the volume into print. Superb editorial, research, and clerical assistance was received from Nomi Lazar, Laura Lawrie, and Alice Kustenbauder. I am grateful to them all.

The Flight from Reality in the Human Sciences

Fear of Not Flying

IN MEDIEVAL ENGLAND there was a curious gap between the study and practice of law. From the thirteenth century to the seventeenth, the main language used for pleading in common law courts was Law French. It seems to have developed because Latin, the language of formal records, carried too much historical freight from Roman law for the peculiarities of English circumstances, whereas medieval English was insufficiently standardized for official use. Law French was a hybrid dialect, owing more to Picard and Angevin influences than to Norman French, in which French vocabulary was combined with the rules of English grammar. The common lawyers developed it for their pleadings in the courts, passing it down from generation to generation.[1]

This evolving vernacular of the common law courts had little, if any, impact on the academic study of law. Latin was the language of jurisprudence in Oxford and Cambridge, and, although Law French could reportedly be learned in ten days or fewer, the professors of jurisprudence appear not to have thought it worth their while. This might have been, as Fortescue said, because Latin was the language of all scientific instruction.[2] It might have been, as Blackstone claimed, because the civil law—taught and studied in Latin—was embraced in the universities and monasteries after the Norman Conquest but resisted in the

---

[1] See J. H. Baker, "The Three Languages of the Common Law," *McGill Law Journal*, Vol. 43 (January 1998), pp. 5–24.

[2] Sir John Fortescue, *De Laudibus Legum Anglie*, S. B. Chrimes, ed. (Cambridge, UK: Cambridge University Press, 1942 [c. 1460]), p. 114.

courts.[3] It might have been, as contemporary historians such as J. H. Baker maintain, because English Law was thought insufficiently cosmopolitan to merit serious study.[4] Whatever the reason, English jurisprudence developed in literal ignorance of the practice of English law.

A comparable disjunction afflicts the human sciences today. In discipline after discipline, the flight from reality has been so complete that the academics have all but lost sight of what they claim is their object of study. This goes for the quantitative and formally oriented social sciences that are principally geared toward causal explanation. Following economics, they have modeled themselves on physics—or at any rate on a stylized version of what is often said to go on in physics. But it also goes for many of the more interpretive endeavors that have been influenced by fashions in the humanities—particularly the linguistic turn in philosophy and developments in literary hermeneutics. Practitioners in these fields often see themselves as engaged in interpretation rather than explanation, thereby perpetuating a false dichotomy. Hence my use of the term *human sciences* here to encapsulate both endeavors. This book is my attempt to chronicle the extent of their flight from reality, and to combat it.

I should say at the outset that I do not believe the flight from reality has a single source or cause. It results, rather, from various developments that share elective affinities—developments that all too often are mutually reinforcing. Some of their sources are intellectual, having to do with the ebb and flow of academic fashion. Some of them are institutional, reflecting the structure of academic professions and the incentives for advancement in an era of exhausted paradigms and extensive specialization. This can be bolstered by a perverse sense of rigor, where the dread of being thought insufficiently scientific spawns a fear of not flying among young scholars. Some are political in the broadest sense, having to do with the relations between disengaged human sciences and the reproduction of the social and political order. The flight from reality is not without consequences *for* reality as we will see. At best it marginalizes the potential effects of political and social criticism, and sometimes it contributes to the maintenance of oppressive social relations—however unwittingly.

---

[3] William Blackstone, *Commentaries on the Laws of England* (Chicago: University of Chicago Press, 1979 [1765]), Vol. 1, pp. 16–32.

[4] In correspondence.

I begin making this case, with the help of Alexander Wendt, in the opening chapter. We expose the limitations of empiricist and interpretive methods of social research, showing how they bias the enterprise in method-driven ways, and we argue for a realist view in their stead. Rather than do this in the abstract, we pursue it by reference to a concrete phenomenon that has attracted a good deal of attention in the human sciences: the study of consent. Empiricism as we describe it here encompasses two different approaches to social inquiry—both bastard stepchildren of David Hume. The first we dub *logicism* to call attention to the fact that its proponents embrace the view, made famous by Carl Hempel, that good explanations are sound deductive arguments. For logicists, an hypothesis is scientific only if it is derived from a general theory. Such theories often rest on simplifying assumptions about reality, or even "as if" assumptions that are not valid empirically at all.

It is conventional to defend this practice on the grounds that these theories do a good predictive job in accounting for empirical reality. This might sound reasonable in principle, but in practice logicists often formulate their claims so generally that they turn out to be compatible with all possible empirical results—in effect rendering the empirical world epiphenomenal to the theory. We show how this vitiates the study of consent in practice, when theorists of rational consent have sought to explain away apparent anomalies by concocting redescriptions that render them compatible with their preferred theories. This was understandable with theorists of the early Enlightenment because, as I have argued elsewhere, they embraced the view that certainty is the hallmark of science—making the toleration of counterexamples unacceptable.[5] However, mature Enlightenment views of science assume knowledge generally to be corrigible, with the implication that scientists will not take hypotheses seriously if they cannot be falsified—and, indeed, if the conditions under which they will be rejected cannot be specified in advance. The irony, then, is that although contemporary logicists often like to think of themselves as the only genuinely rigorous practitioners of social science—"if you ain't got a theorem you ain't got shit!" as a partisan of this view once put it to me—in reality they are wedded a view of science that most practicing scientists have not taken seriously for centuries.

---

[5] Ian Shapiro, *The Moral Foundations of Politics* (New Haven: Yale University Press, 2003), chap. 1.

Hume's other bastard stepchildren discussed in chapter 1 are empiricists of a particular stamp—those who became known in the 1950s and 1960s as behavioralists. Often skeptical of the breathtaking theoretical ambition characteristic of logicists, these empiricists were partisans of Hume's insistence that knowledge is grounded in observation of events and that causal knowledge inheres in observing their constant conjunction. Whereas the logicist derives comfort from the certainty that seems to inhere in the deductive relations between premises and conclusions, the Humean empiricist looks to observation for reassurance. We show how, in the political science power literature, this biased research away from attending to factors that coerce people into apparently consensual behavior—whether by surreptitious manipulation of agendas, structuring people's perceptions of alternatives, or even shaping their preferences. The focus on observed behavior was conceived as a corrective to elite theories of politics put forward by Gaetano Mosca, Robert Michels, Vilfredo Pareto, and C. Wright Mills. They had been cavalier in their treatment of observable behavior, ignoring it or explaining away any tensions between it and what Michels described as the "iron law" of oligarchy. Ironically, the behavioralists ended up with a different kind of method-drivenness, one in which the realm of observed behavior was assumed to be the only pertinent realm in accounting for consent.

If behavioralists bias research in favor of the phenomenal realm in one way, partisans of interpretation do it in another. By interpretivism I mean the research agenda that came into vogue in the human sciences during the 1970s, largely because of dissatisfaction with various failed reductionist enterprises. Prominent among these was Marxism, by then famous for its inability to account for the major political developments of the twentieth century. Instead of spawning revolutionary socialist proletariats, the advanced capitalist countries had experienced tenacious nationalism and working-class conservatism—not to mention the rise of Nazism in Germany and Fascism in Italy. Communists who did come to power either did so in peasant societies such as Russia and China contra Marx's prognostications, or they were forcibly imposed by the Soviets after World War II. In any case, by the 1950s it was obvious that, at best, communism as practiced rested on grotesque distortions of Marx's principles.

Attempts to rescue Marxism from an unhelpfully recalcitrant reality produced more noise than light over the succeeding decades. One motivation for those who found the interpretive turn attractive was to get away from the sectarian bickering over how to save Marx's materialism—even when it was conceded that this could operate only "in the last instance."[6] The interpretive turn involves treating articulated beliefs and ideas as elemental to human interaction. They are seen not as part of an epiphenomenal superstructure, to be understood, however circuitously, by reference to its links with the "underlying" material base. Rather, to use one of the buzz words of the day, they constitute reality—or at least human social reality—through language. Social reality is linguistic reality on this view. When human beings do things like create obligations or social contracts they do this through language, not by some other means that is then described by language. Understanding social reality means understanding the linguistic processes that give rise to it.

The interpretive turn thus went hand in glove with the ascent of ordinary language philosophy associated with the later Wittgenstein and J. L. Austin in the 1950s and with developments in literary hermeneutics in which understanding social processes was modeled on the interpretation of texts.[7] It was but a small step from this to the view that society should be conceived of *as* a text, whose meaning is best recovered by exploring the web of linguistic conventions within which social agents operate as collective authors. We are locked within a prison-house of language, as Frederick Jameson colorfully put it, the implication being that it is better to try to understand linguistic reality from the inside than to indulge vain fantasies of escape.[8] Different theorists had different views of how such understanding is best achieved, but they all agreed that the point of the exercise is to elucidate social meanings by exploring the linguistic conventions—the language games, as Wittgenstein had it—within which people inevitably operate. Social reality arises out of conventional linguistic usage, and the key to understanding it lies in recovering the conventions so as to see how people use them to act in the social world.

---

[6] Louis Althusser's phrase in "Ideology and Ideological State Apparatuses," in *Lenin and Philosophy, and Other Essays,* Ben Brewster, trans. (New York: Monthly Review, 2001), pp. 127–88. See also "Contradiction and Overdetermination," in *For Marx* (London: Verso, [1965] 1996), pp. 87–128. For a flavor of the polemics, see E. P. Thompson, "The Poverty of Theory or an Orrery of Errors," *The Poverty of Theory and Other Essays* (New York: Monthly Review Press, 1978), pp. 1–210.

[7] Ludwig Wittgenstein, *Philosophical Investigations* (Oxford: Blackwell, 1953) and J. L. Austin, *How to Do Things with Words* (Cambridge, MA: Harvard University Press, 1962).

[8] Frederick Jameson, *The Prison-House of Language: A Critical Account of Structuralism and Russian Formalism* (Princeton: Princeton University Press, 1974).

Elsewhere I have discussed the interpretative turn's impact on the historical study of political theory by examining the contextual theories of the Cambridge school—John Dunn, J.G.A. Pocock, and Quentin Skinner.[9] There is much to commend their approach to the study of the texts in the history of ideas. In particular, their insistence that contextual knowledge is essential to recover what an author meant to do in writing a text was an important corrective to prevalent methodologies that had assumed reading the text "over and over again" to be sufficient. Some of their contextual rereadings of particular authors are debatable and have been debated, but one would be hard pressed to dispute that important correctives to received interpretations have resulted from this scholarship. Skinner's rereadings of Hobbes have stood the test of time especially well—displacing a tired stereotype of him as "the monster of Malmesbury."[10] Dunn's relocation of Locke's political writings in the theological disputes that were his lifelong preoccupation have revolutionized Locke scholarship for a generation, and the careful contextual researches of Peter Laslett and Richard Ashcraft have established that the *Two Treatises of Government* were written the better part of a decade before the Glorious Revolution of 1688—rubbishing an older conventional wisdom that they were written to justify it.[11] Locke's contradictory views on slavery have received definitive illumination through the contextual analysis of James Farr.[12] Pocock's magisterial recovery of the civic humanist tradition has spawned a revival of interest in republican ideas, complicating, at least, our picture of liberalism's emergence and evolution.[13] This is to say nothing of the revisions of

---

[9] Ian Shapiro, "Realism in the Study of the History of Ideas," *History of Political Thought*, Vol. 3, no. 3 (November, 1982), pp. 535–78.

[10] Quentin Skinner, "Thomas Hobbes and His Disciples in France and England," *Comparative Studies in Society and History*, (1965/1966) vol. 8, pp. 153–68, and "The Context of Hobbes's Theory of Political Obligation," in Maurice Carnston and R. S. Peters, ed., *Hobbes and Rousseau: A Collection of Critical Essays* (New York: Doubleday, 1972), pp. 109–42.

[11] John Dunn, *The Political Thought of John Locke* (Cambridge: Cambridge University Press, 1969); Peter Laslett's "Introduction" to John Locke, *Two Treatises of Government*, Peter Laslett, ed. (Cambridge: Cambridge University Press, 1988), pp. 61, 123–26; and Richard Ashcraft, "Revolutionary Politics and Locke's 'Two Treatises of Government': Radicalism and Lockean Political Theory," *Political Theory*, Vol. 8, No. 4 (November 1980), pp. 429–86, and *Locke's Two Treatises of Government* (London: Allen & Unwin, 1987).

[12] James Farr, " 'So Vile and Miserable an Estate': The Problem of Slavery in Locke's Political Thought," *Political Theory*, vol. 14, no. 2 (May 1986), pp. 263–89.

[13] J.G.A. Pocock, *The Machiavellian Moment: Florentine Political Thought and the Atlantic Republican Tradition* (Princeton: Princeton University Press, 1974). For a review essay of the civic

received interpretations of medieval and early modern natural law theory at the hands of Richard Tuck and James Tully, or the accounts of Adam Smith and David Ricardo's politics from Donald Winch, Shannon Stimson, and Murray Milgate.[14]

It is one thing to say that understanding what an author was trying to do depends critically on recovering the context in which he was writing; quite another to turn this into an a theory of politics and political change. It is this vastly more ambitious agenda, most self-consciously articulated by Quentin Skinner, with which I take issue. I agree with Skinner that any plausible account of political reality must take account of the role political ideas play in shaping it. But making this move inevitably puts large causal questions on the table about what ideologies are, how they shape and are shaped by political conflict and change, and how—if at all—they might be related to the ideas of political theorists.

Skinner ducks these questions by eschewing all causal analysis in favor of the "interpretation," but I argue that in effect this means he does his causal analysis behind his back, which he insists that we should not. He equates the meaning of a text with what an author intended to convey, and he gets at this by seeing how the author's ideas were received by his intended audience. But this overlooks gamuts of relevant possibilities once we are studying their ideas as ideologies. What people overlook might be more important, ideologically, than what they discern. People might be misled, whether for malevolent or accidental reasons. They might supply inadvertent legitimation for practices that they perceive dimly, if at all. How people's ideas are appropriated or misappropriated by subsequent generations might be more important than their intentions as communicated to contemporaries. By assuming that an "internal" reading, geared to recovering authorial intention, is synonymous with studying the history of ideas as the history of ideologies, Skinner affirms a new—rather whiggish—reductionism without ever acknowledging it.

---

humanist scholarship spawned by Pocock, see my "J.G.A. Pocock's Republicanism and Political Theory: A Critique and Reinterpretation," *Critical Review*, Vol. 4, No. 3 (Summer 1990), pp. 433–71.

[14] Richard Tuck, *Natural Rights Theories: Their Origin and Development* (Cambridge: Cambridge University Press, 1979); James Tully, *A Discourse Concerning Property: John Locke and his Adversaries* (Cambridge: Cambridge University Press, 1980); Donald Winch, *Adam Smith's Politics: An Essay in Historiographic Revision* (Cambridge: Cambridge University Press, 1978); Murray Milgate and Shannon Stimson, *Ricardian Politics* (Princeton: Princeton University Press, 1991).

In contrast, I argue for openness to "external" readings. These are geared to locating subjective accounts in larger causal processes without prejudging what those processes might consist in, without deciding in advance whether and how much they might shape or be shaped by political interests, agendas, and events, and without assuming anything a priori about how—if at all—they might be subsumable into a general theory of politics. These are all subjects for research that cannot be settled before it begins. The scientific outlook requires a commitment to discovering what is actually going on in a given situation without prejudging what that is. Opting for the recovery of what a particular political theorist meant to say involves one of many possible cuts at accounting for ideology's role in politics. It has to be justified by comparison with the going plausible alternatives, not smuggled in by the backdoor under the guise of eschewing the world of causation for that of interpretation. Partisans of interpretation often see themselves as fundamentally at odds with behavioral social scientists. So it is ironic that they end up embracing a reductive view that makes them cousins of the behavioralists. Both rule out looking behind the world of appearances. This biases the study of consent by taking some of the most significant possibilities off the table before research begins.

My call for attention to the "external" dimensions of political action as well as the "internal" ones is embedded a realist view of science. It owes much to the work of Rom Harré, Roy Bhaskar, Richard Miller, and others, and I harbor no ambition to offer a full-blown defense of it here. Rather, my goal is to underscore the commitments that are embodied in the realist outlook, explain their significance for the conduct of social inquiry, and show why they should be expected to lead to better results than the going alternatives. To be sure, I mean to portray the realist outlook in an attractive light in these pages, but I try to do this more by illustrating its felicitous consequences for social and political inquiry than by arguing for it from the ground up. Some prefatory remarks are nonetheless in order here to indicate what I take to be involved in the commitment to scientific realism, and to differentiate it from doctrines with which it is sometimes confused.[15]

I take the core commitment of scientific realism to consist in the twofold conviction that the world consists of causal mechanisms that

---

[15] Philosophers and social theorists who consider themselves scientific realists differ on various particulars, and not every one of them shares my view on all particulars. Aspects of these differences are taken up in chapter 1, although for the most part they are not germane to the present

exist independently of our study—or even awareness—of them, and that the methods of science hold out the best possibility of our grasping their true character. Adherents to this view are sometimes characterized as "transcendental" realists.[16] This cumbersome and loaded term perhaps obscures more than it illuminates. I take it to underscore the fact that the realist commitment is implicit in the conduct of science, not a product of it. Unless scientists assumed it to be valid, as they generally do, they would have no good reason to see their enterprise as superior to religion, superstition, tradition, and other pretenders to authority in accounting for reality. This is not to say that the realist commitment implies fidelity to any particular theories or hypotheses about reality's causal structure. Rather, embracing the commitment is necessary for thinking it worthwhile to develop theories and hypotheses, and to evaluate them by reference to the methods of science.

Wendt and I show how, in the study of consent, a realist commitment opens up research agendas to the study of causal questions that are ruled out of court by the behavioral and interpretivist schools. Yet it does this without dismissing behavior and subjective understanding as epiphenomenal, or affirming a reductionist view that is impervious to the demands of evidence so characteristic of logicist ventures. We discuss John Gaventa's *Power and Powerlessness* as exemplifying social science conducted in a realist spirit, both in its attempt to illuminate opaque causal mechanisms that produce consent—"quiescence" is Gaventa's term—in circumstances of domination, and in explaining the relations between those mechanisms and the realms of subjective perception and behavior. From a realist perspective it thus becomes plain that behavioral and interpretive methods exemplify the flight from reality, even though their proponents often resist the ambition to develop general theory.

Perhaps as a reaction against the behavioral and interpretive hostility to general theory, logicist enterprises have won a new lease on life in recent decades. The main vehicle has been the import of microeconomic models into the noneconomic human sciences—notably to political science, sociology, and law—under the banner of rational choice theory. Donald Green and I explore this development as it relates to

---

volume. They are explored more fully in my *Political Criticism* (Berkeley, Los Angeles: University of California Press, 1990), chapter 8.

[16] The term is Roy Bhaskar's, as elucidated in *A Realist Theory of Science* (Sussex: Harvester, 1978) and *The Possibility of Naturalism* (Sussex: Harvester, 1979).

political science in chapter 2, by responding to critics of our book *Pathologies of Rational Choice Theory*.[17] Although logicist ventures are wanting from a realist perspective, we show here that they also collapse under their own weight—largely because of their quixotic theoretical ambition. Taken on their own terms, rational choice theories have, for the most part, degenerated into elaborate exercises geared toward saving universalist theory from discordant encounters with reality. Belying the fanfare about theoretical rigor that often accompanies their claims, we show how rational choice theorists play fast and loose with the definition of rationality in developing hypotheses, in specifying their empirical implications, and in testing them against the evidence.

The litany of failures that we identify includes elaborating sufficient accounts for political phenomena without showing how or why they should be preferred to the going alternatives; "explaining" stylized facts that turn out on close inspection not to bear much relationship to any political reality; post-hoc fiddling with theories in ways that amount to little more than thinly disguised curve-fitting; specifying theories so vaguely that they turn out to be compatible with all empirical outcomes; scouring the political landscape for confirming illustrations of the preferred theory while ignoring the rest of the data; and projecting evidence from the theory by coming up with tendentious descriptions of the political world. Even when rational choice theorists back away from pure universalist claims, they do so in ad-hoc and in unconvincing ways that reinforce their reluctance to entertain the possibility that their theory is incorrect. It is as if someone, on observing one day that red apples no longer fell toward the ground when dropped, asserted that the theory of gravity is fine; we must just accept that it does not apply to red apples.

As this example might suggest, when all else fails the universalist impulse leads rational choice theorists to take refuge in the philosophy of science. Accusing their critics of being "naïve falsificationists," they appeal to the arguments of Thomas Kuhn and Imre Lakatos in vindication of their procedures. Those who appeal to Kuhn seem innocent of his notorious inability to distinguish developing research paradigms, when knowledge is advancing, from decaying ones, when it is not. Given the failure of rational choice theorists to identify unambiguous advances in empirical knowledge, this is a serious worry. Indeed, as

[17] Donald P. Green and Ian Shapiro, *Pathologies of Rational Choice Theory: A Critique of Applications in Political Science* (New Haven: Yale University Press, 1994).

Kuhn was careful to insist, the human sciences have yet to reach the stage where there is a dominant paradigm within which normal science can proceed by puzzle-solving. Hence his description of them as "pre-paradigmatic." Those rational choice theorists who acknowledge that this is the true state of affairs sometimes see it as their mission to provide a remedy—as my discussion of David Laitin's agenda for political science in chapter 6 reveals. They would be well advised to take note of Kuhn's insistence that "I claim no therapy to assist the transformation of a proto-science to a science, nor do I suppose that anything of the sort is to be had."[18]

Rational choice theorists who appeal instead to Lakatos make heavy weather of the claim that you can't beat something with nothing; that theories are not falsified by being tested against "the facts," but rather when a better theory comes along—one that explains what was known before and then some. This is concededly a good account of what often happens in science, yet the difficulty we identify is that in political science rational choice theorists operate is if it applies to their critics but not to themselves. Their characteristic proclivity is to ignore previous scholarship on the topics they study, to create trivial null hypotheses when any are considered at all, and to translate existing knowledge into their preferred terminology rather than add to it. Rational choice theorists operate more like brief-writers for their universal theories, not Lakatosian scientists who try to add to the inherited stock of knowledge by developing theories that perform better empirically than those that have been tried before. If rational choice theorists took their Lakatosian protestations seriously, they would abandon the logicist impulses that flow from Hempel's theory of science and engage seriously in comparative empirical evaluation of their arguments against the most plausible going alternatives. We note that the few of them who have done this have, indeed, contributed to the study of politics. For most, however, the impulse to flee from problem-driven theory to method-driven theorem proves irresistible.

In chapters 3 and 4, I turn from the explanatory to the normative dimensions of the flight from reality. One way in which commentators have sought to link positive and normative theory is to try to derive principles for action and policy from their accounts of how the world

---

[18] Thomas S. Kuhn, "Reflections on My Critics," in Imre Lakatos and Alan Musgrave, eds., *Criticism and the Growth of Knowledge* (Cambridge: Cambridge University Press, 1970), pp. 244–45.

works. Another is to try to intervene in the world to get it to conform to one's normative ideal better than presently it does. Richard Posner, a United States appellate court judge since his appointment to the Seventh Circuit by Ronald Reagan in 1981, engages in both. I provide an assessment of his efforts in chapter 3.

Getting from explanation to prescription means getting from is to ought. Posner's attempt to do this is elusive and ultimately unsuccessful, but it reveals one of the ways in which the flight from reality can have an impact on reality. Posner posits a functionalist account of the common law's evolution, according to which it operates over time to maximize economic efficiency. His is an invisible-hand account in that this process is alleged to occur beyond the ken of common-law judges, who typically do not perceive—let alone understand—the ways in which their decisions contribute to this result. Indeed, as if to underscore this point, Posner upbraids some judges who have sought to apply his theory of wealth-maximization in the course of adjudication. Yet Posner nonetheless delivers a series of nostrums about how judges should behave and proposes various reforms to the administration of courts in the United States based on appeals to his efficiency arguments.

Attention to Posner's invisible-hand account reveals good reasons for skepticism, but even if we bracket them it is far from clear that we should regard it as benign. Consider Posner's efficiency-based account of why the criminal law disproportionately punishes harmful acts committed by poor people.[19] Criminal sanctions become necessary, on his account, when the threat of compensation through the torts system fails to deter potential wrongdoers. Because poor people typically lack the resources to compensate victims that would be sufficient to deter potential perpetrators, the threat of incarceration is needed instead. This "efficiency" based account of a system that discriminates against the poor entails nothing about its moral attractiveness, unless supplemented by an argument showing efficiency to be more desirable than equitable treatment. This becomes obvious when we recall that scholars in the critical legal studies movement have argued for the same evolutionary thesis as Posner's, but to make a rather different normative point.[20] Claims about neutrality to the contrary notwithstanding, they argue, the law operates to sustain capitalist market relations. Oliver

[19] Richard Posner, "An Economic Theory of the Criminal Law," *Columbia Law Review,* Vol. 85, No. 6 (October 1985), pp. 1193–231.

[20] Roberto Unger, *The Critical Legal Studies Movement* (Cambridge, MA: Harvard University Press, 1986).

Wendell Holmes might have been right that the Fourteenth Amendment "does not enact Mr. Herbert Spencer's *Social Statics,*" but they think that it creeps into the common law nonetheless.

The functionalist case does not get Posner from *is* to *ought* any more than it gets Unger and his colleagues from *is* to *ought not.* Nor does it exhaust the possibilities for pressing explanatory theory into the service of normative argument. Another strategy Posner deploys is to point to gaps between purposes he alleges to be immanent in the law and the reality on the ground, thereby supplying impetus to the suggestion that reality stands in need of reform. This is strategy is at least as old as Jeremy Bentham's market-failure theory of the need for government because of the possibility of free riding, tragedy-of-the-commons problems, and other by-products of selfish individual behavior.[21] A different variant was pursued by the legal realists, who pointed to yawning gaps between the professed ideals of American law and the brutal realities of criminal prosecution during the 1930s and after. This eventually spawned a wide range of reforms to criminal procedure and defendants' rights by the Warren Court, designed to bring reality into better conformity with professed constitutional ideals.

Posner's modus operandi is to identify inefficiencies in the law and the administration of the courts, thereby generating impetus for reforms oriented to bringing them into better conformity with his efficiency ideal. Passing over the difficulty, already noted, that it is far from clear that his efficiency ideal is in fact immanent in American law, I show how his appeals to efficiency all involve reifying contestable economic theories as "the" economic theory or the law. This enables Posner to mask a particular ideological agenda in the garb of abstract theory. For instance, close inspection reveals that Posner's unhappiness with the increase in litigation in federal courts in recent decades does not depend on his—or any—general theory of the optimal level of litigation or judicial services. Rather, it reflects a conservative antipathy for government.

These proclivities extend to Posner's activities on the bench. Through an analysis of his labor law and antitrust opinions in his first five years as a federal appellate court judge, I show that he imports his version of the *Social Statics* into judicial opinions in predictable ways, all the while portraying them as uncontroversial economic theory—if not unassailable common sense. The truth, as I show, is that different economic

---

[21] See Shapiro, *The Moral Foundations of Politics,* chapter 2.

theories than the ones Posner invokes would produce different results in these cases; yet he never supplies us with principled reasons for preferring the ones he advocates. The logicist's variant of the flight from reality involves misrepresenting the world by confusing it with dubious models that flow from a pet general theory. Posner's academic writing exemplifies this pathology at every turn. More troubling is that his position on the bench gives him the power to try to reshape reality in accordance with his models—to the arbitrary detriment or benefit of litigants who happen to have their cases appealed to his court.

Dramatically arresting as Posner's reification of efficiency might be, I argue in chapter 4 that he is scarcely alone in his general approach. Political theorists often fail to appreciate that any claim about how politics is to be organized is bound to be a relational claim involving agents, actions, legitimacy, and ends. If they did, they would resist many of the standard contending views in the controversies that preoccupy them. I demonstrate this by reference to contemporary debates concerning the nature of right, law, autonomy, utility, freedom, virtue, and justice. Rather than confront the complexities implicit in the relational logics of these and other political ideals, all too often political theorists appeal to *gross concepts*—my term for ideas that feed into and promote misleading dichotomies. By appealing to gross concepts, political theorists reduce what are actually relational claims to claims about one or another of the terms in a relational argument. I explain how this systematically obscures the phenomena they purport to analyze, diverting attention from first-order questions about the world to second-order conceptual debates that can never be settled because they rest on category mistakes. Gerald MacCallum Jr. pointed this out a long time ago in connection with the arguments about liberty. He showed that debates between "negative" and "positive" libertarians are not really about kinds of freedom, as protagonists since Isaiah Berlin have supposed, but rather about *who* is free, *from what* constraints or *because of what* enabling conditions, *to perform which* actions.

Despite a good deal of ritualistic genuflecting to MacCallum in the literature, my analysis reveals that his reasoning has penetrated little. This is partly because taking it seriously would entail coming to grips with contentious empirical debates about human psychology and the causal structure of the social world—which theorists are loath to do. In arguments about freedom, as in numerous other controversies that exhibit a similar structure, gross concepts are instead presented as dichotomous alternatives. Protagonists on both sides defend their views mainly by pointing to the demerits of the supposed alternative—about which they are invariably right. The result is to perpetuate debates that lurch among gross concepts without getting anywhere.

The activity thrives nonetheless, partly because it is rewarded by professional incentives in the academy but partly, I argue, because many people find gross concepts appealing. They are comforting and simplifying devices that function, as ideologies, to legitimate things that people want to believe. Recognizing the alluring power of gross concepts, I defend an account of the political theorist's vocation that revolves around resisting it. Our job is to reel in gross concepts, not to traffic in them. Rather than try to find the right gross concept to champion, we do better to operate as principled social critics whose goal is embellish political argument with political reality. We should be roving ombudsmen for the truth rather than partisans of any particular message. What this means for the conduct of political theorists within the political science discipline is explored in the final two chapters.

This question is taken up in chapter 5 in the context of a critique of the impulse toward, and rewards for, reductionist explanations in political science. My point of departure is the observation—often leveled at my argument with Green in *Pathologies*—that all observation is theory-laden. Because there is no theoretically unsullied account of "the facts," so the argument goes, we were naïve in supposing that any particular explanation can be evaluated simply by how well it does empirically. Agreeing that Green and I attended insufficiently to this question, I make the case here that it does not stand in the way of a view of the social-scientific enterprise geared to getting at the truth, that this is unlikely to be achieved by any of the going reductionist ventures in political science, and that the endemic availability of alternative descriptions of political reality creates an important ongoing responsibility for political theorists in the division of labor within political science.

The assertion that all observation is theory-laden turns out on close inspection to merit the retort that some types of theory-ladenness are nonetheless more plausible than others. Once the headlights are turned up on particular cases, it becomes plain that there is a world of difference between theory-driven description, in which tendentious accounts are projected onto the problems in order to vindicate pet theories, and situations where there are persuasive reasons, while taking account of previous attempts to study a problem and their limitations, for preferring an alternative construction of it. This is to say nothing of method-driven work, where the construction of the problem is contaminated by the methods available to the researcher. A study in which John Huber and Charles Shipan try to measure Congress's desire to confer discretion on administrative agencies by the number of words in the relevant statutes is easier to comprehend once one is reminded of the "word count" feature of modern word-processing programs.[22] No matter that it would seem to suggest that the countless reams of the Internal Revenue Code are there to limit the discretion of IRS agents. Try telling that to your accountant.

Moreover, whereas some disagreements about explanation are really disagreements about competing descriptions in drag, many are not. When a particular description *is* recognized as apt, there is then a truth of the matter as far as explanation is concerned—even if no one yet knows what it is. That is the realist presumption on which the conduct of all science, on my account, rests. The mistake is to suppose that explanations are scientific only when they flow from a single general theory, which then leads scholars to shoehorn the construction of every problem into terms that are compatible with it. Antireductionist priors, that build toward feasible generality rather than take it for granted prior to empirical research, may well involve descriptions that are theory-influenced. But they will not be theory-driven.

This is not to deny that significant challenges are posed for political science by the theory-ladenness literature. Different ways of characterizing social phenomena predispose researchers to reach for different explanatory arguments, raising questions about how appropriately to choose among them. The conventional answer is prediction. If we can better predict the ways in which judges will decide cases by looking at which outcome maximizes wealth rather than at their jurisprudential commitments, then we should opt for the efficiency-based characterization. But prediction is not all that it is cracked up to be. It can lead us to the misconception that playing basketball makes people taller. More consequentially, I show that because prediction is so difficult in the human sciences, excessive preoccupation with it can drive researchers to focus on trivial but tractable questions—three points to the right of the decimal. Alternatively, it can lead them endlessly to refine predictive instruments that are never going to work. The result? Immensely complicated clocks that neither tick nor tell the time.

---

[22] See John D. Huber and Charles Shipan, *Deliberate Discretion: Institutional Foundations of Bureaucratic Autonomy* (Cambridge: Cambridge University Press, 2002).

Political theorists have important roles to play in political science just because there is no algorithm that dictates the correct descriptive cut at the social world. Among our central tasks is to identify, criticize, and suggest plausible alternatives to the theoretical assumptions, interpretations of political conditions, and above all specification of problems that underlie prevailing empirical accounts and research programs, and to do it in ways that can spark novel and promising problem-driven research agendas. And, especially when esoteric forms of redescription are involved, they must elucidate the links to more familiar understandings of politics.

If the study of politics is inherently contentious, how should it be taught to the next generation of students? This is the subject of my final chapter, a critique of David Laitin's recent proposal to standardize political science teaching to undergraduates. His goal is to do for political science what Samuelson did for economics by creating an orthodox curriculum, and he proposes a model syllabus for its introductory course. I make the case that Laitin's proposal is wrongheaded in ways that both reflect and encourage the flight from reality.

Laitin's proposal reflects the flight from reality by conflating the discipline with its object of study, calling to mind the economist's reputed answer to a student query that economics is "what economists do." Undergraduates typically become political science majors because they are interested in politics, not the political science discipline. It should be troubling if these students are presented, as Laitin believes that they should be, with an account of political science that is sanitized to obscure its controversial character. The impulse to do this has more to do with professional incentives to get grants and public recognition for the discipline, as Laitin comes close to conceding, than with any plausible account of how to teach students to think systematically about the fundamentals of politics. Even when scholars believe they have the One True Theory or the One Best Method—indeed, particularly in that case—they do students a disservice not to tell them about the others.

Laitin's proposal is liable to encourage the impulse to flee reality by detaching scholars from a particular kind of discipline that undergraduate teaching offers. His reasoning depends on the illusion that an initial political science course can get students up to speed in the same way that essentials are covered in introductions to physics, chemistry, and math. These disciplines differ from the social sciences in that there is little, if any, disagreement among their practitioners on what the appropriate descriptive cut on the world actually is. Against Laitin, I argue that the economists' decision to standardize their discipline as he recommends and would emulate has had the disastrous consequence of divorcing introductory teaching from controversies at research frontiers of their discipline. This famously alienates undergraduates from what they are required to study in introductory economics courses. It also reinforces the powerful disincentives for active research scholars to teach the introductory courses, turning them over instead to adjunct faculty and flunkies.

This is a loss for the students, but also for the researchers. Bright undergraduates often have noses for important problems and a refreshing desire to cut to the chase about what difference the theories they are being asked to understand make in the actual world. They are not hostage to academic literatures that may be little more than rotten boroughs in the ways that graduate students so often are. If scholars in political science were to free themselves from the discipline that comes with having to teach undergraduates as completely as economists have done in recent decades, they would have yet one more reason to succumb to their—already overdeveloped—fear of not flying.

CHAPTER ONE

The Difference That Realism Makes:

Social Science and the Politics of Consent

Ian Shapiro and Alexander Wendt

ALL FORMS of social inquiry rest on beliefs about what counts as an explanation of social phenomena. Should explanations of social life be deduced from observable facts? Should they be grounded on peoples' self-understandings? Should they be based on whatever enables us to intervene with effect in the world? Most of the time, social scientists go about their research without worrying about these issues, which primarily interest philosophers of social science. This may be unavoidable and even desirable given the intellectual division of labor, but it becomes problematic when bad philosophical assumptions contaminate the conduct of social science.

Since the 1950s, philosophical debates about social explanation have been dominated by two mutually antagonistic schools of thought: logical empiricism and interpretivism. The former, which was dominant from the heyday of the Vienna Circle until the early 1960s, rested on the view that observation is theory-neutral and that the task of science is to come up with law-like generalizations about these observations. Interpretivism coalesced around a series of critiques of this view during the 1960s. Whether inspired by Thomas Kuhn's work on conventionalism in the history of science or by the linguistic turn in philosophy and literary theory, interpretivists share the belief that "all observation is theory-laden" and that science therefore cannot be the objective inquiry that logical empiricists took it to be.

In recent decades, the terms of this debate have been challenged by a group of self-styled scientific realists. Realists contend that theory-ladenness is a matter of degree and that the fact that observation is theory-laden does not mean that it need be theory-determined. More-over, they claim that social inquiry informed by both logical empiricism and interpretivism is more theory-laden than it should be, closing off important lines of causal argument before experience. Realism im-poses fewer a priori constraints on scientific practice. A commitment to it makes it possible for the researcher to consider a greater range of possible explanations.[1]

A notable feature of much of the debate among empiricists, inter-pretivists, and realists is that it is conducted at a high level of abstraction in technical jargon that is accessible and of interest only to initiates. For those of us who have been concerned to press the realist case, the ques-tion arises, therefore, what difference it makes to anyone other than metatheorists of method. That is the question motivating this chapter. The goal is to illustrate the difference that realism makes in the human sciences by reference to arguments about the nature of consent. We proceed in two stages. First, we venture to make good on the realists' critical claim that both logical empiricist and interpretivist views of social explanation are theory-laden in ways that are at odds with the requirements of good scientific practice. Then we go on to show that analyses of consent that rest on a realist view of explanation are com-paratively less theory-laden, inviting consideration of a wider array of questions and explanations than do alternative views. Thus, although we do not offer a philosophical defense of realism, we do aspire to bolster its plausibility by demonstrating its comparative advantages for interpreting and explaining consent.

We begin with a brief discussion of some of the problems that studying consent presents to social scientists. Next, we argue that logi-cal empiricism has degenerated in practice into two truncated forms, logicism and empiricism, and we show how these place artificial con-straints on the study of consent. Next, we consider interpretivist ap-proaches to understanding consent. The gravamen of our claim is that logical empiricist and interpretivist assumptions about science often bias studies of consent toward accepted and uncritical understand-ings; that is, in ways that obscure the operation of certain kinds of power. Finally, we discuss the study of consent in light of a realist conception of social science. Arguing first that realism does not, as is

---

[1] A useful introduction to the three-way debate among logical empiricists, interpretivists, and realists is Russell Keat and John Urry's *Social Theory as Science*, 2nd ed. (London: Routledge & Kegan Paul, 1982).

sometimes thought, entail any particular social or political theory, we go on to demonstrate its greater openness to possible explanations by reference to a discussion of John Gaventa's book, *Power and Power-lessness*.[2] We conclude by revisiting the differences that realism do and do not make.

CONSENT

The ideal of consent, that is, the consent to be governed, is a linchpin of Western political consciousness. The modern liberal tradition revolves around commitments to it, whether in the contractarian tradition traceable to the seventeenth century or in the market-based theory of revealed preference that has dominated utilitarianism since the 1800s. So captivating are the moral intuitions behind commitments to consent that even those hostile to liberalism usually embrace some variant of it. Edmund Burke affirmed his traditionalism by describing it as an agreement among the dead, the living, and those yet to be born, and much of the Marxist critique of bourgeois ideology reduces to the claim that its apparent roots in consent are spurious. Among twentieth century political theorists as different as John Rawls, Robert Paul Wolff, Robert Nozick, and Jürgen Habermas, a commitment to consent operates as the basic legitimating device of moral arguments.[3]

Not all apparent agreement is authentic, however, and perhaps none is entirely so. The powerful often cloak relations of domination in the language of consent, and the powerless often insist that conditions to which they have agreed are tainted by duress. Activists and critical theorists may go further, arguing that the dispossessed only agree to what they do because they are confused about their interests—whether because they are victims of hegemonic ideologies, subject to structural coercion of which they are unaware, or are otherwise deceived.

It is among the tasks of those who study consent to distinguish the more from the less plausible among such competing assertions, to get beyond the conflicting ideological claims and rationalizations to the

---

[2] John Gaventa, *Power and Powerlessness: Quiescence and Rebellion in an Appalachian Valley* (Urbana: University of Illinois Press, 1980).

[3] John Rawls, *A Theory of Justice* (Cambridge, MA: Harvard University Press, 1971), pp. 118–93; Robert Paul Wolff, *In Defense of Anarchism* (New York: Harper & Row, 1970), pp. 3–68; Robert Nozick, *Anarchy, State and Utopia* (New York: Basic Books, 1974), pp. 3–147; Jürgen Habermas, *Communication and the Evolution of Society* (Boston: Beacon, 1979), pp. 3–69.

truth about consent in specific situations. Yet they often disagree with one another about consent no less than the political agents whom they study. Most observers would agree that modern liberal societies rest on the at least tacit agreement of most of their members. Yet libertarians claim this agreement reflects the uncoerced choices of free individuals; theorists of liberal corporatism see it as negotiated and managed by state officials; Gramscian neo-Marxists think it masks the hegemony of ruling ideas that prevents the ruled from conceiving of alternatives to existing arrangements; and poststructuralists argue that it is part of a coercive process of individualization.[4]

Sometimes, such differences can be resolved by appealing to the facts of the case at hand, particularly when two theories are articulated within the same epistemological tradition. More often, however, they turn on competing conceptions of what the relevant facts are. Do we count self-understandings as facts, and if so, should we treat them as authentic or as symptoms of "false consciousness"? What about forms of coercion that may not be directly observable, like those involved in keeping issues that provoke overt conflict off the political agenda or in constituting the powers and interests of actors? Should we be interested in the alternative courses of action available to an agent in determining the authenticity of consent?

Disagreements about the authenticity of consent that turn on different answers to such questions cannot easily be settled by appeals to the empirical record because what that record consists in is part of what is at issue. It is fashionable to respond to this situation by treating competing theoretical claims as incommensurable, but it is part of our thesis here that skepticism toward that response is almost always in order. Actual circumstances often do not warrant such a radical response, and usually it only appears to people to be mandated because of faulty assumptions about the overdetermining character of theory. For a realist, whether and to what degree competing explanations are incommensurable is a question for investigation, not philosophical fiat. Part of the business of science is to devise criteria by reference to which we can adjudicate apparent incommensurabilities.

---

[4] Friedrich Hayek, "Law, Legislation and Liberty," in *The Mirage of Social Justice*, Vol. 2. (Chicago: University of Chicago Press, 1976), pp. 107–32; Leo Panitch, "The Development of Corporatism in Liberal Democracies," *Comparative Political Studies*, Vol. 10, No. 1 (April 1977), pp. 61–90; Antonio Gramsci, *Prison Notebooks: Selections* (New York: International Publishers, 1971), pp. 3–219; Michel Foucault, *Discipline and Punish* (New York: Random House, 1979), pp. 135–94.

LOGICAL EMPIRICISM AND THE ANALYSIS OF CONSENT

The prevalence of incommensurability talk is rooted in the failures of logical empiricism; it is with these that one must begin. Empiricism emerged as a philosophy of observation. For Hume and his followers, the limits of what can be said to exist—"the real"—were thought to be exhausted by what is given in or deducible from direct sensory experience. On this view of knowledge, it is not legitimate to infer from putative effects the existence of entities, be they quarks or utilities, that cannot directly be observed. It does not exclude incorporation of unobservable "theoretical entities" into scientific theories, but it does lead logical empiricists to conceive of those entities and theories instrumentally (as instruments for organizing and predicting experience) rather than realistically (as referring to real entities or structures in the world).[5]

Proponents of this ontology, sometimes described as "event-centered," define causation in Humean terms by reference to constant conjunctions of events. In Hume's view, the commonsense idea that causal mechanisms exist in the world, producing the regularities and other phenomena we observe, was no more than metaphysical superstition. We see regularities that lead us to posit causal arguments, but we never actually observe causal mechanisms.[6] With the commonsense view of causation denied to them, logical empiricists sought other grounds for conceptualizing the relation between cause and effect that is the basis of scientific explanation. They found them in the structure of theoretical arguments through which scientists advance causal claims. Theorists such as Carl Hempel argued that scientists try to subsume particular causal claims under more general lawlike theories, so that the relation between particular instances of lawlike arguments and the arguments themselves can be conceived of deductively.[7] Hempel's deductive-nomological (D-N) model gave logical empiricists a measure of security against the perceived dangers of commonsense inference. Deductions

[5] On instrumentalism see Milton Friedman, "The Methodology of Positive Economics," *Essays in Positive Economics* (Chicago: University of Chicago Press, 1953), pp. 8–14, and Ernst Nagel, *The Structure of Science,* 2nd ed. (Indianapolis: Hackett, 1979), pp. 129–52.

[6] David Hume, *A Treatise on Human Nature,* Vol. 1. (New York: Dutton, 1974), pp. 73–175.

[7] Carl Hempel, "The Function of General Laws in History," *Journal of Philosophy,* Vol. 39, No. 2 (15 January 1942), pp. 35–48. For a good discussion of the deductive-nomological model in the social sciences, see John Gunnell, *Philosophy, Science, and Political Inquiry* (Morristown, NJ: General Learning Press, 1975), pp. 60–96.

from lawlike generalizations would generate predictive claims that could be tested against future experience, tending to confirm, undermine, or reveal the need for modifying a theory. Science was thought to advance by this process of subsuming particular causal claims under more general covering-law arguments.

Hempel and his followers believed that the D-N model was a reconstruction of the logic of scientific explanation, not a description of scientific practice. As Abraham Kaplan points out, even in the physical sciences the practice of explanation was almost never conducted by reference to this reconstructed logic.[8] This fact was apparently lost on many behavioral revolutionaries in the social sciences, however, who, in their well-intentioned efforts to enhance the epistemic authority of their enterprises, adopted it as a description of scientific practice to which social scientists should try to conform. Perhaps not surprisingly, early behavioralists failed to come up with law-like generalizations rich enough to generate predictive theories of social action.[9] This seemed to suggest either that the human sciences were in their infancy or that a scientific understanding of the social world was impossible. Most social scientists, of course, took the former view but did so while rejecting strict adherence to logical empiricism in favor of more amorphous doctrines like "postbehavioralism." This crisis of logical empiricism produced two characteristic responses—one more logicist, the other more traditionally empiricist. These two bastardized versions of logical empiricism have shaped much contemporary social scientific practice, and it is to the analyses of consent they have rationalized that we turn next.

LOGICISM AND EPIPHENOMENAL THEORIES OF CONSENT

What we describe as the the logicist response is most often taken in economics and the social sciences influenced by it, where the prestige of rational choice models of human behavior remain highest. In place

---

[8] Abraham Kaplan, *The Conduct of Inquiry* (New York: Harper & Row, 1964), pp. 3–11. For a good discussion of some implications of Kaplan's distinction for methodological debates within the social sciences, see R. Little, "International Relations and the Methodological Turn," *Political Studies*, Vol. 39, No. 3 (September 1991), pp. 463–78.

[9] For further discussion of the difficulties attending the search for lawlike regularities in the social sciences, see Alasdair MacIntyre, *After Virtue* (Notre Dame, IN: University of Notre Dame Press, 1984), pp. 88–108, and Richard Miller, *Fact and Method* (Princeton: Princeton University Press, 1987), pp. 15–59.

of lawlike generalizations about observable phenomena, logicists ground their theories on assumptions that may or may not reflect observations about the world, with the suggestion that we proceed on the premise that reality behaves "as if" those assumptions held. Such a move might have seemed defensible because of the logical empiricist's instrumentalist view of theory: If theory is merely an instrument for organizing experience rather than a reference to real causal mechanisms, then the character of the propositions from which explanations are derived is irrelevant as long as we satisfactorily organize experience or "save the phenomena."[10] Yet it creates important problems.

Instrumentalism made sense within the original D-N framework because prediction of events was intended as a check on the validity of the underlying propositional base. When prediction no longer plays such a role and assumptions are no longer held empirically accountable, however, theory takes on a nominalist quality in which a view of reality is projected from the theory rather than measured against it. Despite the scientific pretensions of microeconomics and rational choice theory, for example, it is difficult to imagine what would count, for many of their proponents, as decisive evidence against their theories. For logicists, social inquiry is too often an exercise in trying to derive an ever widening class of phenomena from the theory rather than an attempt to validate the theory empirically. The logicist response to the crisis of logical empiricism, then, is to seek epistemic security in the deductive elements of the D-N model, but the failure of the model's nomological constraints to be instantiated in the human sciences means that in practice their theories often project the reality they purport to explain.

Logicism has the effect of reducing instances of consent to an epiphenomenal status, to a logical artifact "read off" of theoretical assumptions. In this regard, logicist analyses of consent share much in common with other reductionist theories of consent that from time to time masquerade as science. Hobbes argued that all human motivation finds its ultimate source in the fear of death, and although he appealed to consent as the basic legitimating norm of his politics, this was derived from an account of what it must be rational for everyone to agree to in light of this reductive theory of motivation. The cruder

---

[10] As instrumentalists pointed out, initially implausible premises sometimes turn out to be true, and an epistemology that disprivileges them seems unreasonably conservative; see Friedman, "The Methodology of Positive Economics," pp. 8–14. On the empiricist's limited objective of "saving the phenomena," see Bas van Fraassen, *The Scientific Image* (Oxford: Clarendon, 1980), pp. 41–69.

variants of historical materialism treat consent in a similar epiphenomenal fashion: If workers fail to see that the employment relations
to which they agree are exploitative, this must be a product of false
consciousness deriving, ultimately, from workers' failure to grasp the
truth of the theory. In an analogous vein, Bentham argued that the
proposition that people seek pleasure and avoid pain is an axiom that
could not and—he thought—need not be validated empirically, insisting that every effort to disconfirm it could be redescribed as exemplifying it. Bentham went so far as to deny by definition the possibility
of free will in every circumstance in which it might conflict with his
assumptions about human motivation.[11] In all these cases, claims
about instances of consent are read off from assumptions that are not
themselves subject to evidential considerations.

Some contemporary utilitarians have tried to reduce the amount of
contestable empirical psychology contained in their assumptions by
treating people as preference (rather than utility) maximizers. Yet they
often retain a Bentham-like mania for taking an explanation and running with it in ways that are, for all the talk about science, uncon-
strained by any requirements of confrontation with evidence. "Economic" rationales are constructed for apparently perverse acts, as when
people consent to go to more or less certain death in war or when
poor single women have large numbers of children, even when this
motivation has never been documented empirically.[12]

The epiphenomenal status of consent is also apparent in the work of
law-and-economics theorists such as Richard Posner. Arguing that the
common law evolves in ways that maximize the production of wealth
(whether judges understand this or not), Posner holds that consensual
transactions are buttressed by the law over time because they serve that
end. He appears unperturbed by the fact that the law proscribes many
consensual transactions where the link between proscription and
wealth maximization is less than evident, as in laws against obscenity,
pornography, and the taking of drugs. When the law does buttress consent, but in ways that appear unrelated to wealth maximization, Posner
goes to great lengths to rescue his explanatory thesis. Perhaps the limiting case of this is his claim that the reason why there are laws against

---

[11] Jeremy Bentham, *A Fragment on Government and an Introduction to the Principles of Morals
and Legislation,* W. Harrison, ed. (Oxford: Blackwell, 1960 [1789]), p. 125.

[12] For an example of such moral hazard arguments, see Charles Murray, *Losing Ground: American Social Policy, 1950–1980* (New York: Basic Books, 1984), pp. 157–66, and Christopher Jencks,
"How Poor Are the Poor?" *New York Review of Books* (9 May 1985), pp. 41–48 for criticism.

rape is that an "implicit market" of dating—in which sexual gratification requires mutual consent—is comparatively more efficient than a coercive system. So all-encompassing is the explanatory endeavor that it is often difficult to tell whether wealth maximization is being used to explain the evolution of law or being defined by reference to however the law evolves.[13]

This is not to say that logicist ventures are entirely without value for the human sciences. Taking an explanation and running with it, driving an as-if causal theory to the hilt, may reveal as faulty the assumptions that hitherto had been taken for granted and may generate research problems and hypotheses for investigation that otherwise would not have been considered.[14] Furthermore, no one can do everything and it is often true that those with great skill at exploring the formal properties of analytical models will often not be adept empirical investigators and vice versa. There is nothing in principle objectionable about division of labor in the human sciences, but it carries risks that proponents of logicism have neglected. By confusing what can never be more than devices for hypothesis generation with the conduct of social science itself, they often lose sight of the phenomena that their theories purport to explain, and the disputes about the fine points of analytical models that occupy much of their attention often reside so deeply in a world of counterfactuals that they could never be evaluated empirically.

The idea that correct scientific practice involves the ever more widespread application of a set of assumptions that is not itself empirically grounded permeates much of the rational choice scholarship in contemporary social science.[15] It is method- rather than question-driven, a tendency reinforced by the fact that logicists no longer seem to expect social science to generate predictive theories. Tellingly, one logicist suggests that "we must not be lulled by apparent empirical successes into believing that scientific knowledge can be attained without

---

[13] Richard Posner, "An Economic Theory of Criminal Law," *Columbia Law Review*, Vol. 85, No. 6 (October 1985), pp. 1193–231.

[14] The literature on the logic of decision rules since Arrow exemplifies all these phenomena. For an overview, see Dennis Mueller, *Public Choice II* (Cambridge and New York: Cambridge University Press, 1989), pp. 43–178.

[15] Note here that the argument is not against general theory but rather against the idea that generality itself is an indicator of a theory's plausibility; whether a general theory is in fact valid depends on its ability to resist falsification, not on its ability to provide an interpretation of more and more events.

the abstract, rigorous exercise of logical proof."[16] Although logicist scholarship is not always ideologically motivated (and when so motivated not always from the political right), it often seems to be geared more toward saving the thesis than explaining the piece of social reality in question—toward protecting and elaborating on the paradigm than using it to illuminate our understanding of the world. Genuine science is driven by the desire to understand reality; logicist endeavors frequently exhibit the self-sealing quality of ideologies because at root they are so often motivated instead by advocacy of a theory, paradigm, or point of view.

EMPIRICISM AND BEHAVIORAL THEORIES OF CONSENT

A different kind of bastardization of logical empiricism also results from the failure of the D-N model to generate a deductive social science. Avowedly less theoretically ambitious than the logicist response, it typically revolves around setting ever more modest explanatory goals within the general framework of a Humean approach to causation.[17] Social scientists in this empiricist subtradition usually are question driven and sensitive to the requirements of evidence. As a consequence, they are often hostile to logicism. Yet their arguments are also influenced by the skeptical epistemological assumptions built into logical empiricism, which generate a worldview in which observable events are conceived as the basic units of social reality. In contrast to the logicist's propensity to secure inferences in the logical certainty of deductive relations between premise and conclusion, empiricists seek to ground inferences in the confidence that comes from the direct presentation of events to the senses.

The consequences of taking this tack are well illustrated in the behavioral literature on power and consent, in which observable dissensus was seen as the basic datum for arguments about the conditions under which we might claim an agent's agreement to have been coerced.[18] The

---

[16] Bruce Bueno de Mesquita, "Toward a Scientific Understanding of International Conflict: A Personal View," *International Studies Quarterly,* Vol. 29, No. 2 (June 1985), p. 129.

[17] For a useful discussion of empiricism's progressive explanatory modesty over time, see Roberto Unger, *Social Theory: Its Situation and Its Task,* Vol. 1 (Cambridge and New York: Cambridge University Press, 1987), pp. 135–44.

[18] The classic of this genre is Robert Dahl, "The Concept of Power," *Behavioral Science,* Vol. 2, No. 3 (July 1957), pp. 201–15.

behavioralists' arguments prompted criticism that they had failed to consider forms of power that might be exercised via the manipulation of agendas, the formation of preferences, and the constitution of identities—all of which might be expressions of latent conflict and structural power relations that are not themselves directly observable.[19] By appealing to such phenomena, critics rejected the behavioralists' claim that power is plurally dispersed in liberal societies. Not surprisingly, however, behavioralists brushed such complaints aside as unscientific and ideologically motivated.[20] This reluctance to take the critics seriously reflected two related features of Humean empiricism: hostility toward unobservables (which makes the reference to unexpressed interests or powers seem inherently suspect), and event-centeredness (which is unfriendly to relational dimensions of social reality like structural power). Empiricism's self-imposed limits on what may count as a warranted causal inference ruled out of consideration the counterphenomenal claims for which critics of behavioralist theories of consent argued, making the debate as much about epistemology and ideology as about substance.

In short, empiricism privileges a different sense of the familiar than does logicism. Whereas logicism predisposes the explanatory enterprise toward prevailing theory, empiricism predisposes it toward the views of everyday agents and the institutional practices they support. To either sense of the familiar, Richard Miller's observation is applicable: "Whether the bias toward the familiar is in fact scientifically good depends on whether the institutions in which we live are biased toward the reasonable, when they make certain beliefs respectable and routine."[21] How unobservables and a non-Humean view of causation might inform explanations of consent is discussed later; at this point, we claim only that the empiricist's characteristic skepticism about unobservables has the effect of privileging everyday explanations of consent by default. In the end, these reduce to the claim that if one wants to know whether an agent's evident agreement was coerced in a given situation, one should ask that person.

[19] Peter Bachrach and Morton Baratz, "The Two Faces of Power," *American Political Science Review,* Vol. 56, No. 4 (December 1962), pp. 947–52; Steven Lukes, *Power: A Radical View* (London: Macmillan, 1974); Jeffrey Isaac, *Power and Marxist Theory* (Ithaca, N.Y.: Cornell University Press, 1987).

[20] Nelson Polsby, *Community Power and Political Theory,* 2nd ed. (New Haven: Yale University Press, 1980), pp. ix–xvii.

[21] Richard Miller, *Fact and Method,* p. 514; Miller's observation is applied by him only to the first sense of familiar.

This is not to say that social science limited to empiricist conceptions of legitimate practice has been without value in the study of consent. Robert Dahl's claim that the American polity exhibits circulating elites rather than a single ruling class—defended abstractly in his *Preface to Democratic Theory* and explored empirically in *Who Governs?*[22]—was developed as a response to the elite theorists of democracy, namely, Mosca, Michels, Pareto, and C. Wright Mills. Much of the latter work had been informed by the "iron law of oligarchy"—a post-Marxian reformulation of the old Hobbesian argument that power is indivisible and always resides in one place, no matter what the ostensible institutional political structure. Dahl's important insight was that the elite theories relied less on evidence than on theoretical or ideological attractiveness for their appeal; in the present terminology, they exemplified forms of logicism. By confronting their arguments with a combination of anomalous evidence and theoretical skepticism, Dahl upped the ante. Not only did he supply troublesome examples (such as the fact that in New Haven in the period he studied, different groups shaped decision making in different arenas) that proponents of elite theory had to explain, he rightly pointed out that the burden of persuasion was theirs. Critics of Dahl and other behavioralists were right to say that the exclusive focus on visible behavior biases inquiry against the possibility that some critical theories might be true. But Dahl was right to insist that proponents of these theories confront and explain his data from New Haven in a credible way. Indeed, it is doubtful that the more sophisticated empirical work on consent that grew out of the faces-of-power debates (some of which is discussed later) would have been attempted but for Dahl's behavioral critique.

The moral of this story is that although studies of social life that confine themselves to the requirements of an empiricist approach to explanation may exhibit systematic biases that lead their proponents to ignore the opaque dimensions of causal relations, they also can make useful contributions to the study of the phenomena to which they are addressed. But in the study of a phenomenon as causally complex as consent in a world riddled with more and less opaque power relations, such practice is likely to generate problematic instances that require new explanations. The acuity with which Dahl undermined the claims

[22] Robert Dahl, *A Preface to Democratic Theory* (Chicago: University of Chicago Press, 1956) and *Who Governs?* (New Haven: Yale University Press, 1963). See also Dahl, "The Concept of Power."

of the elite theorists never established the truth or even plausibility of his own pluralist thesis. This should not surprise us; any causal theory of the place of power in consensual relations that restricts itself to the realm of observable events will likely miss a good deal of what is really going on.

INTERPRETING CONSENT: THE TURN TO HERMENEUTICS

By a curious convergence, although by a quite different route, students of consent who have been influenced by the interpretive turn in social theory also bias their investigations toward the phenomenal realm. To understand why this is so requires attention to the hermeneutic critique of logical empiricism. Interpretivisms come in various forms; what they share in common is resistance to the logical empiricist notion that theories are true insofar as they correspond to facts that exist in the world out there. The philosophical groundwork for this resistance was laid by the later Wittgenstein who insisted, in opposition to the correspondence theory of truth, that the meanings of propositions are artifacts of the conventional rules governing their use.[23] This move opened the way for a shift in focus away from the relationship between language and reality toward language as reality, to a preoccupation with what J. L. Austin described as the performative dimensions of language. In his famous example, when someone says "I promise to x" he thereby becomes obligated; he is not describing an action that is performed in another way.[24] The ordinary language philosophers who followed Wittgenstein and Austin argued that language constitutes social reality via such performative devices. As a result, they conceived of the task of understanding the social world as elucidating the norms and rules governing linguistic use.[25] This move had elective affinities with Kuhn's subsequent argument that, even in the hard sciences, observation is overdetermined by theory; that what counts as evidence for a scientist is an artifact of the system of rules and expectations governed by the prevailing paradigms or beliefs rather than by anything external to that

---

[23] Ludwig Wittgenstein, *Philosophical Investigations* (Oxford: Blackwell, 1953), sec. 139.

[24] J. L. Austin, *How to Do Things with Words* (Cambridge, MA: Harvard University Press, 1962).

[25] Austin himself had been unsure how much language was performative, a subject about which he changed his mind; see the papers by Walter Cerf, Max Black, and L. W. Ferguson in K. T. Fann, ed., *Symposium on J. L. Austin,* (New York: Humanities Press, 1969), pp. 351–79, 401–19.

system.[26] Much of philosophy has since moved on under the influence of Saul Kripke and others, but the assumptions behind ordinary language philosophy still inform a good deal of interpretive scholarship in the human sciences.[27]

Why does the interpretive turn bring with it a bias toward the phenomenal realm? The answer varies with the type of interpretivism at issue and the explanatory status that is claimed for it, but the sources of such bias are invariably traceable to an internal preoccupation with the language and beliefs of social agents. This follows naturally from the Wittgensteinian equation of meaning with use. Consider the following "consensual" acts:

1. A man and a woman say "I do" at the appropriate times in a conventional wedding ceremony in the contemporary United States.

2. A worker who would otherwise be unemployed for reasons beyond his control gratefully agrees to an employment contract in which he receives half the minimum wage.

3. A battered wife voluntarily chooses to return home knowing that she will face more abuse and may be killed.

Example 1 illustrates that more than one action may be performed simultaneously. The participants in a wedding ceremony are self-consciously committing themselves to one another through the marriage contract, but they are also reproducing the social structure of the nuclear family even if they are utterly unaware of this. Example 2 illustrates that people can be structurally coerced without knowing what the source of the coercion is or even that they are being coerced; the worker may blame his circumstances entirely on himself. Example 3 illustrates that the kinds of processes illustrated in examples 1 and 2 can occur simultaneously: People can be coerced into consenting to arrangements by forces that they do not understand, and in doing so, they can produce and reproduce social structures of whose existence they may be entirely unaware. The battered wife may be the victim of a psychological syndrome that causes her to interpret abuse as a sign

---

[26] Thomas S. Kuhn, *The Structure of Scientific Revolutions* (Chicago: University of Chicago Press, 1962), pp. 10–51. Note that Kuhn never thought that his arguments applied to the human sciences, which he regarded as "preparadigmatic."

[27] See Saul Kripke, *Naming and Necessity* (Cambridge, MA: Harvard University Press, 1982), and *Wittgenstein on Rules and Private Language* (Cambridge, Ma: Harvard University Press, 1984).

of her husband's affection; in acting on this belief, she may be inadvertently reproducing an exploitative relationship.

Interpretive accounts of human action are generally inadequate for analyzing these types of cases because of the centrality they ascribe to the meaning of an action for the performing agent. As Quentin Skinner, one of the most sophisticated defenders of this method describes it, the interpretivist tries to understand human action "not in causal and positivist terms as a precipitate of its context, but rather in circular and hermeneutic terms as a meaningful item within a wider context of conventions and assumptions." The goal is to "elucidate" the "meaning" of a "social action . . . for the agent performing it."[28] Different practitioners of interpretivism employ different methods for pursuing this elucidation (for Skinner, agents' intentions are to be "decoded" from the prevailing linguistic context of conventional assumptions), but the task invariably revolves around trying to recover the significance of actions for the performing agents. Thus Skinner distinguishes the motives for which an action was performed from the agent's intentions in performing it. The former may be the causes of actions, but they are merely contingently related to them; the essence of any action is its meaning, and this is divined by getting into the performing agent's mind and discovering its significance for him or her. In Skinner's words, no agent can be said "to have meant or done something which he could never be brought to accept as a correct description of what he had meant or done."[29]

This method has serious limitations for the analysis of the preceding three examples and others like them because it is constitutionally predisposed to miss phenomena like ideological distortion, dimensions of actions that involve overlooking and neglecting, unconscious intentions, and the functional dimensions of actions for social structures that may or may not be evident to agents. Because ideology and power relations often operate via the more opaque dimensions of language on agents' self-understandings, any method of investigating consensual actions in a power-laden world that limits the inquiry to those

---

[28] Quentin Skinner, "Hermeneutics and the Role of History," *New Literary History*, Vol. 7, No. 1 (Autumn 1975), pp. 215–16, and "Social Meaning and the Explanation of Social Action," in Peter Laslett, W. G. Runciman, and Quentin Skinner, eds., *Philosophy, Politics, and Society*, Fourth Series (Oxford: Blackwell, 1972), p. 136.

[29] Quentin Skinner, "Motives, Intentions, and the Interpretation of Texts," *New Literary History*, Vol. 3, No. 2 (Winter 1972), p. 401, and "Meaning and Understanding in the History of Ideas," *History and Theory*, Vol. 8, No. 1 (1969), p. 29.

self-understandings potentially involves bias. This is not to say that every act of apparent consent really masks some underlying functionalism or determinism (to go that route would be to lurch back toward logicism). It is to say that we cannot assume, before inquiry into particular cases begins, that it does not. Herbert Marcuse's claim that the consensual norms in modern liberal societies mask and facilitate "repressive tolerance" cannot even be evaluated from the interpretivist's standpoint, which is indicative of its built-in bias.[30] It is this dimension of interpretive social science that has led critics to describe it as "linguistic behaviorism."[31]

How serious these flaws are depends on the explanatory status that is claimed for an interpretive account of an action. If, for example, elucidations of individual and collective meanings are regarded as simply one component of a fuller explanation of an action, no objection to them as necessarily biased may be in order. Or if an interpretivist claims in advance only to be interested in the meaning for the relevant agent (as in some schools of literary exegesis) and not in other (e.g., causal) aspects of the situation, the method also can be defended, perhaps, from the present charge.[32] So long as no generalizations about their broader epistemic significance or completeness are made for interpretive accounts, "weak" interpretivism may be unobjectionable.

However, this is not what many practitioners in the human sciences have in mind when they advocate or deploy interpretive methods. Most of the interpretive work done in the social sciences and history of ideas since the 1960s was inspired by one of two versions of "strong" interpretivism: that interpretive elucidations of meanings are by definition the best explanations of actions, or that, because causal explanation is impossible in the human sciences (so that they are not "sciences" at all), interpretive elucidations of meaning are the only explanation of

---

[30] Herbert Marcuse, "Repressive Tolerance," in Robert Wolff, Barrington Moore, and Herbert Marcuse, co-authors, *A Critique of Pure Tolerance* (Boston: Beacon, 1965), pp. 81–123. Note that a charge of bias is not the same as one of conservatism, which defenders of interpretivism correctly resist on the grounds that it can bring to the surface competing interpretations of the practices prevalent in a culture and unmask contradictions within dominant interpretations; see Michael Gibbons, "Interpretation, Conservatism, and Political Practice," *Polity*, Vol. 17 No. 4 (1985), pp. 777–94; and Georgia Warnke, *Gadamer: Hermeneutics, Tradition and Reason* (Stanford, CA: Stanford University Press, 1987), chaps. 1 and 2.

[31] Charles Chihara and J. Fodor, "Operationalism and Ordinary Language: A Critique of Wittgenstein," in George Pitcher, ed., *Wittgenstein: The Philosophical Investigations* (London: Macmillan, 1966), pp. 384–419.

[32] The present chapter does not discuss other objections to such methods.

their significance.[33] Just what the status of the knowledge gained from such analyses is supposed to be is a subject of dispute among interpretivists, but if any claim is made that it is genuine by virtue of being interpretive—that interpretive accounts are "true" accounts of actions that agents perform—then the difficulties of built-in bias to which we have pointed arise.

Often, it is difficult to get a grip on what status is being claimed for an interpretive account. For instance, much of Quentin Skinner's rhetoric about method (his equation of "causal" with "positivist" accounts and his description of interpretivist accounts as alternatives to them) suggest that he takes the radical view that all causal explanations in the history of ideas fail. But his own substantive work belies this claim. He has resolutely insisted that the history of ideas should be studied as the history of ideologies and that his interpretive method makes this possible. On reflection, it should be evident, however, that studying the evolution of ideologies while ignoring causal questions is not possible. We should be unsurprised, therefore, to discover that his substantive work is laced with implicit causal claims and assumptions.

Consider Skinner's treatment of modern ideologies of individual rights that lie at the core of liberal conceptions of consent. These he traces to the Huguenot theory of resistance developed during the later sixteenth century. Skinner concedes that to understand Huguenot ideology during this period, it is "essential to begin by considering the nature of the situation in which they found themselves at the start of the civil wars in 1562,"[34] and he consequently devotes an entire chapter to a discussion of these wars before analyzing the political works of the Huguenots themselves.

Examination of the chapter on the Huguenot revolution reveals that Skinner is only concerned to analyze the events surrounding the revolution "internally," that is, as they appeared to the participants. Thus the Huguenots' moderate attitude toward the de Medicis before 1572 is explained in terms of Catherine de Medici's recognition, during the 1560s, that the imposition of religious conformity was politically unviable and that her best hope of retaining power lay in granting the Huguenots a measure of religious toleration; they in turn realized that it

---

[33] For a discussion of the varieties of interpretivism, see Bryan Wilson, ed., *Rationality* (Oxford: Blackwell, 1974) particularly the papers by Peter Winch, Ernest Gellner, Alasdair MacIntyre, and Steven Lukes, pp. 1–49, 78–111, 112–30, and 194–213.

[34] Quentin Skinner, *Foundations of Modern Political Thought*, vol. 2 (Cambridge: Cambridge University Press, 1978), p. 241.

would be impolitic not to take advantage of this fact.[35] The entire chapter is written on this plane of explanation; the political ideas of the Huguenots and their opponents are invariably treated as subjective rationalizations for actions. Skinner never mentions the structural transformations then occurring in European society or that the development of a generalized individual right to resist contributed importantly to the growth of an ideology of consent that could legitimate the transition to a market-based society. That there may be some causal link between the emergence of this ideology and the transition from feudalism to capitalism is never considered. The present concern is not to establish that some such causal link exists but only that Skinner's interpretive method prevents his even considering it.[36]

Enough has by now been said to establish that there is a built-in bias toward the phenomenal realm when interpretivists claim (or assume) that their accounts are the only adequate (or the best) causal accounts of human actions, or when—eschewing the possibility of causal analysis—they nonetheless insist that their elucidations are the only adequate (or the best) ways in which human actions can be understood. Interpretivist epistemic commitments are by their nature wedded to prevailing interpretations, and, to the degree that these misdescribe what is actually going on, so will the interpretive accounts that are based on them. When people engage in seemingly consensual acts it is possible that their agreement is uncoerced, but this is only one possibility. Interpretivists are not inclined to ask the question which, if any, of prevailing interpretations of a voluntary act is the correct one due to their commitment to the priority of commonsense interpretations and their rejection (or at least disinterest in) causal explanation.

This is not to say that interpretivist explanations are without value. Like empiricist accounts, they often generate problematical pieces of evidence for existing theories that up the ante in constructive ways, and they may lead to the discovery of causal explanations that might otherwise not have been discovered or, at least, to new grist for the mill of hypothesis generation. This possibility can be discerned, for example, in James Scott's interpretive work on the "hidden transcripts" of subordinate groups. As a field-based political anthropologist in Southeast

---

[35] *Ibid.*, pp. 241–44; 249–54.
[36] Parts of the preceding paragraph are adapted from Ian Shapiro, "Realism in the Study of the History of Ideas," *History of Political Thought,* Vol. 3, No. 3 (Winter 1982), pp. 568–69.

Asia, he documented in rich detail the fact that the languages of subordinate groups change radically with context. Their "scripts" when they are "off stage" in one another's company differ dramatically from their "public transcripts" in their masters' presence. On this basis, Scott was able to expose Gramscian conceptions of hegemony as too simpleminded in ways that exhibit some parallels with Dahl's critique of the elite theorists discussed earlier. Just as Dahl upped the ante by producing anomalous findings for conventional elite theory, so Scott's work suggests that at least some instances of apparent hegemony are illusory.

And just as Dahl's work was better at indicating weaknesses in prevailing explanations than in generating new ones, so, too, with Scott's. It is, indeed, difficult to extract a clear causal story from Scott's work or even a series of causal hypotheses to explain the phenomenon he describes, although it is evidently pregnant with causal significance. One might imagine someone, having read Scott, trying to test the hypothesis that the size of the gap, somehow measured, between the public and private transcripts of subordinate groups is a consequence of the degree of their objective powerlessness, somehow measured. Doing this would involve moving beyond the interpretive realm, but in ways that would not have been attempted were it not for Scott's interpretive work.[37]

To sum up, it is right to insist that the phenomenal realm should not be granted a privileged status that delimits the bounds of inquiry, but neither should it be arbitrarily disprivileged. That is the vice of logicism. Whether and to what degree peoples' beliefs and self-understandings explain their actions is a subject for scientific investigation, not armchair reflection.

SCIENTIFIC REALISM AND CONSENT

Like empiricists and interpretivists, realists embrace assumptions about the kinds of inferences that we are warranted in making about the world. Commonsense realism is the belief that the world of everyday objects exists independently of the mind; in this respect it is opposed to philosophical idealism and allied to empiricism. Scientific realism involves the additional presumption that the unobservable entities and

---

[37] James Scott, *Weapons of the Weak* (New Haven: Yale University Press, 1985), pp. 314–50, and *Domination and the Arts of Resistance* (New Haven: Yale University Press, 1990), pp. 70–107 and 136–82.

causal mechanisms often posited in scientific theories exist.[38] This aspect of realism distinguishes itself from empiricism, which is agnostic about unobservables, and from most versions of interpretivism, which deal with causal matters implicitly when they deal with them at all.

REALISM ON INTERPRETIVISM AND LOGICAL EMPIRICISM

The interpretivist critique of the possibility of social science took as its target a logical empiricist conception of what such a science entailed, focusing on its assumption that there is a bedrock of observed but uninterpreted facts on which knowledge claims could rest. Realists do not assume the existence of any such bedrock, yet they argue that the fact that human action is linguistically constituted is not a barrier to the possibility of social science.[39] Realists criticize interpretivists for treating the intentional realm and the linguistic rules constituting it as unproblematic givens. For realists, this obscures the truth that self-understandings and social conventions are themselves results of causal processes such as socialization and power relations. Realists think that it is the task of social science to investigate these processes.

If realists differ from interpretivists in their attempts to provide an epistemic space for causal explanation, they differ from logical empiricists in the criteria they regard as appropriate for what counts as such an explanation. For realists, the epistemological skepticism on which traditional empiricism rests is unwarranted. The disagreement here stems from the confidence that empiricists have placed in observation as a bedrock for theory. Realists agree with interpretivists that there is no theory-neutral observation language of the kind that empiricists take for granted. All observation is informed by the existing

---

[38] The following discussion ignores differences within the realist tradition, focusing only on the commitments that set realists apart from empiricists and interpretivists. Like many treatments of social scientific realism, ours owes much to Roy Bhaskar, *A Realist Theory of Science* (New York: Humanities Press, 1975) and *The Possibility of Naturalism: A Philosophical Critique of the Contemporary Human Sciences* (New York: Humanities Press, 1979), as well as to Miller, *Fact and Method*. The chapter also draws on the more extensive discussion of realism in the philosophy of the natural sciences, including Jarrett Leplin, ed., *Scientific Realism* (Berkeley and Los Angeles: University of California Press, 1984) and Paul Churchland and Clifford Hooker, eds., *Images of Science: Essays on Realism and Empiricism* (Chicago: University of Chicago Press, 1985).

[39] For a good statement of this argument, see John Greenwood, "The Social Constitution of Action: 'Objectivity and Explanation,'" *Philosophy of the Social Sciences*, Vol. 20, No. 2 (June 1990), pp. 195–207.

stock of knowledge embodied in past successful theories—whether background assumptions about how the world works or technical knowledge about how to build observational aids like microscopes and telescopes. By itself, observation is not an adequate foundation for knowledge: Existence claims always involve a combination of observation and theory-based inference. Observation, however, is not determined by theory or discourse. Unlike interpretivists, realists contend that well-established theories do refer to, and are constrained by, external reality.[40]

Realists also differ from empiricists in the status they accord to unobservables. Scientists routinely assume the existence of unobservables, depending on them both to predict novel facts and to intervene successfully in the world. This poses two challenges for philosophies of science: accounting for the fact that much scientific practice is "realist" in character, and explaining its success.[41] Realists argue that the best explanation for both is that science provides at least partly true descriptions of the causal structure of the world. Were this not the case, the ability of science to get us to the moon would be an inexplicable miracle.[42]

This illustrates a basic realist device: abduction or "inference to the best explanation"—reasoning on the basis of mature theories from observed effects to unobservable causes. Abduction to unobservables is a way of generating knowledge in which theory plays a vital role, and the

[40] On the debate between realists and postmodernists over the nature and possibility of reference, see Sollace Mitchell, "Poststructuralism, Empiricism and Interpretation," in Sollace Mitchell and Michael Rosen, eds., *The Need for Interpretation* (London: Athlone, 1983), pp. 54–89; Christopher Norris, *Contest of Faculties* (London: Methuen, 1985), pp. 47–69; and Michael Devitt and Kim Sterelny, *Language and Reality: An Introduction to the Philosophy of Language* (Cambridge, MA: MIT Press, 1987), pp. 199–220.

[41] Most natural scientists are realists except in quantum mechanics; on the challenge posed by the latter to realism, see Henry Krips, *The Metaphysics of Quantum Theory* (Oxford: Clarendon, 1987), and Miller, *Fact and Method*, pp. 515–603. It is less true in the social sciences, in part because of the pervasive influence of logical empiricism on social scientists' conceptions of what constitutes "scientific" practice. Even here, however, much of what practicing social scientists actually do in their research can best be understood on a realist as opposed to empiricist conception of science. For a good realist critique of what is wrong when it is not so informed, see David Dessler, "Beyond Correlations: Toward a Causal Theory of War," *International Studies Quarterly*, Vol. 35, No. 3 (September 1991), pp. 337–56.

[42] On the "miracle argument" for realism, see Richard Boyd, "The Current Status of the Issue of Scientific Realism," in Leplin, ed., *Scientific Realism*, pp. 58–63; and Alison Wylie, "Arguments for Scientific Realism: The Ascending Spiral," *American Philosophical Quarterly*, Vol. 23, No. 3 (July 1986), pp. 287–97. On the realist assumptions implicit in scientific practice, see Thomas Cook and David Campbell, "The Causal Assumptions of Quasi-Experimental Practice," *Synthese*, Vol. 68, No. 1 (July 1986), pp. 141–80.

empiricist-realist debate turns on their epistemic legitimacy.[43] Empiricists and interpretivists disallow it, arguing that the history of science is replete with failures that undermine any claim that scientific knowledge about unobservables is progressive, whereas realists depend on it. They argue that even though fallible, our knowledge of the underlying structure of reality can reasonably be assumed to be cumulative, so there are good reasons for trusting the strategy's claims.

The emphasis on abduction underlies realism's non-Humean assumptions about causal explanation. In the realist view, causation is a relation between mechanism and outcome rather than premise and conclusion as in the deductive-nomological model.[44] Giving a causal explanation consists in using observation and abductive inference to describe how causal mechanisms work. It is not a matter of deriving events from lawlike generalizations; for realists, explanation and prediction are not symmetrical.[45]

On the realist view, science should be driven by questions rather than methods, and the scientist's goal should be to describe accurately the causal mechanisms by reference to which his questions about reality can be answered. Scientists start with questions about the world, usually (but not always) with some aspect of it that seems to be counterintuitive or difficult to comprehend, and they try to explain these apparent facts or anomalies. Why do bodies fall to earth? Why does the horizon appear to be curved? Why do we see lightning before we hear thunder? Why do prices rise during recessions when we expect them to fall? Why do millions of people choose to go to almost certain death in war? How do institutions shape peoples' preferences and beliefs? These are the kinds of questions that motivate practicing scientists. They begin neither with a method nor with a theory but with an aspect of reality that they are trying to understand. The ways in which

---

[43] Brian Ellis, *Truth and Objectivity* (Oxford: Blackwell, 1990), p. 110.

[44] Useful contrasts of the empiricist and realist conceptions of causation include Ernan McMullin, "Two Ideals of Explanation in Natural Science," in Peter French. Theodore E. Uehling Jr., and Howard K. Wettsetein, eds., *Causation and Causal Theories*, Midwest Studies in Philosophy, Vol. 9 (Minneapolis: University of Minnesota Press, 1984), pp. 205–20; and Dessler, "Beyond Correlations."

[45] On the incoherence of explanatory-predictive symmetry, see Philip Kitcher, "Explanatory Unification and the Causal Structure of the World," in Philip Kitcher and Wesley Salmon, eds., *Scientific Explanation*, Minnesota Studies in the Philosophy of Science, Vol. 13 (Minneapolis: University of Minnesota Press, 1989), pp. 411–13.

scientists show how outcomes are produced by causal mechanisms depend on the nature of the question being asked.[46] Sometimes, quantitative, cross-sectional analysis will provide strong material for good abductive inferences. In other contexts, qualitative or historical analysis will be more appropriate. Sometimes, more theory will be required and sometimes less. The injunction to describe how causal mechanisms work entails no fixed set of methodological implications for the practice of science; there is no single correct method of causal analysis. Choices about causal explanation should rest on pragmatic criteria, not a priori commitments.[47]

The question-oriented, pragmatic character of realists' methodological commitments is reflected in their approach to evaluating causal claims. Realists are not hostile to logical empiricists' reliance on predictions of empirical regularities as evidence for the validity of claims because in perfectly closed systems, causal powers should usually produce such regularities.[48] They are skeptical, however, that such a one-dimensional approach toward falsification will be helpful in the open systems that dominate social life. As a result, realists rely on three additional criteria for assessing causal claims: whether they conform with our existing understanding of the phenomenon in question (those that do not merit greater skepticism); whether they enable us to predict novel facts unforeseen by existing theories; and whether they allow us to intervene successfully in the relevant environment. What these criteria mean in practice is taken up next.

[46] Alexander Wendt, "The Agent-structure Problem in International Relations Theory," *International Organization,* Vol. 41, No. 3 (Summer 1987), pp. 361–65; Alan Garfinkel, *Forms of Explanation* (New Haven: Yale University Press, 1981), pp. 21–48. For a good example of how sensitivity to the nature of the question being asked can affect what counts as an "explanation," see Hidemi Suganami, "Bringing Order to the Causes of War Debates," *Millennium,* Vol. 19, No. 1 (Spring 1990), pp. 19–35.

[47] For good overviews of realist approaches to causal analysis, see Andrew Sayer, *Method in Social Science: A Realist Approach* (London: Hutchinson, 1984), pp. 79–107, 211–34; Ray Pawson, *A Measure for Measures: A Manifesto for Empirical Sociology* (London: Routledge & Kegan Paul, 1989), pp. 157–96.

[48] This convergence of views about causation has led some critics of realism to argue—mistakenly, in our view—that it is parasitic on logical empiricism. See Brian Fay, "General Laws and Explaining Human Behavior," in Daniel Sabia and Jerald Wallulis, eds., *Changing Social Science* (Albany: State University of New York Press, 1986), pp. 103–28; cf. McMullin, "Two Ideals of Explanation."

Realism and the Study of Consent

Some realist philosophers of social science have suggested that realism yields particular substantive conclusions about the social world; most frequently, these conclusions are illustrated by "structurationist" conceptions of the relationship between agents and social structures or by Marxist conceptions of the nature of capitalism.[49] This leap from philosophy to social theory is a mistake. Structurationist social theory and Marxist political economy quite probably presuppose realism because only on such a foundation can their appeals to unobservable causal mechanisms be justified. It is one of the comparative virtues of realism that it is open to such critical theorizing about society; to that extent, it permits students of social life to go beyond the boundaries of the familiar in ways that social inquiry framed in logical empiricist and interpretivist terms typically do not. But this does not mean that realism presupposes or entails the truth of such theories. Realism requires only that the task of social science is to describe causal mechanisms. It says nothing about what these mechanisms are, nor does it tell us whether we should be pluralists, elitists, or Marxists when seeking to explain particular instances of consent. To think otherwise is to fall into the same trap of method-driven social science for which logical empiricists and interpretivists have been criticized and thus to misunderstand the "difference that realism makes." That difference is permissive, not prescriptive.

The difficulties of identifying and choosing among causal accounts are thrown into sharp relief by the study of consent. They arise from the existence of such latent factors as the structural conditioning of cognitions, interests, and identities, and they are compounded by the problems associated with studying open systems where experimental closure usually is not feasible. Nonetheless, creative social scientists who are not tied to the varieties of empiricism and interpretivism discussed here have found ways to address these problems empirically. They do this by formulating tentative explanations for the phenomena in question and then attempting to supply descriptions of the causal mechanisms posited by the proffered explanations.

A classic of this genre is *Power and Powerlessness*, John Gaventa's study of quiescence in the mining communities of central Appalachia.

---

[49] See, for example, Bhaskar, *The Possibility of Naturalism*, pp. 31–55, and *Scientific Realism and Human Emancipation* (London: Verso, 1986), pp. 103–223; David Dessler, "What's At Stake in the Agent-Structure Debate?" *International Organization*, Vol. 43, No. 3 (Summer 1989), pp. 441–74;

Writing as a social scientist rather than a philosopher, Gaventa does not trace his disagreements with behaviorialist students of power back to the differences between their event-centered ontology and his realist assumptions. Yet he clearly wants to question an event-centered view of things. As a result, he tries to problematize what its proponents take as given. Instead of assuming that inaction or inertia is natural and activism is problematic, he argues that inertia is what has to be explained, so that "the study of quiescence in a situation of potential conflict becomes the task, rather than the study of conflict in a situation otherwise assumed to be conflict-free."[50] More specifically, the questions motivating Gaventa's study are the following:

> Why, in a social relationship involving the domination of a nonelite by an elite, does challenge to that domination not occur? What is there in certain situations of social deprivation that prevents issues from arising, grievances from being voiced, or interests from being recognized? Why, in an oppressed community where one might intuitively expect upheaval, does one instead find, or appear to find, quiescence? Under what conditions and against what obstacles does rebellion begin to emerge?[51]

Gaventa's tentative explanation for the existence of quiescence in such situations is that it is a product of power relationships, that "in situations of inequality the political response of the deprived group or class may be seen as a function of power relationships, such that power serves for the development and maintenance of quiescence of the non-elite."[52] If apparent consent is hypothesized to be the consequence of such power relationships, the empirical task is to discover and describe the mechanisms by which this occurs. If no such mechanisms can be discovered, we would have to call into question the hypothesis that but for the existence of the specified power relationships the dominated group would rebel.

Gaventa employs four strategies to try to identify the relevant causal mechanisms: one historical, one comparative, one structural, and one quasi-experimental. The first proceeds from the assumption that if quiescence is manufactured, there should be historical traces of this in overt conflicts of the past. His historical analysis provides evidence for the proposition that there were major conflicts of interest between the

---

Jeffrey Isaac, "Realism and Reality: Some Realistic Reconsiderations," *Journal for the Theory of Social Behaviour,* Vol. 20, No. 1 (March 1990), pp. 5–6.

[50] Gaventa, *Power and Powerlessness,* p. 26.

[51] *Ibid.,* p. 3.

[52] *Ibid.,* p. 4.

miners and the corporation that owned the mines during the 1920s and 1930s, that the miners failed to prevail in these conflicts, and that these failures contributed to a quiescent mentality in which opposition was thought to be pointless. Comparatively, Gaventa adduces evidence in support of his thesis by showing that in other comparable circumstances—except that the relevant power relations were different—miners were more rebellious. Structurally, Gaventa describes the mechanisms by which power imbalances were maintained by the role of corrupt unions in keeping mine workers in a dependent state and their almost total lack of resources to challenge the existing order. Quasi-experimentally (as a participant-observer), he studies the miners' propensity toward oppositionalism when power relations begin to break down or change in other ways.[53]

By pursuing these four lines of inquiry, Gaventa makes a strong case for his thesis that the quiescence of Appalachian miners cannot be explained by behavioralist conceptions of power that rely exclusively on overt coercion as a criterion for drawing inferences about the presence or absence of consent. Instead, he establishes that it is in large part due to the effects of the less easily observed second and third "dimensions" of power: the mobilization of institutional biases against the emergence of overt conflict and the conditioning of the miners' understandings of their interests. The result is a richly textured account of how all three forms of power interact to neutralize potential opposition to the dominance of the mine owners, one that incorporates the insights provided by the behavioralist's preoccupation with observable events while at the same time digging beneath them.

How might logical empiricists and interpretivists criticize Gaventa's analysis? Perhaps surprisingly, few have denounced it as "antiscientific" or "ideological"; indeed, the book has been widely acclaimed. One reason for this acceptance is probably the richness of its empirical analysis. Whereas many challenged Steven Lukes's abstract discussion of the third dimension of power that inspired Gaventa, he suppresses the potentially most problematic aspect of that discussion (the notion of "real interests") and brings so much direct and indirect evidence to bear on his claims that the epistemic gap between what we all can observe and his causal inferences is minimized. The absence of systematic challenge

---

[53] For the historical and comparative analysis, see *ibid.*, pp. 47–121; for the structural analysis, see pp. 125–201; and for the quasi-experimental analysis, see pp. 207–51.

also suggests a second reason for the book's acceptance: that the inferential leaps that Gaventa does take conform to the epistemic sensibilities of most practicing social scientists. Notwithstanding the logical empiricist introduction to the philosophy of social science that most social scientists receive in graduate school, the more flexible, question-driven standards of causal inference articulated by realists seem better able to describe day-to-day research practices. Most scientists are not as relentlessly skeptical in their efforts to root out quasi-science as logical empiricists would like them to be.

That said, what might a dyed-in-the-wool logical empiricist or interpretivist say about Gaventa's argument? An interpretivist who believed that causal arguments were entirely inappropriate in the social sciences would reject any effort to explain the miners' quiescence in terms other than communities of discourse and meaning. Because Gaventa is trying to explain the nature and evolution of those communities causally, a strong interpretivist would perforce have to reject his theory. Some interpretivists do not reject causal explanation per se so much as empiricist conceptions of causation, with which it is hard to reconcile notions of human freedom and subjectivity.[54] They might find Gaventa's realist approach to causal claims more acceptable, particularly because he supplies a narrative that links these claims to the self-understandings of agents.

The logical empiricist's concern with grounding causal inferences on the epistemically secure foundations of direct experience or logical deduction suggests at least three reasons to be skeptical about Gaventa's claims. The first concerns his effort to escape the thorny problem of imputing to subordinate actors real, but unobservable, interests on the basis of which they would act were it not for the effects of second- and third-dimensional forms of power. Gaventa argues that rather than impute real interests to actors, it is sufficient to show that subordinate actors are prevented from acting on or conceiving certain interests.[55] As David Howell points out, this may beg the question if the source of prevention lies in unobservable forms of power, the existence of which Gaventa is trying to establish by appeals to the observable record.[56] On what independent basis can one plausibly say that in the absence of

---

[54] John Greenwood, "Agency, Causality, and Meaning," *Journal for the Theory of Social Behaviour,* Vol. 18, No. 1 (March 1988), pp. 95–115.

[55] Gaventa, *Power and Powerlessness,* p. 29.

[56] David Howell, "Docile Diggers and Russian Reds: Contrasts in Working-class Politics," *Political Studies,* Vol. 29, No. 3 (September 1981), pp. 457–58.

direct coercion the miners would have revolted but for unobservable second- and third-dimensional forms of power? A prior, well-grounded theory of human interests would seem necessary to answer this question (playing, in effect, the role of lawlike generalizations or assumptions in deductive-nomological theories), and at present we lack such a theory. The problem of real interests, in other words, can be suppressed but not eliminated, a fact that calls into question the epistemic basis of Gaventa's whole research strategy of trying to explain the "nonevent" of quiescence.[57]

Pressing this issue, a second feature of Gaventa's study to which a logical empiricist might object is that it does not systematically address a number of rival explanations for the miners' quiescence. Gaventa does show convincingly that first- and second-dimensional forms of power cannot account for his findings, but he does not deal directly with the behavioralist's fallback position, to which he refers several times, that the miners were quiescent because of a "culture of apathy." To be sure, Gaventa seeks to explain the miners' "apathy," but his research design and evidence do not allow him to determine whether such a culture actually exists or what its roots, beyond power relations, might be. As a result, he has no independent basis for claiming that the behavioralist theory is mistaken. It may be that systematic disempowerment contributes to such a culture, but so might other factors that he does not address. At most, the skeptic might argue, Gaventa's monocausal account shows that the miners' quiescence is consistent with his theory of unobservable power mechanisms, but this does not establish causation. To make strong causal claims would require a multivariate research design that tested his claim against a number of rival hypotheses.

The logical empiricist might close out this critique by noting that Gaventa's use of a single-case-study research design has inherent limitations as a basis for causal inference. Gaventa does try to broaden his inferential base through comparative and historical methods, but the former are casual and unsystematic, and the latter are insufficient to rule out rival hypotheses (were they even considered). What is missing, in short, is any basis for establishing the existence of observable regularities between cause and effect, and without these we cannot have much confidence that what we think is causation is in fact causation. To generate such "constant conjunctions" would at the very least require a comparative case study in which cases were selected on the basis of

[57] *Ibid.*, p. 458.

the independent variable and, ideally, of course, many cases on which appropriate statistical operations could be performed.

Scientific realists and perhaps Gaventa himself would probably agree with the logical empiricist's warnings about rival hypotheses and case studies. Realists do not deny the possibility, even likelihood, of multiple causal mechanisms or the need to construct research designs that will rule out claims about some in order to heighten confidence about others. Realists also favor identifying empirical regularities as one kind of evidence for the existence of causal mechanisms. But they would remind social scientists working in open systems not to conflate regularities with mechanisms and, in particular, not to take the absence of regularities as decisive evidence against a proposed causal theory. Because they regard the primary task of science to be the description of how causal mechanisms work, realists tend to favor qualitative research methods, such as information-intensive case studies, that permit such description even if this means weakening the inferential base for considering rival hypotheses.[58]

So, there are good, logical empiricist reasons for skepticism about Gaventa's conclusions; moreover, given the kinds of questions about consent that he asked, there will probably always be such reasons. The issue is whether we should risk asking such questions anyway, using whatever techniques we can devise under the inferential circumstances to deal with rival hypotheses, or whether we should eschew them because we cannot hope to find the kinds of lawlike answers found in laboratory studies. Regarding science as question rather than method driven, realists respond in the affirmative and are willing, if necessary, to tolerate the persistent epistemic insecurity that this entails. Realists argue against the logical empiricist belief that without regularities we have nothing. This belief demands a level of epistemic guarantees that would foreclose most social inquiry and ignores the possibilities of using a variety of inferential techniques to adjudicate among competing knowledge claims even when such guarantees are absent. The empiricist's skepticism should be a source of ideas for improving on research designs such as Gaventa's in the future, not a reason to abandon his questions.

[58] On the interest of realists in case studies, see Sayer, *Method in Social Science*, pp. 211–34; and Alexander George and Timothy McKeown, "Case Studies and Theories of Organizational Decision Making," in R. Coulam and R. Smith, eds., *Advances in Information Processing in Organizations* (Greenwich, UK: JAI, 1985), pp. 21–58.

Even without empirical regularities that take all rival hypotheses into account, Gaventa's conclusions are comparatively persuasive. Two reasons for this shed light on the kinds of considerations that realists and many practicing social scientists take as evidence for the existence of putative causal mechanisms, and thus for the possibility of rational adjudication of knowledge claims within open systems. The first is that the evidence that Gaventa marshals conforms to many widely accepted assumptions about human behavior. It is scarcely counterintuitive to argue that politically disempowered and economically dispossessed people will become quiescent with repeated defeats in overt conflict and, conversely, rebel when given the chance. This conformity with preexisting assumptions is important because in the realist view, all observation is theory-laden to a degree. Scientists compare theories not with "the evidence" as empiricists claim but with alternative theories and background understandings about how the world works. Conformity of a theory with those understandings is never a sufficient reason to accept it, but a theory wildly at odds with them will inevitably bear a heavier burden of proof. Simply put, Gaventa tells an intuitively plausible causal story.

The second form of evidence in support of his claims is closer to being decisive. It concerns what happened when "interventions" occurred in the system of dominant-subordinate relations, first in the form of an externally induced weakening of corporate power in the early 1930s, and later, when a documentary on the Appalachian miners was made for British television in the early 1970s. The former prompted a violent but short-lived "rebellion" of the miners against the owners. Although not shown on American television, the documentary (which included numerous interviews with miners, poor farmers, and their families speaking freely about their political and economic situation) was widely distributed in videotaped form throughout Appalachia. It did not provoke armed rebellion, but in conjunction with ongoing efforts to organize the population, its discernible effects were almost immediate, altering perceptions of interest and helping to mobilize a population that had been politically quiescent for decades for collective action against corporate power. Although this collective action ultimately failed to produce the changes the miners sought, it did reinforce new perceptions of interest and was taken sufficiently seriously by local government and corporations that significant reforms were implemented.

Such instances of intervention considerably strengthen the plausibility of the counterfactual claim. Gaventa recognizes that this is vital to his case that the miners would not be quiescent in the absence of the causal mechanism of third-dimensional power, so that what might look to the behavioralist like "consent" was in fact an effect of power relations. A logical empiricist would probably dismiss the evidence for third-dimensional power from such interventions, arguing that absent systematic consideration of rival hypotheses, it does not "prove" anything. Realists, who seldom regard any single type of test as decisive, would resist this conclusion, arguing that it rests on unrealistic expectations about theory confirmation. For realists, ability to intervene successfully in the world is one argument to accept a theory; in this case, it reasonably buttresses Gaventa's conclusions.

CONCLUSION

Questions generate research domains. Sometimes, these domains are so complex that regularities are impossible to document, and the only way of testing claims about the presence of putative causal mechanisms is to remove them and see what happens. This raises normative questions about the conduct of science that cannot be escaped, as the discussion of intervention in the case of the Appalachian miners makes clear. Use of intervention as a criterion of theoretical success encourages (though it does not require) social scientists to build "critical" theories, that is, theories that can only be assessed by calling into question the institutional structures that generate the observable regularities of everyday society. The "problem," of course, is that this is a politically charged act that seems to violate the often stated goal of value neutrality in the conduct of social science. However, if we eschew intervention as a criterion of theory choice in favor of trying to find empirical regularities, we may limit social inquiry to "problem solving" theories that can only be used for the purpose of reproducing or perhaps reforming that order.[59] As Brian Fay made clear in his critique of logical positivism, this is no less a political stance than one premised on critical scrutiny of existing institutional structures.[60] All questions that social scientists might ask or decline to ask about society are political in the uses to

[59] The distinction between critical and problem-solving theories is offered by Robert Cox, "Social Forces, States and World Orders: Beyond International Relations Theory," in Robert Keohane, ed., *Neorealism and its Critics* (New York: Columbia University Press, 1986), pp. 204–54.

[60] Brian Fay, *Social Theory and Political Practice* (London: Allen & Unwin, 1975), pp. 18–69.

which their answers can be put. We do not presume to tell social scientists what questions to ask, only to encourage them not to adopt a philosophy of science that prevents certain questions from being considered at all.

The objective of our discussion was to explain why and how epistemological commitments should structure the practice of social inquiry as little as possible. A twofold argument was presented. On the one hand, we argued that the difference that realism makes is less than some of its proponents claim. Realism does not prevent social scientists from doing bad social science, it does not give them substantive conclusions about the structures of social life, and it certainly does not tell them whether they should be liberals, Gramscians, or Foucauldians about particular instances of consent. Realism is a philosophy of social science, not a theory of society. On the other hand, realism does undermine the philosophical justifications for the limiting conceptions of social scientific practice implied by logical empiricism and interpretivism. These doctrines impose a priori constraints on the kinds of questions that social scientists ask of social life and on the kinds of theories they are likely to entertain. The genuinely scientific study of consent must be open to the possibility that any theory about its nature might be true. The realist intervention in debates about epistemology in the social sciences is worthwhile for clearing away misleading constraints on social scientific practice, but it does not tell us what such practice should discover. That is a job for social scientists, not philosophers.

CHAPTER TWO

Revisiting the Pathologies of Rational Choice

Donald Green and Ian Shapiro

THE SOCIAL SCIENCES were founded amid high expectations about what could be learned through systematic study of human affairs, and perhaps as a result social scientists are periodically beset by intellectual crises. Each generation of scholars expresses disappointment with the rate at which knowledge accumulates and yearns for a new, more promising form of social science. The complexity of most social phenomena, the crudeness with which explanatory variables can be measured, and the inability to perform controlled experiments may severely constrain what *any* form of social science can deliver. Nevertheless, nostrums that seem to put social science on the same path as the natural and physical sciences have great appeal. One can scarcely attend an academic conference in the social sciences without hearing someone, young or old, wax eloquent about the need for more linguistic precision, analytic refinement, and rigorous theorizing.

Into the breach steps rational choice theory, the essence of which is that people maximize utility in formally specifiable ways. As we point out in *Pathologies of Rational Choice Theory,* variants of rational choice theory impose different assumptions about the sorts of utilities people maximize, the nature of the beliefs they possess, and the manner in which they acquire and process information.[1] All share in common, however, a concern with the existence and nature of equilibria resulting from strategic interaction. A given work of rational choice scholarship may be

---

[1] Donald Green and Ian Shapiro, *Pathologies of Rational Choice Theory: A Critique of Applications in Political Science* (New Haven: Yale University Press, 1994), pp. 17–30.

more or less formal in presentation, but its claims about social equilibria must in principle be deducible from a logic of instrumental behavior.

Only by dint of haute mathematiques snobbery or technical aversion could one fail to be impressed by the analytic achievements of rational choice theory in political science. Each passing year witnesses some new extension or refinement in what has become a vast web of interconnected logical propositions. To all appearances, this immense deductive system would seem to furnish the rigorous, cumulative theory that has long been the El Dorado of social science.

But what has this theoretical apparatus contributed to the stock of knowledge about politics? The central claim of our book is that very little has been learned by way of nonobvious propositions that withstand empirical scrutiny. One encounters arresting propositions that are not sustainable (e.g., that changes in collective incentives have little effect on rates of participation in large groups; or that majority rule engenders voting cycles over redistributive questions). And one encounters sustainable propositions that are not arresting (e.g., that rising selective incentives increase participation in collective action; or that supermajoritarian voting rules limit opportunities for policy change). But seldom does one encounter applications of rational choice theory that are at once arresting and sustainable.

It is customary for proponents of rational choice theory to meet this charge by shifting the burden of persuasion. They will defy the critic to show that rational behavior plays no role whatsoever in politics or, in the case of particular anomalies, to establish that no conceivable rational choice logic could account for the phenomenon in question. Neither rejoinder suffices to vindicate rational choice theory. Alternatively, defenders of rational choice theory will lay claim to intuitions that are widely shared by nonrational choice theorists, reminding us that behaviors like voting become less frequent as they become more costly. The idea that human action is to some degree price elastic, although important and empirically sustainable, nonetheless runs afoul of what Robyn Dawes calls the Grandmother Test: "Is the sustainable proposition one of which Robyn's grandmother is unaware?" As we noted in *Pathologies*, virtually all students of politics, past and present, harbor causal intuitions consistent with rational choice theory.[2] The question is whether the advent of rational choice scholarship has *added* to the existing stock of knowledge.

---

[2] *Ibid.*, p. 147.

Of course, as Bernard Grofman points out in an essay entitled "On the Gentle Art of Rational Choice Bashing," it is one thing to assert that little has been learned, another to build a case based on a careful inspection of existing literature.[3] We therefore set ourselves the task of reviewing what are widely regarded as the most well-developed and sophisticated literatures, those concerning mass collective action, legislative behavior, and party competition. These literatures contain many works that claim to furnish theoretically advanced and empirically supported propositions. But the vaunted reputation of rational choice applications fades when these works are subjected to the kind of close reading they receive in *Pathologies*.[4] After one cuts through the tendentious and uninformative empirical work, post-hoc theoretical embellishments, and clever attempts to sidestep discordant facts, what remains does not warrant the fanfare with which rational choice contributions are so often advertised.

One would hardly expect proponents of rational choice theory to accept this claim without putting up a fight, and a number of our critics allege that *Pathologies* fails to acknowledge legitimate empirical contributions. We respond to this charge, and its accompanying bill of particulars, in the next section. First we wish to reiterate that that, while contending that that rational choice has added little to the stock of nonobvious, empirically sustainable propositions about politics, our book did not address the extent to which traditional forms of political science have done so.[5] One of the most frequent reactions to our book among those with whom we have spoken is, "Why isn't this book *Pathologies of Social Science?* Why pick on rational choice?" The answer is

---

[3] Bernard Grofman, "On the Gentle Art of Rational Choice Bashing," in Bernard Grofman, ed., *Information, Participation and Choice* (Ann Arbor: University of Michigan Press, 1993).

[4] See Green and Shapiro, *Pathologies*, chs. 4–7.

[5] Diermeier proposes that we sample articles at random from leading journals in an effort to compare the quality of rational choice and other forms of political science. This research design changes the inquiry to, "What is the likelihood that a given RC article advanced our stock of knowledge, and how does this compare to the likelihoods for non-RC scholarship?" First, the evaluative criterion should properly be what has been learned in toto, not article-for-article efficiency. Second, literatures represent a more defensible sampling unit than articles. Besides leading to a critique that would have been scattered and disjointed, random sampling of articles along the lines he suggests would surely have opened us to the charge that we had managed to miss the best work. As it happens, despite Diermeier's qualms about our literature review, he does not believe rational choice to be "empirically more successful than the collection of mutually inconsistent middle-level approaches that had dominated political science before the advent of rational choice theory." See Daniel Diermeier, "Rational Choice and the Role of Theory in Political Science," *Critical Review: An Interdisciplinary Journal of Politics and Society,* Vol. 9, Nos. 1–2 (Winter/ Spring 1995), p. 68.

twofold. It is our impression, first, that traditional research in political science, although often trivial, uninspired, and ill-conceived, is more flatfooted than tendentious. Examples of the kinds of theory-saving biases described in chapter 3 of *Pathologies* can be found in traditional political science, but for the most part its shortcomings are what we describe as pedestrian.[6] Tellingly, pathological research tends to turn up in precincts of political science inhabited by those who cling to theories comparable in scope and ambition to rational choice theory: classical Marxism, elite theory, systems theory, structural-functionalism, and the like. Second, traditional political science, for all its defects, is not similarly bereft of empirical accomplishments. Key's encyclopedic account of how the racial hierarchy of the South shaped its political institutions, Stouffer's pathbreaking demonstration that intolerance of socialists and communists had more to do with insulation from cosmopolitan ideas than fears concerning the threats posed by international communism, the account by Campbell et al. of the central role that social-psychological attachments play in shaping political perceptions and evaluations represent but a small sample of the works unknown to the growing cadre of political scientists who lack graduate or undergraduate degrees in political science.[7] *Pathologies* does not purport to contrast the accomplishments of rational choice and traditional political science, but that should not be taken to mean that we believe no contrast exists.

What explains the gap between rational choice theory's formidable analytic advances and its lackluster empirical applications? Our view is that empirical progress has been retarded by what may be termed method-driven, as opposed to problem-driven research. Rather than ask "What causes X?" method-driven research begins with the question "How might my preferred theoretical or methodological approach account for X?" Framing the research endeavor in this way sets in motion the methodological biases to which *Pathologies* calls attention, such as the tendency to ignore alternative explanations, make slippery predictions, or dwell on confirming illustrations.

The method-driven proclivities of rational choice scholars may, in turn, be accounted for by their universalistic aspirations: to construct a unified, deductively-based theory from which propositions about politics—or, indeed, all human behavior—may be derived. One of our

---

[6] Green and Shapiro, *Pathologies*, p. 33.

[7] V. O. Key, *Southern Politics in State and Nation* (New York: Knopf, 1949); Samuel Andrew Stouffer, *Communism, Conformity, and Civil Liberties* (Garden City, NY: Doubleday, 1955); Angus

central objections to the way in which rational choice is applied in political science concerns its proponents' drive to show that *some* variant of rational choice theory can accommodate every fact, an impulse that is not accompanied by an equally strong drive to test the proposed account against new evidence. The rational choice approach inspires great commitment among its adherents, and too often this leads to scientific practices seemingly designed to insulate rational choice theories from untoward encounters with evidence.

Our book ascribes the methodological deficiencies of rational choice scholarship to universalism and the method-driven science it engenders, but an abundant supply of alternative hypotheses exist. Flawed empirical research could be the product of inadequate training: unfamiliarity with the principles of research methodology, insufficient knowledge of the day-to-day workings of politics, or lack of exposure to nonrational choice literatures and explanations. Alternatively, one could attribute the empirical track record of rational choice theory to problems more basic than methodological miscues. It could be that the psychology of choice presupposed by rational choice models cannot adequately characterize decision making within a political context. It could be that strategic interaction of the sort found in politics gives rise to multiple equilibria and that rational choice theory will remain at an impasse until these theoretical indeterminacies are worked out. It could be that the laws that govern human conduct do not accord with the rules of deductive logic.

None of these hypotheses can be ruled out a priori, and only time will tell whether our diagnosis stands up. Ours is an optimistic view. We do not suppose that every rational choice proposition is doomed to fail, nor do we regard the methodological deficiencies we identify as inevitable features of rational choice theorizing. Furthermore, we believe that applied scholarship can be improved in the short run by greater attentiveness to the methodological concerns we raise. The long-term question is whether these problems can be corrected without attending to what we suppose to be the root cause: the tenacious *commitment* rational choice theorists seem to have to their preferred method of political analysis. Some of our critics assure us that universalism is less evident among younger generations of rational choice scholars, who are doing correspondingly better empirical work. This

Campbell, Philip Converse, Warren Miller, and Donald Stokes, *The American Voter* (New York: John Wiley & Sons, 1960).

upward trajectory would be consistent with our thesis, and we hope it continues. By contrast, if we should look back twenty years hence only to discover that little had been learned despite the move away from universalism, we would conclude that the causes of failure run deeper than we supposed.

This chapter is structured as follows. After responding in detail to the charge that *Pathologies* fails to acknowledge important empirical achievements of rational choice scholarship, we rebut the charges put forward by Susanne Lohmann, Morris Fiorina, Michael Taylor, and Dennis Chong that we get the rational choice literature on collective action wrong in ways that lead us to undervalue its theoretical and empirical achievements. Next we meet the charge that our ignorance of "modern philosophy of science" causes us to criticize unfairly the achievements of rational choice scholarship.[8] We respond that neither Imre Lakatos nor Thomas Kuhn supplies the conceptual resources to salvage the rational choice enterprise as it is construed by our critics who appeal to their views. Then we revisit the distinction between problem-driven and method-driven research in the course of responding to various criticisms of what we say about universalism in *Pathologies*. Building on our earlier discussions of partial and segmented universalism, as well as useful points made by some of our critics, we describe five types of domain restriction that, we hypothesize, are likely to delimit the range of successful rational choice applications. Then we briefly take up Peter Ordeshook's call for an engineering-based conception of political science. We hesitate to follow his advice, which in any case begs important questions that are thrown into sharp relief by discussion of the effects of rational choice experimental research on the subjects studied. In a concluding section we sum up the reasons for our conviction that advances in political science should be expected to come at the level of the hypothesis or the middle-level generalization rather than that of the architectonic theory or paradigm.

WHAT HAS BEEN LEARNED?

A basic objection to our argument is that, through oversight or thick-headedness, we fail to acknowledge the legitimate empirical accomplishments of rational choice scholarship in political science. As against

---

[8] Diermeier, "Rational Choice and the Role of Theory," p. 60.

our claim that little has been learned from rational choice theorizing that is both nonobvious and empirically sustainable, a number of our critics praise a list of rational choice applications or at least wave approvingly in the direction of certain literatures. Our critics tend not to spell out precisely what has been learned from the works they laud.[9] Indeed, they at times seem satisfied merely to call attention to the existence of empirical research, without commenting on its quality.[10] Nevertheless, upon reading a dozen or so references to putative accomplishments, the fairminded reader might well begin to wonder whether *Pathologies* gave short shrift to a body of carefully executed empirical work grounded in formal analysis of instrumental behavior.

This impression is quickly dispelled once the elements of this body of work are evaluated seriatim. Although they may be said to include empirically sound, substantively significant, and formally rigorous applications of rational choice theory, no one piece of scholarship meets all of these criteria. Consider first Donald Horowitz's *A Democratic South Africa?*, which Ordeshook praises as an exception to the rule that rational choice scholarship tends to be empirically uninformative.[11]

---

[9] Fiorina, for example, refers to Norman Frolich, Joseph Oppenheimer, and Oran Young, *Political Leadership and Collective Goods* (Princeton: Princeton University Press, 1971); Terry Moe, *The Organization of Interests* (Chicago: University of Chicago Press, 1980); Jack L. Walker Jr., *Mobilizing Interest Groups in America* (Ann Arbor: University of Michigan Press, 1991). Frohlich et al. are instances in which scholars were led to "think harder about the importance of leadership or entrepreneurship in the formation of groups" in the wake of Mancur Olson Jr., *The Logic of Collective Action* (Cambridge, MA: Harvard University Press, 1971 [1965]). See Morris P. Fiorina, "Rational Choice, Empirical Contributions, and the Scientific Enterprise," *Critical Review: An Interdisciplinary Journal of Politics and Society*, Vol. 9, Nos. 1–2 (Winter/Spring 1995), p. 91. Daniel Diermeier chides us for failing to discuss James M. Snyder Jr., "Campaign Contributions as Investments: The U.S. House of Representatives, 1980–1986," *Journal of Political Economy*, Vol. 98, No. 6 (December 1990), pp. 1195–227 and "On Buying Legislatures," *Economics and Politics*, Vol. 3, No. 2 (July 1991), pp. 93–109, which he describes only as "important." See Diermeier, "Rational Choice and the Role of Theory," p. 68, note 12. The prize for the most opaque reference goes to Kenneth Shepsle, who questions why we did not discuss "the continuing series of books by Paul Abramson, John Aldrich, and David Rohde on change and continuity in elections." Kenneth A. Shepsle, "Statistical Political Philosophy and Positive Political Theory," *Critical Review: An Interdisciplinary Journal of Politics and Society*, Vol. 9, Nos. 1–2 (Winter/Spring 1995), pp. 216, n. 5.

[10] See Norman Schofield, "Rational Choice and Political Economy," *Critical Review: An Interdisciplinary Journal of Politics and Society*, Vol. 9, Nos. 1–2 (Winter/Spring 1995), p. 194, n. 10, and p. 195, n. 12; Susanne Lohmann, "The Poverty of Green and Shapiro," *Critical Review: An Interdisciplinary Journal of Politics and Society*, Vol. 9, Nos. 1–2 (Winter/Spring 1995), pp. 127–54. This is not to mention the converse tactic of applauding findings that are unobservable for the reason that they do not yet exist in print (e.g., Schofield, "Rational Choice and Political Economy," p. 204, n. 20; Fiorina, "Rational Choice, Empirical Contributions," pp. 85–94).

[11] Donald Horowitz, *A Democratic South Africa?* (Berkeley: University of California Press, 1991); Peter C. Ordeshook, "Engineering or Science: What is the Study of Politics?" *Critical*

Like Ordeshook, we think this an excellent book, but it contains no empirical test of any theory (nor does it purport to), and in any case Horowitz's is not a rational choice argument (nor does it purport to be). True, he believes that the design of electoral systems should be based on the assumption that aspiring politicians will try to win elections. No minimally literate political scientist would ever have suggested differently, and if that were Horowitz's contribution, it would run afoul of the Grandmother Test. But it is not. On the contrary, his contribution is to propose an electoral system for South Africa premised on the idea that variables other than the strategic calculations of politicians, most important the depth of ethnic antipathies, determine the viability of electoral institutions.[12] Whether or not Horowitz is right about South Africa, his argument does not draw discernibly upon the insights of rational choice theory.

By the same token, Jane Mansbridge's analysis of the campaigns for and against the Equal Rights Amendment, which Fiorina regards as an insightful application of Mancur Olson's *Logic of Collective Action*, can only with some imagination be called a piece of rational choice scholarship.[13] Granted, Mansbridge prefaces her discussion by arguing that the logic of collective action may explain why involvement in these campaigns tended to be sporadic and largely the province of those with deep ideological commitments. But this thought is neither the subject of empirical analysis nor central to the thrust of Mansbridge's argument, which is that the pro-ERA movement lost as a result of lapses in leadership, tactical problems in coordinating a divisive coalition of backers, and the difficulty of formulating persuasive reasons why lawmakers should back the amendment. Why one mass movement should lose to another in this instance cannot readily be explained by reference to Olson, particularly since these two groups did

---

Review: An Interdisciplinary Journal of Politics and Society, Vol. 9, Nos. 1–2 (Winter/Spring 1995), p. 176.

[12] Specifically, Horowitz thinks that winner-take-all electoral systems that might be expected to work in pluralist political cultures (in which cleavages are cross-cutting) will not work in "deeply divided" cultures such as he takes South Africa's to be, and he proposes a different system that is designed to take account of the ethnic divisions there.

[13] By citing this work, Fiorina attempts to catch us coming and going. At one point he takes us to task for criticizing the work of Carole Uhlaner (who attempts to apply rational choice propositions) on the grounds that she is not a rational choice theorist. However, here he takes us to task for not taking up the work of Jane Mansbridge, who is no more a rational choice theorist than Uhlaner. See Fiorina, "Rational Choice, Empirical Contributions," pp. 91 and 87, nn. 3 and 91. See also Jane J. Mansbridge, *Why We Lost the ERA* (Chicago: University of Chicago Press, 1986), ch. 10; Olson, *Logic of Collective Action.*

not, by Mansbridge's account, differ appreciably with regard to selective incentives. Like Horowitz, Mansbridge makes no attempt to link the relevant actors' tastes, beliefs, and strategic options to game-theoretic propositions. Indeed, passages in which Mansbridge highlights the strategic blunders that resulted from ideological rigidity and self-deception lead one to question whether she regards political behavior as the product of utility maximization.[14]

William Riker's *Liberalism Against Populism* is at least billed by its author as an application of rational choice theory.[15] Ordeshook calls this work a "discussion of populist democracy [that] provides both a warning about naive political 'reforms' and insights into the practical side of social choice theory."[16] The empirical basis for Riker's "warning" is a collection of historical narratives about the cycle-prone and manipulated character of majoritarian politics. As we document at some length in *Pathologies*, however, these narratives are not only tendentious but fraught with factual inaccuracies.[17] Ordeshook makes no mention of these difficulties. If Riker is an example of the empirical successes of rational choice theory, one shudders to think of what Ordeshook would regard as its failures.

A self-conscious attempt to apply rational choice analysis to American politics not discussed in *Pathologies* is Fiorina's memorable work, *Retrospective Voting in American National Elections*.[18] Shepsle wonders why we fail to discuss this justly acclaimed book, implying that we tiptoe around an uncomfortable example of an empirical success. Apart from the fact that the subject matter of Fiorina's book—the effects of retrospective performance evaluations on electoral choice and partisan identification—is tangential to the three broad literatures we review, our reasons are twofold.[19] First, it is unclear whether Fiorina's is a rational choice model. Fiorina himself seems at times apologetic about the

---

[14] Mansbridge, *Why We Lost the ERA*, pp. 136–37.

[15] William H. Riker, *Liberalism Against Populism* (San Francisco: Freeman, 1982).

[16] Ordeshook, "Engineering or Science," p. 176.

[17] Green and Shapiro, *Pathologies*, pp. 44, 107–13.

[18] Shepsle, "Statistical Political Philosophy;" Morris P. Fiorina, *Retrospective Voting in American National Elections* (New Haven: Yale University Press, 1981).

[19] There is some disagreement among rational choice theorists about the theoretical coherence of propositions about electoral choice, be they Fiorina's claims about retrospective voting or Ordeshook's assertions about strategic voting in multi-candidate elections. As Ferejohn and Fiorina point out, it is unclear how rational actors should choose among candidates when their ballots have no plausible chance of influencing the election outcome. See John Ferejohn and Morris Fiorina, "To P or Not to P? Still Asking After All These Years," manuscript (Stanford, CA: Stanford University Press, 1993).

ways in which his model departs from what he calls "rational choice, narrowly interpreted," conceding that "whether or not the model is rational, it is realistic" and "if not completely 'rational,' the model at least attempts to be highly reasonable."[20] Second, without in any way denying the extent to which Fiorina's work contributed to conceptual debates, introduced methodological innovations and stimulated subsequent empirical inquiry, his central empirical claim has not, in our view, survived subsequent challenges. As against the social-psychological perspectives on partisanship and voting behavior advanced in the *American Voter*, Fiorina claims to have provided "a great deal of evidence on the side of voter rationality," noting that "undoubtedly, the most important set of findings concerns the accommodation of a voter's party identification to political reality."[21] Elsewhere Green and Palmquist and Green have called into question the empirical basis for the claim that party identification represents a running tally of retrospective performance evaluations, and we did not see the point in rehashing the arcane statistical issues that form the basis of that critique in *Pathologies*.[22] The bottom line is that traditional accounts of partisanship seem to fare better empirically than the one offered by Fiorina.

Like Fiorina's analysis of survey data, Elinor Ostrom's discussion of how a variety of small communities have dealt with common-pool resource problems is thoughtful and engaging.[23] This work, which draws praise from Ordeshook and Fiorina, is largely an inductive empirical inquiry into the conditions under which people can "organize and govern themselves to obtain continuing joint benefits when all face temptations to free-ride, shirk, or otherwise act opportunistically."[24] Ostrom uses her collection of case studies to identify a set of "design principles," or "essential elements or conditions that help to account for the success of these institutions in sustaining [common-pool resources] and gaining the compliance of generation after generation of appropriators to

[20] Fiorina, *Retrospective Voting*, pp. 77, 78.

[21] *Ibid.*, p. 199. See also Campbell et al., *American Voter*.

[22] Donald Philip Green and Bradley L. Palmquist, "Of Artifacts and Partisan Instability," *American Journal of Political Science*, Vol. 34, No. 3 (August 1990), pp. 872–902; Donald Philip Green, "The Effects of Measurement Error on Two-Stage Least-Squares Estimates," *Political Analysis*, Vol. 2 (1990), pp. 57–74.

[23] Elinor Ostrom, *Governing the Commons: The Evolution of Institutions for Collective Action* (Cambridge: Cambridge University Press, 1990).

[24] Ordeshook, "Engineering or Science," p. 176; Fiorina, *Retrospective Voting*, p. 91; Ostrom, *Governing the Commons*, p. 29.

the rules in use."[25] This exploratory approach seems a sensible way to develop hypotheses; indeed, it illustrates the kind of close-to-the-ground theorizing that we advocate in *Pathologies*. But what is the connection with rational choice theory? Are rational choice hypotheses tested and shown to be persuasive? To be sure, the inquiry is inspired by longstanding theoretical interest in the so-called tragedy of the commons and in the logic of collective action, yet the connection between the resulting "framework" of eight design principles and rational choice theory is tenuous. In this vein, Paul Sabatier notes that certain key components of Ostrom's analysis correspond more closely to functional than rational choice analysis, whereas Taylor takes Ostrom to task for relying on an informal analysis that makes no use of recent currents in game theory.[26] As for hypothesis testing, Ostrom herself balks at the idea of calling her design principles causes of successful resource management, a reluctance that seems fitting on conceptual grounds and in light of the inductive manner in which these principles were derived.[27] Whatever its merits, this work cannot be regarded as a successful test of empirical propositions derived from rational choice theory.[28]

Ostrom's subject matter is rather exotic by the standards of American political science. Kiewiet and McCubbins, Cox and McCubbins, and Krehbiel, by contrast, apply rational choice theories to the U.S. Congress.[29] We discussed these works at length in *Pathologies*, characterizing them as praiseworthy attempts to theorize in closer proximity to data.[30]

---

[25] Ostrom, *Governing the Commons*, p. 90.

[26] Paul A. Sabatier, review of *Governing the Commons*, *American Political Science Review*, Vol. 86, No. 1 (March 1992), pp. 248–9; Michael Taylor, review of *Governing the Commons*, *Natural Resources Journal*, Vol. 32 (1992), pp. 633–48.

[27] Ostrom, *Governing the Commons*, p. 90.

[28] Like Ostrom, Steven Brams is interested in the crafting of institutions, in this case voting rules. He argues on behalf of a system of "approval voting" based on a formal analysis suggesting that this voting rule encourages voters to cast "sincere" ballots. The empirical question concerns the extent to which voters in fact respond to these incentives. Brams, to his credit, has made a concerted effort to engage this question but has to date been hampered by the dearth of approval voting systems currently in place at the national and subnational level. It remains to be seen, therefore, whether Brams's work will precipitate an "advance [in] our understanding of electoral systems," as Ordeshook contends. See Steven Brams, "Approval Voting in Multicandidate Elections," *Policy Studies Journal*, Vol. 9, No. 1 (Autumn 1980), pp. 102–8; Ordeshook, "Engineering or Science," p. 176.

[29] Roderick D. Kiewiet and Matthew D. McCubbins, *The Logic of Delegation* (Chicago: University of Chicago Press, 1991); Gary Cox and Mathew McCubbins, *Legislative Leviathan* (Berkeley: University of California Press, 1993); Keith Krehbiel, *Information and Legislative Organization* (Ann Arbor: University of Michigan Press, 1991).

[30] Green and Shapiro, *Pathologies*, pp. 134, 197–202.

Although these works are well-informed and innovative, their (informal) models of congressional politics exhibit certain basic theoretical flaws, and the central hypotheses they generate do not make a strong showing empirically. Nonetheless, Shepsle lavishes praise on these works, applauding the way in which they combine "extremely sophisticated theory" with "equally sophisticated empirical examination."[31] Yet Shepsle neither tells us what has been learned from these works nor grapples with the specific criticisms we advance. The careful reader will have noted that, like Shepsle, neither Fiorina nor Daniel Diermeier—who also praise these works—explain why they find their central arguments persuasive. A different approach is taken by Ferejohn and Satz, who do not dispute our empirical evaluation of these works but try to circumvent it by arguing that they offer *interpretive* insights:

> A wide range of congressional actions can be understood as instances of underlying general causal mechanisms. Even if none of these studies had provided an improved statistical account of any specific behavioral phenomenon, they would remain outstanding additions to our understanding of congressional behavior and organization.[32]

To be sure, congressional behavior *can* be understood in terms of utility maximization. But why should we believe this particular interpretation?

We come finally to three venerable pieces of congressional scholarship by Richard Fenno, David Mayhew, and Lawrence Dodd. They resemble rational choice scholarship insofar as they interpret congressional politics by reference to the ways in which purposive actors negotiate their strategic environments.[33] Notice, however, that they contain no theorems, no game-theoretic models, and no formal exposition of any kind. The contrast between the Spartan stylizations of contemporary rational choice scholarship (e.g., Baron and Ferejohn; Weingast

---

[31] Fiorina seems equally enthusiastic but does not spell out what has been learned from these works. Drawing instead on what would appear to be the labor theory of value, Fiorina exclaims: "Who in the legislative subfield has put together a wider array of data on the Congressional Parties than RC scholars Cox and McCubbins, and who in the legislative subfield is a more painstaking empirical worker than RC scholar Keith Krehbiel?" See Shepsle, "Statistical Political Philosophy," p. 218; Fiorina, "Rational Choice, Empirical Contributions," p. 93.

[32] John Ferejohn and Debra Satz, "Unification, Universalism, and Rational Choice Theory," *Critical Review: An Interdisciplinary Journal of Politics and Society*, Vol. 9, Nos. 1–2 (Winter/Spring 1995), p. 76.

[33] Richard F. Fenno Jr., *Congressmen in Committees* (Boston: Little, Brown, 1973); David Mayhew, *Congress: The Electoral Connection* (New Haven: Yale University Press, 1974); Lawrence C.

and Marshall) and the descriptive richness of *Congressmen and Committees* and *Congress: The Electoral Connection* calls to mind Ordeshook's Dilemma: "comprehensive models that treat the full complexity of politics will necessarily require long strings of ad-hoc assumptions and qualitative analysis. If we try to maintain deductive rigor, the requirements of tractability will draw us away from comprehensive reasoning."[34] It is doubtful that even the most technically proficient rational choice theorists could fashion a formal rendering of Dodd's oscillating equilibria of legislative-executive balance, Mayhew's depiction of multifaceted and continually evolving reelection strategies, or Fenno's account of how reelection-influenced policy seekers come to adhere to the endogenous and often self-contradictory "strategic premises" of the committees on which they sit. To frame these works as examples of rational choice is to abandon the very features of rational choice scholarship—parsimony, formal precision, deductive rigor—that are so often touted as its principal selling points.

Two conclusions emerge from this brief review of the successes our critics attribute to rational choice theory. First, one cannot but be impressed by the paucity of sustainable empirical analysis flowing from rational choice theory, particularly in relation to the vast corpus of analytic rational choice scholarship that has developed over the past three decades. That our critics should have to resort to examples such as Mansbridge and Horowitz attests to the dearth of empirical accomplishment; all the more so, references to Fenno and Mayhew which antedate many of the most important analytic developments within rational choice theory. And, of course, it is far from clear that these authors would characterize their own work as examples of rational choice. Like patients undergoing psychoanalysis, these authors would have to learn that they harbor rational choice proclivities of which they are unaware.[35]

Dodd, "Congress and the Quest for Power," in Lawrence C. Dodd and Bruce I. Oppehheimer, eds., *Congress Reconsidered* (New York: Praeger, 1977).

[34] David P. Baron and John Ferejohn, "Bargaining in Legislatures," *American Political Science Review*, Vol. 83, No. 4 (December 1989), pp. 1181–206; Barry Weingast and William Marshall, "The Industrial Organization of Congress; or, Why Legislatures, Like Firms, Are Not Organized as Markets," *Journal of Political Economy*, Vol. 96, No. 1 (February 1988), pp. 132–63; Ordeshook, "Engineering or Science," p. 180.

[35] On reading Satz and Ferejohn, one might add Jim Scott to the list of scholars alleged to be suffering from this particular disorder. See Debra Satz and John Ferejohn, "Rational Choice and Social Theory," *Journal of Philosophy*, Vol. 91, No. 1 (February 1994), pp. 71–87, 80.

Second, the list of exemplars contains no instances in which rigorous formal modeling combines with careful and insightful empirical work. On the contrary, the handful of empirical successes that turn up tend to exhibit weak connections, at best, with rational choice theory. It is no small irony that after one peels away the claims that are made on behalf of the formal precision and theoretical depth of rational choice analysis, the putative accomplishments turn out to be works like Dodd's or Ostrom's. We regret that rational choice scholars have not aspired to produce the sort of meticulously researched, inductively-based political science characteristic of Fenno or Mayhew. Had they done so, there would have been no need to write *Pathologies*.

What of Fiorina's charge, echoed by Diermeier, that our standards for evaluating scholarship are so stringent that even works like *Congressmen in Committees* cannot meet them?

> Fenno's book is highly empirical, but it is not based on random samples of committees or members, contains no multivariate equations or even significance tests, and doesn't explicitly consider and reject alternative explanations. Moreover, the theoretical account is built on the same data that it is used to explain. By the standards used in *Pathologies*, it is pretty clear that Fenno's study makes no empirical contribution.[36]

Only a superficial reading of both books can sustain this conclusion. The main empirical contribution of Fenno's work is to establish an empirical connection between the dispositions of members and the character of the committees on which they serve. It is not necessary to draw a random sample in order to sustain this claim. And far from failing to consider alternatives, Fenno grapples repeatedly with the issue of whether committee differences may be attributable to policy content, rather than goals, norms, and external environment. It is true that Fenno derives his hypotheses inductively, and he is careful to point out that the transformations afoot at the time of his writing will subject his analysis to a more demanding test.[37]

Nor would we take Fenno to task for conducting qualitative research or failing to conduct statistical tests. Both Fiorina and Shepsle seem to believe that we advocate the exclusive use of quantitative methods in political science, despite the fact that this view is nowhere expressed in

---

[36] Fiorina, "Rational Choice, Empirical Contributions," p. 90.
[37] Fenno, *Congressmen in Committees*, pp. 280–81.

Pathologies.[38] Our objection to method-driven political science extends to categorical recommendations of quantitative over qualitative methods. Some political phenomena will be more amenable to statistical analysis than others, and the decision of how to study politics should follow the choice of which problem to study. Like Fiorina and Shepsle, we sense that method-driven insistence on the use of quantitative techniques leads to inferior political science. Our injunction is that empirical research in political science be systematic, whether the mode of inquiry be ethnographic or statistical. At a minimum, systematic inquiry requires attentiveness to the manner in which cases are selected, constructs measured, and inferences drawn.[39]

COLLECTIVE ACTION

We cannot be said to be in a position to evaluate rational choice scholarship if we fail to understand rational choice theory or appreciate its implications for collective action in politics. This charge, advanced in various forms by Lohmann, Taylor, and Chong, is directed at chapters 4 and 5 of *Pathologies*, which address the adequacy of rational choice explanations of mass political participation. The premise of these chapters is as follows. Each year millions of Americans are asked to contribute money to political parties, candidates, or interest groups. Millions are invited to participate in the policy-making process at some level, whether by attending city council meetings, contacting elected officials, or voting. And, in a given year, large numbers of people engage in one or more such forms of collective action.[40] Doubtless, some proportion

[38] Fiorina, "Rational Choice, Empirical Contributions," p. 90; Shepsle, "Statistical Political Philosophy," p. 214.

[39] We should perhaps mention Robert Lane and James Murphy, both of whom implicitly criticize us on the "What Has Been Learned?" question for failing, as a result of restricting ourselves to political science, to discover that even less has been learned than we claim. As we say in *Pathologies*, we are agnostic about this matter, though it should be plain from our discussion below that we think it is the type of problem under study, rather than anything to do with disciplinary divisions, that determines what sort of explanations are appropriate. In economics no less than in politics, rational choice explanations should be expected to do better in some circumstance than others. See Robert E. Lane, "What Rational Choice Explains," *Critical Review: An Interdisciplinary Journal of Politics and Society*, Vol. 9, Nos. 1–2 (Winter/Spring 1995), pp. 107–26; James Bernard Murphy, "Rational Choice Theory as Social Physics," *Critical Review: An Interdisciplinary Journal of Politics and Society*, Vol. 9, Nos. 1–2 (Winter/Spring 1995), pp. 155–74; Green and Shapiro, *Pathologies*, pp. 179–80.

[40] Steven J. Rosenstone and John Mark Hansen, *Mobilization, Participation, and Democracy in America* (New York: Macmillan, 1993), pp. 42, 51.

of those considering whether to devote time or money find political participation exciting or personally rewarding. A larger proportion, one suspects, regard hours spent attending meetings or dollars given away to political causes as a sacrifice, in the sense that they can easily imagine more gratifying uses for this time and money.

The challenge of creating and sustaining voluntary public participation in democratic institutions has long been a concern among political philosophers. More than a century before Anthony Downs, Hegel predicted the collapse of voter turnout in large democracies, where no individual's ballot is likely to make a difference.[41] Rational choice theorists such as Mancur Olson extended this logic to a wide variety of situations in which large groups of people are asked to make sacrifices for collective causes but have only a vanishingly small probability of making a pivotal contribution.[42] As Chong explains:

> Instead of assuming, as in earlier group theories, that individuals will naturally take action that is in their collective interest, rational choice theory implied that, paradoxically, individuals will refrain from contributing even if they stand to benefit from the collective good. Since people can potentially receive the benefits of such goods without paying for them, they will not readily contribute to their provision.[43]

An equally arresting implication is that in large groups potential participants cannot be stirred to action by blandishments that take the form of collective incentives; only incentives that flow solely to those who participate are predicted to work.

As game theory has become increasingly sophisticated, this underlying argument has been embellished in ways that take into account repeated interaction over time, various beliefs about the expected behavior of others, and so forth. From an analytic standpoint, Fiorina might be right to assert that "The working out of the prisoner's dilemma/ collective action logic has as strong a claim as any to being the most important political science contribution of the twentieth century."[44] But

---

[41] G.W.F. Hegel, *Philosophy of Right*, T. M. Knox, trans. (Oxford University Press, 1942 [1821]).

[42] Granted, the probability that one will cast the decisive vote in a national election, alter the course of history through one's participation in a mass demonstration, or tip the scales in a policy dispute through one's volunteer work on behalf of a political cause is not precisely zero. The odds, however, are long—arguably longer than the odds of sustaining injury or financial loss as a result of one's political involvement.

[43] Dennis Chong, "Rational Choice Theory's Mysterious Rivals," *Critical Review: An Interdisciplinary Journal of Politics and Society*, Vol. 9, Nos. 1–2 (Winter/Spring 1995), p. 40.

[44] Fiorina, "Rational Choice, Empirical Contributions," p. 90.

as an empirical matter, rational choice theorists have been unable to resolve a broad array of anomalies without reformulating rational choice propositions in ways that make them empirically banal. The conclusion we draw in *Pathologies* is that rational choice models of collective action have yet to deliver nonobvious, empirically sustainable predictions. This conclusion does not sit well with some of our critics.[45]

Paradox? What Paradox?

As may be inferred from the title of her critique Lohmann objects strenuously to our discussion of rational choice models of voter turnout and collective action. The central objective of her essay is to dispel the impression that rational choice theory is incapable of accounting for high levels of political participation by showing that it is *logically possible* to craft models that make this prediction. Lohmann believes that demonstrating the existence of just one such model—regardless of how ludicrous its underlying assumptions—enables her to pronounce high levels of collective action "qualitatively consistent" with rational choice theory. This gambit culminates in a series of snappy rejoinders: we do not understand rational choice theory; we present a logically flawed account of collective action; we foolishly render examples of anomalies that are in fact consistent with some variant of rational choice theory.

We do not deny for a moment that it is logically possible to formulate a rational choice model that implies large-scale collective action among self-interested actors. *Pathologies* summarizes an assortment of such models. Some presuppose that citizens engage in collective action because they each expect to cast the decisive vote in a national election or throw the decisive fist in the air during a political demonstration; others, that citizens are enticed or blackmailed into political participation by local officials, interest groups, or nosy neighbors.[46] And this by no means exhausts the range of logical possibilities. The constraints of logic in no way prevent one from imputing to voters the belief that failure to engage in political participation will dislodge the earth from its orbit. We cannot be criticized for failing to recognize that *some* rational choice model can be constructed to explain mass collective

---

[45] Green and Shapiro, *Pathologies*, pp. 47–97.
[46] See Lohmann, "The Poverty," p. 146.

action, as well as every other form of human conduct; no one appreciates more than we the rational choice theorist's capacity for mercurial theoretical invention.

The question is whether to take seriously any proposed model that rests on preposterous assumptions, such as the notion that each eligible voter possesses complete information about the tastes and beliefs of the rest of the electorate. As Lohmann herself concedes, "under incomplete information, voter turnout is vanishingly low if the electorate is large," and since "incomplete information about voter preferences or voting costs is a closer approximation to reality than is the complete information assumption," this result trumps the very models she lays out.[47] In the end, her survey has done nothing more than to "establish the empirical irrelevance of rational choice theory (defined narrowly as a theory that does not allow for noninstrumental motivations) as an explanation of high voter turnout."[48] Notwithstanding the sharp rhetoric that infuses her essay, the bottom line to Lohmann's exegesis of formal theories of collective action is the same as ours: rational choice models that account for high levels of mass participation strain credulity.

The refrain throughout Lohmann's essay is the *logical* error of likening problems of collective action to an n-person prisoner's dilemma. Analogies of this sort are variously denounced as "erroneous" or "false," as though the proper way to model an empirical phenomenon were an analytic rather than synthetic question. "Many rational choice theorists share the view that rational choice theory predicts no voluntary contributions to public goods," Lohmann reminds us, "But this only demonstrates that rational choice scholars can be wrong about their theory. What rational choice theory implies is a matter of logic, not of what claims well-known political scientists at high-status research departments have made in leading political science journals."[49] It should be obvious that this claim begs the question of what substantive premises will undergird rational choice logic. Modeling social phenomena inevitably means focusing attention on certain causal factors rather than others. The question of which factors go farthest in explaining the phenomenon under study is an empirical one. Why should a model that fails to incorporate any number of plausible influences upon the

[47] *Ibid.*, p. 146.
[48] *Ibid.*, p. 146.
[49] *Ibid.*, p. 138.

turnout decision necessarily concern itself with the tiny existential possibility that a voter could cast the decisive ballot in a national election?[50]

Lohmann avoids entirely the issue of how to achieve verisimilitude between rational choice models and actual cases of collective action. Each of the examples she supplies is artificial and concededly unrealistic.[51] And rather than take up any of the real instances of political action described in *Pathologies*, Lohmann dwells instead on an ancient fable that we use to introduce chapter 5.[52] The only point during which Lohmann's essay intersects with planet earth occurs when she takes up some of the experimental evidence we discuss in that chapter. But there, Lohmann offers up a series of misinterpretations that can only be ascribed to the pathology we dub "projecting evidence from theory."

First, Lohmann charges that we draw the "false conclusion" that experimental evidence of prosocial behavior is at variance with rational choice theory due to our "erroneous belief that defection is necessarily a dominant strategy on the part of rational, self-interested individuals in a collective dilemma."[53] So determined is Lohmann to emphasize the rational choice insight that cooperation may be a rational strategy when players have the potential to make a pivotal contribution, she fails to realize that the conclusions we draw are supported by evidence from experiments in which, *by design, each player has no opportunity whatsoever to make a pivotal contribution*.[54] The fact that defection constitutes a

[50] To put it another way, why should "logic" necessarily dictate an analogy between voter turnout and contributions to a collective cause? One could liken political participation instead to rooting for sports teams or to acts of religious piety, and, indeed, rational choice theorists have trotted out these very analogies from time to time.

[51] *Ibid.*, pp. 141–42, 144–45.

[52] Lohmann wanders off into an extended formal analysis of the barge parable without ever taking notice of the tenuous link between her algebra and the subject matter of chapters 4 and 5 of *Pathologies*. Repeatedly in these chapters we advise readers that the political phenomena under discussion are cases in which large numbers of people must independently and under conditions of imperfect information decide whether to sacrifice valued resources on behalf of a collective undertaking that their contributions are unlikely to influence to any appreciable degree. As applied to the case of mass politics, the barge parable ought to have conjured up in Lohmann's mind an image of a supertanker being pulled against the current of a mighty river through the efforts of millions of citizens each tugging a line.

[53] *Ibid.*, p. 140.

[54] Compare Robyn M. Dawes, Jeanne McTavish, and Harriet Shaklee, "Behavior, Communication, and Assumptions About Other People's Behavior in a Commons Dilemma Situation," *Journal of Personality and Social Psychology*, Vol. 35, No. 1 (January 1977), pp. 1–11; William C. McDaniel and Frances Sistrunck, "Management Dilemmas and Decisions: Impact of Framing and Anticipated Responses," *Journal of Conflict Resolution*, Vol. 35, No. 1 (March 1991), pp. 21–42; John M. Orbell, Alphons J. C. Van de Kragt, and Robyn M. Dawes, "Explaining Discussion-induced Cooperation," *Journal of Personality and Social Psychology*, Vol. 54, No. 5 (May 1988), pp.

dominant strategy in such games renders Lohmann's criticisms entirely irrelevant. Next, Lohmann turns her attention to the effects of communication in social dilemma games. "Rational choice theory," she explains, "implies that pre-play communication cannot affect the outcome of a prisoner's dilemma game, in which each player's dominant strategy is to defect."[55] But noting that "there are many social dilemma situations in which communication can further cooperation," Lohmann questions our interpretation of one experiment, apparently not realizing that *this study presented players with incentives that made defection a dominant strategy.*[56] Again, Lohmann launches into a theoretical exegesis designed to show that we fail to appreciate the subtleties of game theory, when in fact none of her arguments speak to the anomalies we cite or in any way undermine our interpretation of them.[57]

One senses that grappling with the complex array of empirical phenomena charted in chapters 4 and 5 is a motivation of secondary importance for Lohmann, who, like Norman Schofield, is animated primarily by indignation at the notion that we "make no reference to the last decade of theoretical work on the prisoner's dilemma."[58] One need not be a rational choice theorist to understand why Lohmann and Schofield would prefer to see more credit assigned to the latest currents in game theory. However, the purpose of *Pathologies* was to assess the empirical performance of rational choice theory, not chart its analytic refinements. This objective led us to say relatively little about the kinds of models Lohmann describes, which generate multiple equilibria and

---

811–19; John M. Orbell, Alphons J. C. Van de Kragt, and Robyn M. Dawes, "Covenants Without the Sword: The Role of Promises in Social Dilemmas," in Kenneth Koford and Jeffrey Miller, eds., *Social Norms and Economic Institutions* (Ann Arbor: University of Michigan Press, 1991); Alphons J. C. Van de Kragt, Robyn M. Dawes, John M. Orbell, S. R. Braver, and L.A. Wilson II, "Doing Well and Doing Good as Ways of Resolving Social Dilemmas," *Experimental Social Dilemmas* in Henk A. M. Wilke, David M. Messick, and Christel G. Rutte, eds. (Frankfurt am Main: Verlag Peter Lang, 1986).

[55] Lohmann, "The Poverty," p. 140.

[56] *Ibid.*, p. 140. See Dawes et al., "Behavior, Communication, and Assumptions." See also Orbell et al., "Explaining Discussion-induced Cooperation"; Orbell et al., "Covenants Without the Sword"; Peregrine Schwartz-Shea and Randy T. Simmons, "The Layered Prisoners' Dilemma: Ingroup versus Macro-Efficiency," *Public Choice*, Vol. 35, No. 1 (April 1990), pp. 61–83; Van de Kragt et al., "Doing Well and Doing Good."

[57] Likewise, Taylor believes he has found a "flaw" in our discussion of interpersonal communication, noting that it can be important when the game is not a one-shot prisoner's dilemma. We never claim otherwise and in fact attempt to forestall this very criticism. See Michael Taylor, "Battering RAMS," *Critical Review: An Interdisciplinary Journal of Politics and Society*, Vol. 9, Nos. 1–2 (Winter/Spring 1995), p. 228, n. 4; Green and Shapiro, *Pathologies*, p. 89.

[58] Schofield, "Rational Choice and Political Economy," p. 206.

therefore diffuse empirical predictions.[59] It should be clear from the myriad of studies cited on pages 89 through 93 of *Pathologies* that the models Lohmann proposes do not even begin to accommodate the range of anomalies that turn up in the laboratory. Rather than wheel out ever more elaborate analytic structures, rational choice scholars should endeavor to construct models of collective action that are empirically sustainable. Otherwise, it is not obvious to the empirically-minded social scientist why the models Lohmann refers to should be termed "important" or "powerful."

The Motive Power of Collective Incentives

Michael Taylor is on the whole sympathetic to the claims made in *Pathologies* but, like Lohmann, believes we misunderstand rational choice theories of collective action.

> According to Green and Shapiro's reading of the RCT of collective action, collective benefits are irrelevant to an individual's decision. This is wrong. Whether or not any particular theorist believes this, the correct rational-choice formulation must be that free-riding occurs if the costs to the individual of making a contribution exceed *the benefits to him of the increased amount of the non-excludable good which results (directly or indirectly) from his contribution,* plus the selective benefits contingent on his contribution, if there are any.[60]

This corrected decision rule turns out to be the same one that we discuss at length in chapters 4 and 5 of *Pathologies*. Taylor is evidently not thinking, as we do, about mass-based collective action, where the expected collective benefits flowing from any one person's contribution are likely to be minute. Even if an individual would in principle trade $10,000 to determine unilaterally the outcome of a presidential election, the likelihood that she will cast the decisive vote in an actual election is vanishingly small. If we were to post odds of such an occurrence at one-in-a-million, the *expected value* of the collective good in question is a penny. Expected values are not mentioned in Taylor's formulation, and this obscures what rational choice theories imply about how

[59] See Lohmann, "The Poverty," p. 136.
[60] Taylor, "Battering RAMS," p. 228, n. 4, Taylor's italics.

changes in the value of collective goods are likely to influence decisions to participate.

As the odds of influencing collective outcomes become infinitesimal, the motive force of collective incentives becomes severely attenuated. Consider again the case in which the probability that one's participation will be decisive is .000001. Increase the personal value of an election or social cause from $100 to $100,000, and one has merely increased the expected benefit from one tenth of a mil to a dime. Because it is difficult to imagine that a dime's worth of incentive would stimulate any appreciable increase in collective action, it follows that even implausibly large changes in collective incentives will have little effect on behavior. Indeed, it is this comparative statics proposition that makes rational choice theories of collective action interesting and testable. As it happens, these tests have not tended to concord with theoretical expectations.[61]

COMPARATIVE STATICS AND A BIT OF REVISIONISM

Olson's account of mass based collective action is best remembered for its grim prediction that such efforts can be sustained only through coercion or selective benefits. At least, that is how everyone but Fiorina remembers it. He categorically denies that Olson makes any such point prediction, so to refresh memories, let's hear from Olson himself:

> [U]nless the number of individuals in a group is quite small, or unless there is coercion or some other special device to make individuals act in their common interest, *rational, self-interested individuals will not act to achieve their common or group interests.* In other words, even if all of the individuals in a large group are rational and self-interested, and would gain if, as a group, they acted to achieve their common interest or objective, they will still not voluntarily act to achieve that common or group interest.[62]

> [I]n a large group in which no single individual's contribution makes a perceptible difference to the group as a whole, or the burden or benefit of any single member of the group, it is certain that a collective good will

---

[61] See Green and Shapiro, *Pathologies,* pp. 62–65, 84–85.
[62] Olson, *Logic of Collective Action,* p. 2, Olson's emphasis.

not be provided unless there is coercion or some outside inducements that will lead the members of the large group to act in their common interests.[63]

[T]he rational individual in the large group in a socio-political context will not be willing to make any sacrifices to achieve the objectives he shares with others. There is accordingly no presumption that large groups will organize to act in their common interest. Only when groups are small, or when they are fortunate enough to have an independent source of selective incentives, will they organize to act to achieve their objectives.[64]

Fiorina resists the notion that conventional rational choice analysis predicts the collapse of mass-based collective action. But unlike Lohmann, who seeks refuge in the empirical indeterminacy of multiple equilibria, Fiorina's instincts are to recast Olson's empirical propositions in ways that are amenable to the experimental or quasi-experimental research methods of social science. Out with equilibrium results; in with comparative statics. Forget about point predictions, and focus on predictions about how rates of mass political participation *change* as a consequence of exogenous shifts in the strategic environment. Far from disagreeing with this prescription, we would lay claim to it as a recurrent theme in *Pathologies*. Our disagreement with Fiorina concerns the extent to which rational choice theorists follow this prescription. Perhaps he ought to spread the word among rational choice theorists who, like Lohmann, attach great theoretical and empirical importance to absolute rates of mass political participation. Notice, however, that the retreat to comparative statics robs rational choice theory of much of its cachet. Would Olson have made the same splash if his central prediction had been merely, "other things being equal, the level of collective action within large latent groups ebbs and flows with selective incentives?"[65] Similarly, much of the air goes out of rational choice big-think when its question "why do people vote?" changes to "what factors increase or decrease turnout?"

Having made the move to what we describe as partial universalism, Fiorina nonetheless fails to take up the empirical questions that naturally follow. To what extent does the level of collective action respond

---

[63] *Ibid.*, p. 44.

[64] *Ibid.*, pp. 166–67.

[65] Fiorina mentions Olson's other important proposition concerning the differential organizing capabilities of large and small latent groups. For reasons given by Taylor, this proposition is diffi-

to changes in the incentives identified by rational choice theories, and to what extent do other factors account for changes in turnout? Fiorina has little to say about the comparative statics findings reviewed in *Pathologies*, which, among other things, underscore the anomaly pointed out by Ferejohn and Fiorina that collective incentives attract voters to the polls even when they do not foresee a close election.[66] In an apparent retreat from this more nuanced form of hypothesis testing, Fiorina at one point proposes to require of rational choice propositions only that they make predictions of proper sign, reminiscent of Lohmann's notion that predictions of positive turnout are "qualitatively consistent" with the observation that millions vote in national elections.[67]

THE PATHOLOGIES OF *PATHOLOGIES*

Like most of our critics, Dennis Chong seems to concede the basic thrust of our critique concerning collective action. He does not dispute our claim that much of the empirical evidence gathered to date poses problems for non-banal variants of rational choice theory. His critique focuses instead on three interrelated concerns. First, he charges us with overlooking the fact that rational choice theory "is valuable for specifying a causal mechanism behind the phenomenon in question."[68] Second, he takes us to task for failing to offer alternatives to rational choice

---

cult to test empirically. See Olson, *Logic of Collective Action*; Michael Taylor, *The Possibility of Cooperation* (Cambridge and New York: Cambridge University Press, 1987).

[66] Lohmann, relying on the word of Grofman, seems to think that the comparative statics predictions of rational choice theory fare well empirically. That this conclusion can be drawn in the face of the literatures reviewed in *Pathologies* lends credence to social-psychological theories of consistency bias and persuasion, as applied to the assimilation of scientific evidence. Presumably, if our assessment were correct, this pattern of results would qualify as a genuine anomaly (as opposed to "unsolved problem") by Chong's criteria, as it is consistent with social-psychological theories of group identification. Lohmann also praises Hansen et al., which we too regard as the best work of its kind, but does not address the methodological concern we advance (see *Pathologies*, p. 64). Hansen et al. find turnout in Oregon school district elections to be higher in smaller districts, in which voters are more likely to cast pivotal votes. The authors do not, however, examine whether this same pattern of turnout holds for state and national elections, in which such inter-district variation should be absent. See John Ferejohn and Morris Fiorina, "Closeness Only Counts in Horseshoes and Dancing," *American Political Science Review*, Vol. 69, No. 3 (September 1975), pp. 920–25; Bernard Grofman, "Downsian Political Economy and the Neo-Downsian Agenda" (University of California at Irvine: Unpublished mimeo, 1994); Stephen Hansen, Thomas R. Palfrey, and Howard Rosenthal, "The Downsian Model of Electoral Participation: Formal Theory and Empirical Analysis of the Constituency Size Effect," *Public Choice*, Vol. 52, No. 1 (1987), pp. 15–33; Green and Shapiro, *Pathologies*, p. 64.

[67] Fiorina, "Rational Choice, Empirical Contributions," p. 88.

[68] Chong, "Rational Choice Theory's Mysterious Rivals," p. 41.

explanations of collective action. Finally, he is troubled by what he sees as our attempt to "impose arbitrary rules about the limits of rational choice theory."[69] We address these concerns as they apply to theories of collective action here, saving a more general discussion of them for later.

It is ironic that Chong lauds rational choice for its capacity to furnish a causal mechanism by which social action emanates from individual choice, when during the course of his essay he lists not one but several mechanisms alleged to fall within the penumbra of rational choice explanation.[70] Initially, Chong suggests that the mechanism is a cognitive one in which decision makers determine which of the many courses of action available to them furnishes maximum utility. Putting stock in this mechanism, however, immediately raises the question whether it is plausible to believe that ordinary people can solve the kinds of complex strategic puzzles that may stymie game theorists for months. Recognizing that "no individual has the resources to evaluate thoroughly all the choices he must make," Chong offers another mechanism: "conformity" to the actions advocated by "community leaders" or the "cumulative wisdom of the community."[71] Why conformity, and why "such strong emotional attachments to the patterns of behavior [developed] through socialization"?[72] To answer this requires yet another mechanism, this one structural-functional or evolutionary, by which "blind conformity is adaptive early in life because it improves the rate of information transmission from parents to their offspring."[73] It is far from apparent why this melange of causal mechanisms should inspire confidence in the claims of rational choice theory.

As for the charge that *Pathologies* makes only "half-hearted" reference to alternative theories, our views concerning architectonic theory bear repeating.[74] The fact that there are no alternative theories of comparable scope and generality implies nothing about the empirical serviceability of rational choice theory; it is equally compatible with the view that no single theory can account for the recalcitrant complexity of politics. If pressed to come up with an alternative to rational choice theory, our

[69] *Ibid.*, p. 46.
[70] See Green and Shapiro, *Pathologies*, p. 20–23.
[71] Chong, "Rational Choice Theory's Mysterious Rivals," p. 56.
[72] *Ibid.*, p. 56.
[73] *Ibid.*, p. 56.
[74] See Green and Shapiro, *Pathologies*, pp. 183–88.

immediate inclination is to ask: What is the phenomenon to be explained? Presumably, one must have a clear sense of the object of inquiry before one can canvass the relevant explanations, some of which may involve utility maximization while others stress the role of habit, impulse, or cognitive biases. The formulation of alternative explanations, in other words, should be a problem-driven activity.

It is certainly incorrect to say that *at the level of specific empirical claims* we propose no alternatives. As against the claim that collective action is stimulated by selective incentives or the opportunity to make pivotal contributions, we suggest that mass political behavior may be shaped by enthusiasm for the collective objectives, attitudes toward leaders and prominent symbolic figures in the movement, and feelings of personal adequacy and obligation to participate.[75] Granted, these propositions neither stem from broad-gauge theories nor presuppose that individual action need be irrational; thus, they seem to fall short of Chong's requirement that critics of rational choice theory must show that strategic behavior plays no part whatsoever.[76] Moreover, since Chong seems to believe that everything from conscious calculation to "cultural inertia" may be squared with some variant of rational choice logic, he may regard these alternatives as indistinct from rational choice theory.[77] But then our disagreement becomes largely semantic, and rational choice theory is nothing but an ever-expanding tent in which to house every plausible proposition advanced by anthropology, sociology, or social psychology.

Chong defends post hoc embellishment of rational choice theories on the grounds that such modification "increases the empirical power of a theory and therefore is a progressive development," noting, however, that "ad-hoc modification should generate additional tests of the theory."[78] For us, the question of whether ad-hoc modifications are in

---

[75] The category of alternative hypotheses properly includes methodological objections as well. Chong, for example, alludes to the survey-based finding purporting to show that participants in large-scale collective action perceive their own contributions as pivotal to the success of the cause. An alternative (and testable) view is that *claiming* to be pivotal is part of the ideological discourse of activism and that a more refined survey questionnaire would discern that people do not actually believe that the movement would fail if they were suddenly to become incapacitated. Chong believes this hypothesis commits us to a full-scale indictment of survey research, but advancing a methodological criticism of this sort no more obliges us to embrace this broader critique than does reference to economic class oblige one to embrace Marxism. See Chong, "Rational Choice Theory's Mysterious Rivals," p. 49–52.

[76] Chong, "Rational Choice Theory's Mysterious Rivals," pp. 52, 56.

[77] *Ibid.*, p. 56.

[78] *Ibid.*, pp. 45–46.

fact progressive (since they necessarily imply a tradeoff between predictive accuracy and theoretical parsimony) hinges on the *outcome* of
such tests. This point warrants emphasis, because our critics often take
us to be categorically opposed to post-hoc modification, or they sense
a contradiction between our call for inductive theory-building and our
criticism of post-hoc theory-modification. Both criticisms are mistaken. Inductive theorizing draws on existing evidence and attempts to
understand it; meaningful empirical assessment therefore comes when
the reformulated predictions confront new data. Wood and McClean
take us to task for "ridicul[ing] the way in which rational choice articles
end with calls for more empirical work"; what we object to are disin-
genuous calls.[79] This criticism has special force as applied to rational
choice theories of collective action, where meaningful empirical testing
seldom materializes.

Is it surprising that rational choice theories should encounter difficulty when applied to mass political participation? Each of our critics
furnishes reasons to believe that the answer is no. Fiorina speculates
that "RC [rational choice] models are most useful where stakes are high
and numbers low, in recognition that it is not rational to go to the
trouble to maximize if the consequences are trivial and/or your actions
make no difference"; Lohmann, that "the rational choice approach is
bound to be more useful when applied in domains with high-powered
incentives, where a 'rational' response has high payoffs, than in domains . . . where learning effects or selection pressures are weak"; Taylor, that "rational choice explanations are most likely to work where
. . . much, for the agent, turns on his or her choice"; and Chong, citing
Harsanyi, that "acts of altruism or morality are likely to occur when
the costs of doing so are small."[80] Nonetheless, Chong is right to oppose
the imposition of "arbitrary rules about the limits of rational choice
theory."[81] As we make clear in our discussion of arbitrary domain restriction in *Pathologies*, our position is that propositions about the conditions under which rational choice theories offer powerful explanations must themselves be testable and tested.[82] Indeed, one of the central

---

[79] Stewart Wood and Iain McClean, "Recent Work in Game Theory and Coalition Theory,"
Political Studies, Vol. 43, No. 4 (1995), pp. 703–17.

[80] Fiorina, "Rational Choice, Empirical Contributions," p. 88; Lohmann, "The Poverty," p. 131;
Taylor, "Battering RAMS," p. 225; Chong, "Rational Choice Theory's Mysterious Rivals," p. 46.

[81] Chong, "Rational Choice Theory's Mysterious Rivals," p. 46.

[82] See Green and Shapiro, *Pathologies*, pp. 44–46.

purposes of *Pathologies* is to open up a research agenda in which such middle-range hypotheses are developed and evaluated empirically.

Note, however, that this line of inquiry is undone by the kind of post-hoc theorizing in which Chong engages. To the extent that such propositions as that "values and dispositions that are not acquired through conscious calculation and may even be unresponsive to changes in opportunity costs" are absorbed into rational choice theory, its boundaries become so murky that it becomes difficult, if not impossible, to assess when rational choice theories succeed and when they fail.[83] This problem becomes especially acute when those who advance post-hoc theories are content merely "to show that it is not obvious that social norms and values lie entirely outside of rational choice theory."[84] The universalistic impulse to explain everything by reference to "the operation of interests and more-or-less conscious strategic calculation," often justified in the name of theoretical parsimony and "backed up" by reference to multiple equilibria, is in tension with efforts to understand the circumstances in which interests hold sway or in which calculation conforms to the logic of formal models.[85]

WHY A LITTLE PHILOSOPHY OF SCIENCE IS A DANGEROUS THING

Several critics take us to task for misunderstanding the rational choice enterprise for reasons having to do with the philosophy of science. Different critics make different points in this regard. However, all seem to think that, our earlier discussion of these issues notwithstanding, we are flatfooted positivists whose ignorance about philosophy of science blinds us to the contributions of rational choice theory.

Wingwalking with Lakatos

Ferejohn and Satz, Chong, Fiorina, and Shepsle all take us to task for naïvely supposing that theories are accepted or rejected as a result of a confrontation with the relevant evidence, rather than—as argued—by comparison with alternative theories. Their arguments boil down to two connected claims: You can't beat something with nothing, and

---

[83] Chong, "Rational Choice Theory's Mysterious Rivals," p. 56.
[84] *Ibid.*, p. 57.
[85] *Ibid.*

What's your alternative to rational choice theory? These are both arguments to which we attended in *Pathologies*, but since what we said there
appears not to have persuaded our critics, we take up their claims more
fully here.[86]

The Lakatosian argument that theories are not rejected until something better comes along resurfaces now as Shepsle's "First Law of
Wingwalking" ("Don't let go of something until you have something
else to hold on to").[87] We advanced two considerations as pertinent to
thinking about this claim in the context of the empirical achievements
of rational choice theory. First, given that the alleged achievements of
rational choice theory are so difficult to identify, a whiff of hubris inevitably accompanies the suggestion that the rational choice paradigm oc-
cupies a position in political science analogous to that of Newtonian
physics before the Einsteinian revolution. Shepsle's appeal to the First
Law of Wingwalking might be easier to take seriously if one could develop a degree of confidence that the aircraft in question were in fact
airborne. It is doubtful, after all, that we and our critics would be engaged in the present debate if rational choice theorists could point to a
track record of noteworthy achievements.

Second, in *Pathologies* we insisted that the Lakatosian position be
advanced consistently or not at all. Although rational choice theorists
are sometimes quick to criticize others by reference to Lakatosian reasoning, it is rare that they live up to it themselves. One of our central
complaints concerns the skimpy attention to extant alternative explanations in the rational choice literature. As a result, rational choice theorists are less than well placed to fault others for failing to evaluate rational choice explanations by comparing them with an alternative that can
be shown to do better. Far too often, as we showed, the standard rational choice modus operandi is to adduce sufficient accounts of political
phenomena by reference to rational choice models, with reference either to no alternatives or to trivial ones.[88] Some (such as Elster) think
that rational choice accounts should be presumptively privileged; some
(such as Diermeier) think it unnecessary to consider alternatives; and
some (such as Chong) propose recasting the alternatives as rational
choice explanations.[89]

---

[86] See Green and Shapiro, *Pathologies*, pp. 180–85.
[87] Shepsle, "Statistical Political Philosophy," p. 217.
[88] See Green and Shapiro, *Pathologies*, pp. 37, 84, 88, 121–22, 126, 180–85.
[89] John Elster, ed., "Introduction," in *Rational Choice* (New York: New York University Press,
1986); Diermeier, "Rational Choice and the Role of Theory;" Chong, "Rational Choice Theory's
Mysterious Rivals."

Critics like Chong find the preceding criticism unpersuasive. They believe that, in evaluating the rational choice enterprise, *we* should shoulder the burden of supplying an alternative to rational choice theory. This criticism misses the mark for two reasons. First, we argued in *Pathologies* that there are good reasons for skepticism that there is any such alternative general theory to be found, so disparate in kind are the phenomena that political scientists study. Even a question of the form: "What explains collective action?" seems to us likely to be too general to get very far empirically. The causal variables that explain why some people contribute money to environmental interest groups while others don't, why some people join the Aryan Resistance and others don't, and why some people attend school board meetings and others don't, may well differ from one another. Better to ask more finely honed questions about the circumstances in which certain types of actors engage, or fail to engage, in different sorts of collective action. Our concern is not to reject rational choice theory in toto in favor of embracing some alternative in toto but, rather, to suggest that there are better ways of doing social science. Indeed, as we say repeatedly (and elaborate in the discussion of method-driven versus problem-driven research later), we expect that some rational choice hypotheses can reasonably be expected to do well in certain types of political contexts.

It bears reiterating, second, that, at the level of evaluating particular hypotheses, Chong's argument reflects a misunderstanding of where burdens of persuasion appropriately rest. Someone who points out that a theory has failed to deliver on its claims no more adopts the burden of supplying an alternative than would a mechanic who points out that a car has a broken engine be obliged to have a working engine in his possession. Like Shepsle's charge that we are "not consistent about specifying a null against which a theory is compared," Chong's complaint that the alternatives to rational choice explanations that we mentioned at various points in *Pathologies* are "vague" misses the point.[90] Our aim was not to propose and defend alternatives. Rather, we sought to point out to those who invoke Lakatos that, in case after case, proponents of rational choice explanations have not tried to show that their accounts do better than any alternative, and to indicate the kinds of alternatives we think that they might want to consider.

---

[90] Shepsle, "Statistical Political Philosophy," p. 217; Chong, "Rational Choice Theory's Mysterious Rivals," p. 38.

Now a theory need not triumph over an alternative in order to be considered plausible; indeed some of the work we praised in *Pathologies* is not victorious in this way.[91] However, a proposed explanation will be unpersuasive to the extent that no effort is made to demonstrate that it does better than credible extant alternatives. Consider Chong's discussion of the observation that "collective action piggybacks on existing community organizations. People who were affiliated with churches and fraternal organizations . . . were more likely to be active in the civil rights movement."[92] Chong attributes this relationship to the fact that, within a small group context, cooperative behavior can be "monitored" and "rewarded and punished." But one could hardly come away from the immense literature on political participation without envisioning an alternative hypothesis: That individual differences in proclivities (tastes, senses of obligation, feelings of personal competence) for small group membership might account for both organizational participation and political activism.

This is not to deny that there may be circumstances in which an explanation might prove illuminating even if no alternative is considered, particularly when the phenomenon in question has not previously been studied or the proposed explanation seems counterintuitive. However, explanations of this sort must be conceded to be speculative in a stronger sense than that in which all well-tested explanations are provisional: accepted as the best available account until something better comes along. One might usefully think about the process of considering alternative explanations in a quasi-Baysean fashion: The more there are credible explanations of a particular phenomenon in currency, the heavier is the systematic comparative burden to be shouldered by someone who proposes a new one. Our complaint in *Pathologies* was that, all too often, proponents of rational choice models seem uninterested in—even unaware of—bodies of established scholarship that offer pertinent competing explanations.[93]

Similar misunderstandings infuse Shepsle's reference to George Stiglitz's parable of the opera, in which two opera singers audition for a part and after the first sings the judges instantly award it to the second. This leads Shepsle to the assertion that because we "are unhappy" with rational choice, we "award the prize to some untested contender."[94] The

---

[91] See Green and Shapiro, *Pathologies*, pp. 189–90.
[92] Chong, "Rational Choice Theory's Mysterious Rivals," p. 41.
[93] See Green and Shapiro, *Pathologies*, pp. 181–83.
[94] Shepsle, "Statistical Political Philosophy," p. 218.

analogy is misleading, however, because in science the prize does not have to be awarded to anyone. Before the discovery of chlorophyll scientists did not know why grass is green, but scientifically minded people could nonetheless have good grounds for rejecting a theory that accounted for it on the grounds that the moon is made of green cheese.[95] Likewise, if someone advances a theory that purports to explain the relatively poor performance of blacks in certain fields by reference to alleged genetic inferiority, one does not have to have in one's possession an alternative theory that does account for their poor performance in order to conclude that there is not a shred of credible evidence to support the genetic inferiority view. Of course, one has to know *something* to dismiss these theories as implausible, but it does not have to be much, and certainly one does not have to have an explanation that does account for the phenomenon in question. Often in political science, perhaps typically, no one knows the correct answer. Proponents of particular hypotheses properly adopt the burden of demonstrating that they triumph over the most credible extant alternative. One who is skeptical of their claims properly adopts no analogous burden; after all, a hallmark of the scientific outlook is the presumption it accords to skepticism. To suggest that the burden of providing an alternative should be shouldered by the skeptic would make it possible for theories routinely to appear to be more credible than they really are, and for scholars to claim that they know things when they do not. What more dangerous barrier to the growth of knowledge could there be?

A different variant of the Lakatosian claim is put forward by Ferejohn and Satz, who insist that successful theories in other sciences do not always yield unique predictions. The example they give is of evolutionary theory, which does not predict "a unique evolutionary path."[96] Indeed this is so, not least because most versions of evolutionary theory assume that evolutionary outcomes are critically influenced by random events. But in biology, as we noted in *Pathologies*, evolutionary theory can and does produce testable predictions.[97] For instance, a variant of evolutionary theory might generate the hypothesis that there was a gradual expansion of cranial capacities of a given species during a particular period. This, in turn, would issue in predictions that could be falsified if larger skulls were subsequently discovered that could be

---

[95] We are indebted to Brian Barry for this example.
[96] Ferejohn and Satz, "Unification, Universalism," p. 75.
[97] See Green and Shapiro, *Pathologies*, pp. 22–23.

shown (by independent dating methods) to be older than smaller, younger skulls from the specified period.[98] If evolutionary theory produced no falsifiable predictions of this kind, there would be little reason to take it any more seriously than creationism.

Kuhn to the Rescue?

Diermeier adopts a Kuhnian point of view, thereby placing himself at odds with our Lakatosian critics. On his view, the "normal" science of rational choice legitimately involves "puzzle-solving" within an established paradigm. Diermeier insists that according to "Kuhn's concept of paradigms," what we describe as pathologies "are perfectly acceptable and indeed consistent with characteristic behavior in the most successful natural science." They are "standard" features of "normal research, i.e. research guided by a paradigm."[99] Diermeier's argument boils down to two central contentions, one concerning the relations between theories and tests, the other concerning the appropriate interpretation of empirical anomalies. With regard to the first, Diermeier devotes considerable attention to establishing something we never sought to deny: That assumptions on which theories are built are seldom, if ever, directly tested empirically.[100] To this he adds that because unobservables are by their nature unmeasurable, we must also concede that theories incorporating them cannot be tested.[101] But we no more objected to the use of unobservables than we did to the use of untested assumptions. We did insist that there must be *some* empirical test, a view that Diermeier appears to accept in his essay's opening sentence.

---

[98] Murphy might be right that evolutionary theory has done best empirically when proponents have detached particular evolutionary hypotheses from the method-driven search for equilibrium results. For reasons that are spelled out later, we would, however, dispute what appears to be his concluding claim: that abandoning the search for equilibria is tantamount to abandoning science. See Murphy, "Rational Choice Theory as Social Physics," p. 162–69.

[99] Diermeier, "Rational Choice and the Role of Theory," p. 68, 61.

[100] *Ibid.*, pp. 61–63.

[101] "A general form of Green and Shapiro's argument concerning problems with unobservables goes as follows: By definition, unobservables cannot be measured. Thus, theories that contain unobservables cannot be tested empirically. Because rational choice theories contain unobservables, they cannot be tested empirically. Therefore they are unscientific." As indicated in the text we never contend any such thing. Furthermore, this formulation betrays Diermeier's idiosyncratic view that theories must be dubbed scientific or unscientific. Theories are valid or invalid; it is methods of assessing them that are scientific or unscientific. See Diermeier, "Rational Choice and the Role of Theory," p. 63.

The typical mode of proceeding in science is not to test a theory's assumptions or theoretical terms directly, but rather to test the predictions of hypotheses that are derived from the theory.[102] This is not the only way in which to evaluate a theory's empirical performance, but if neither the predictions nor the set of assumptions on which a theory rests are subjected to an empirical test, it is difficult to see how its empirical performance can be evaluated at all. Diermeier qualifies his comparisons between Newtonian physics and rational choice theory by noting that it would be "absurd" to claim that the latter has been as successful as the former, yet he never tells us what the yardstick is by which he judges their relative achievements.[103]

This brings us to Diermeier's contention that successful theories often continue to be maintained in the face of particular anomalies. Before the discovery of Einsteinian relativity theory, Newton's theory failed to account for the nature of Mercury's orbit, but "it would have been foolish," he notes, "to give up Newton's theory, which worked so well in most areas, just because of one anomaly."[104] We took up this claim in *Pathologies*.[105] Indeed, we discussed Diermeier's much-debated example of the implications of inexplicable planetary "misbehavior" for Newtonian physics, pointing out that it was the accumulated successes of Newtonian theory that made scientists understandably reluctant to give it up in the face of a small number of anomalies. Diermeier's reliance on the analogy assumes just what is in dispute here: that rational choice *is* a successful theory.[106]

As we note in *Pathologies*, would-be defenders of this view confront a substantial challenge.[107] To begin with, they must come to grips with

[102] If, for instance, voting is explained on the grounds that people expect to cast the pivotal vote, the belief itself is unobservable, but it presumably has observable consequences. Interviews or survey data might be employed to determine whether people in fact believe that they are likely to cast pivotal votes. Diermeier claims to be "baffled" at our observation that problems associated with unobservables become more severe as the ratio of unobservable terms to observable indicators increases, but this principle is basic to the standard identification problem in the statistical analysis of latent variables. See *Pathologies*, pp. 40–41.

[103] Diermeier, "Rational Choice and the Role of Theory," p. 60.

[104] *Ibid.*, p. 66.

[105] See Green and Shapiro, *Pathologies*, pp. 180–81.

[106] Diermeier makes much of the fact that our example of red apples (*Pathologies*, p. 44) is a single anomaly. Apart from our response in the text, it should be said that it differs from Mercury's "misbehavior" in that the latter did not matter much, given its peripheral nature to people's concerns at the time. Had they been planning to fly to Mercury they would have been forced to grapple with the reasons for their inability to understand its orbital behavior. See Diermeier, "Rational Choice and the role of Theory," p. 66.

[107] See Green and Shapiro, *Pathologies*, pp. 182–83.

Lakatos's critique of Kuhn, in which he pointed out that if demonstrably superior empirical performance to the going alternatives is not a criterion for the scientific evaluation of theories, it is impossible to distinguish advancing research agendas, where the puzzle-solving is contributing to better understanding, from decaying ones, where it consists of endless post-hoc modifications whose sole function is to rescue a worthless paradigm.[108] That Diermeier never speaks to this question is particularly striking in view of the fact that he fails to adduce a single empirical proposition about politics that he takes to have been established by rational choice theory. One can scarcely enter a debate as to whether or not an anomaly should lead us to abandon a successful theory absent some evidence of the theory's success. Rather than how to cope with this or that "single" anomaly, the question here is what is there besides the anomalies that passes the Grandmother Test?

Perhaps Diermeier would do better to follow his philosophical mentor a little further. Unlike Diermeier, Kuhn realized that there is no established body of theoretical knowledge on which hypotheses in the social sciences can be shown to depend, even though they do "generate testable conclusions."[109] Consequently, he described the social sciences as "proto-sciences" in which "incessant criticism and continual striving for a fresh start are primary forces, and need to be."[110] So far as we have been able to tell, the only evidence so far adduced that rational choice *is* the established paradigm (and entitled to all the special privileges of established paradigms everywhere) is the assertions of its proponents. Furthermore, if the range of opinion among our critics is anything to go by, there seem to be close to as many characterizations of the rational choice paradigm as there are rational choice theorists. Whereas Lohmann distances herself from universalist ambitions, regarding rational choice as little more than a method or approach, for Schofield "what gives rational choice theory coherence is precisely that it *is* an attempt to construct a grand theory of human behavior."[111] Chong declares that

---

[108] Imre Lakatos, "Falsification and the Methodology of Scientific Research Programmes," in Imre Lakatos and Alan Musgrave, ed., *Criticism and the Growth of Knowledge* (Cambridge: Cambridge University Press, 1970), pp. 91–196.

[109] Thomas S. Kuhn, "Reflections on My Critics," in *Criticism and the Growth of Knowledge*, Imre Lakatos and Alan Musgrave, ed. (Cambridge: Cambridge University Press, 1970), pp. 244–45.

[110] *Ibid.*, pp. 244–45.

[111] Lohmann, "The Poverty," pp. 128, 130; Schofield, "Rational Choice and Political Economy," p. 190, Schofield's italics.

rational choice's inherent advantage over other theories is that it supplies us with causal mechanisms, while Satz and Ferejohn insist that
rational choice explanations are "external."[112] Shepsle conceives of rational choice as the best available theory for the moment, to be jettisoned when something better comes along.[113] For Fiorina, by contrast,
it is a badge of honor that he is rational choice "down to my DNA,"
suggesting that its hold over him is rather more profound.[114] To this
Diermeier might respond that such disagreements about the nature of
the enterprise are not indigenous to rational choice; they pervade the
social sciences. This is readily conceded, but the effect is surely to buttress Kuhn's view of them as preparadigmatic.[115]

METHOD-DRIVEN VERSUS PROBLEM-DRIVEN RESEARCH

Because our rational choice critics run the gamut of philosophy-of-
science possibilities, it seems reasonable to infer that what they share
in common is rooted in something else. The argument in *Pathologies* is
that they share a propensity to engage in method-driven research, and
that this propensity is characteristic of the drive for universalism. To be
sure, a commitment to universalism might stem from beliefs about the
philosophy of science, in particular the view that unless one's hypotheses are deduced from equilibrium results that are validated by theorems,
there can be no science.[116] But it might just as easily stem from other

[112] Chong, "Rational Choice Theory's Mysterious Rivals," pp. 41–43; Satz and Ferejohn, "Rational Choice and Social Theory."

[113] Shepsle, "Statistical Political Philosophy," pp. 216–18.

[114] Fiorina, "Rational Choice, Empirical Contributions," p. 85.

[115] Kuhn also warned that "I claim no therapy to assist the transformation of a proto-science
to a science, nor do I suppose that anything of the sort is to be had." Apparently with the likes of
Diermeier in mind, he elaborated as follows: "If . . . some social scientists take from me the view
that they can improve the status of their field by first legislating agreement on fundamentals and
then turning to puzzle-solving, they are badly misconstruing my point. A sentence I once used
when discussing the special efficacy of mathematical theories applies equally here: 'As in individual
development, so in the scientific group, maturity comes most surely to those who know how to
wait.' " Kuhn, "Reflections on My Critics," pp. 244–45.

[116] We did note the curious fact that the covering-law model of science referred to in the text
also requires that the assumptions on which models rest be realistic, a feature that, as Moe pointed
out over two decades ago, is lacking in rational choice models. Unrealistic models are usually
justified, by contrast, on the grounds of their predictive success, which, we argued, is notably
lacking in the case of rational choice theories of politics. In any case, such instrumental views
place no stock in the development of covering laws. See Terry Moe, "On the Scientific Status of
Rational Choice Theory," *American Journal of Political Science*, Vol. 23, No. 1 (February 1979), pp.
215–43. See also Green and Shapiro, *Pathologies*, pp. 30–32.

sources. Some rational choice theorists are universalists because they believe that utility maximization is the wellspring from which all human behavior emanates.[117] Others seem to be universalists almost by default: A lack of interest in, or awareness of, the existence of competing explanations may make rational choice explanations seem compelling. Universalist aspirations may also result from plain intellectual ambition, or—its flipside—ennui with what are seen as the more mundane findings of conventional political science. One has only to attend a rational choice conference to realize that the ambitious pursuit of general theoretical results is more highly prized than empirical research—a status hierarchy that, as we argue in *Pathologies*, has the pernicious effect of reinforcing the division of labor between those engaged theory-building and theory-testing.

The drive for universalism can thus reflect impatience with the journalistic quality of much descriptive political science, or with the less-than-arresting nature of many of the propositions of behavioral political science that do withstand empirical scrutiny. As Charles Taylor pointed out long ago, knowing that Catholics in Detroit tend to vote Democratic (or at least that they did when he wrote) scarcely adds much of profundity to one's knowledge about politics.[118] Leaving aside the fact that the empirically sustainable insights of rational choice theory are not notably more impressive, as in the breathless proclamation that rational choice models have now been developed which predict "positive" voter turnout, it should be said that we have nothing against theoretical ambition. We think it prudent, however, to construct theories in ways that offer some prospect of being empirically sustainable. Otherwise, one runs the risk of sounding like the Monty Python figure who insists ad nauseam to all the world that "this is my theory, and mine alone," without ever indicating why anyone should care. The aim of science, after all, is not to produce theories but, rather, to accumulate

---

[117] See Elster, "Introduction." As we note in *Pathologies*, it is not clear what the defensible basis for this view is. In their critique of us, Ferejohn and Satz appear to think that in the social sciences the merits of rational choice explanations—as a point of departure, at least—are self-evident. The reason for this seems to be that social-scientific explanations must be intentional. Granting this, *arguendo*, it is irrelevant to the issue at hand because, unlike Riker (whose views on this subject are dealt with in *Pathologies*), Ferejohn and Satz concede that rational choice explanations are only one of several types of intentional explanation. See Ferejohn and Satz, "Unification, Universalism," pp. 81–83; Riker, *Liberalism Against Populism*; Green and Shapiro, *Pathologies*, pp. 185–86.

[118] Charles Taylor, "Neutrality in Political Science," in Peter Laslett and W. G. Runciman, eds., *Philosophy, Politics and Society*, Third Series (Oxford: Blackwell, 1967), p. 57.

knowledge. Theories are more or less valuable to the degree that they contribute to that endeavor.

Now one can, of course, be method-driven without being an aspiring universalist. One might be unreflectively so inclined, or motivated by a desire to cash in on the technical virtuosity one has achieved as a formal modeler, or aesthetically attached to using certain methods.[119] Nonetheless, the drive for universalism should be expected to foster method-driven research, because it all too easily transforms the social-scientific enterprise from a dispassionate search for the causes of political outcomes into brief-writing on behalf of one's preferred theory. If one is committed—in advance of empirical research—to a certain theory of politics, then apparent empirical anomalies will seem threatening to it and stand in need of explaining away. Lawyers may properly be committed to vindicating their clients' points of view. For scientists, by contrast, the appropriate professional commitment is to getting at the truth regardless of its theoretical implications.

Stanley Kelley is thus mistaken if he takes it to be our view that the pathologies we identify are the necessary result of employing rational choice models.[120] They are, rather, the characteristic result of universalist ambition, and for that reason should be expected to afflict other equally ambitious theoretical constructions.[121] Fiorina is right when he says that theories of comparable scope and range would likely run into similar difficulties; indeed we made this point ourselves in relation to Marxism, elite theory, systems theory, and structural-functionalism.[122] As Fiorina seems to concede, this is scarcely a reason to emulate them.[123] We have never contended that anything in the maximization postulate itself leads to the pathologies we described. They are generated, rather, by the conviction that some manner of utility maximization must account for all political outcomes or the enterprise of political science is dead.

[119] One wonders, in this connection, about how to interpret appelations like "beautiful" that can sometimes be heard at rational choice conferences if someone supplies an elegant proof or deductive argument.

[120] Stanley Kelley Jr., "The Promise and Limitation of Rational Choice Theory," *Critical Review: An Interdisciplinary Journal of Politics and Society*, Vol. 9, Nos. 1–2 (Winter/Spring 1995), pp. 102–3.

[121] This was evident to at least some readers of *Pathologies*. Ferejohn and Satz characterize our argument on this point accurately in "Unification, Universalism," p. 71.

[122] See Green and Shapiro, *Pathologies*, pp. 189–90.

[123] Noting that Parsons, Truman, and Easton "were not exactly modest" with respect to grand theoretical ambition, Fiorina asserts that "not every scholar who found a structural-functionalist,

A possible response to the preceding argument is that rational choice explanations are no more or less universalistic than other explanations in the social sciences. Among our critics, this view is most forcefully stated by Fiorina. Implicitly or explicitly, he notes, the applicability of all explanations is limited by ceteris paribus clauses. Critics of rational choice accounts "often assume that a monocausal explanation is being offered" as a result of their failure to recognize that rational choice propositions "typically are stated with a ceteris paribus condition. Such an assumption is *always* made whenever there is an attempt to apply a model empirically."[124] Like any other explanations, rational choice explanations are intended to zero in on a particular part of the causal terrain only. Their proponents have never sought, or, at any rate, they should not seek, to deny that other causal factors are covered by ceteris paribus conditions.

We have no difficulty with this formulation; in effect, it is a version of what we described in *Pathologies* as partial universalism. Our worry is that if one approaches explanation in a method-driven way designed to vindicate *some* rational choice explanation, for all one knows one might be dealing with one percent of the problem. As our discussion of such quips as tall men being more likely than short men to bump their heads on the moon was intended to suggest, even if true, rational choice explanations may be rendered utterly trivial by the variables that are embedded in the relevant ceteris paribus clauses.[125] This difficulty can be compounded by the fact that failure to attend to other independent variables may throw off inferences that one draws from the data. Once the world of monocausal explanation has been eschewed, it makes little sense to zero in on one variable and model it, without trying first to get a sense of how important it is in relation to other variables and how it interacts with them. This is why we press the question, What seems most likely to account for X?, as superior to: How can a rational choice model be developed that accounts for X?[126]

---

a groups, or a systems perspective useful shared the universalist ambitions of these theorists." Fiorina, "Rational Choice, Empirical Contributions," p. 87.

[124] *Ibid.*, p. 88, Fiorina's italics.

[125] See Green and Shapiro, *Pathologies*, pp. 61, 193.

[126] Wood and McClean point out that even within one set of ceteris paribus conditions virtually any outcome can typically be retrodicted as an equilibrium result. Like Ferejohn and Schofield, they think that our preoccupation with empirical testability misses rational choice theory's most profound problems. What they appear not to realize is that, even if this theoretical difficulty were resolved, the pathologies that flow from method-driven science would remain. See Wood and McClean, "Recent Work in Game Theory"; John Ferejohn, "Rationality and Interpretation: Parlia-

It is not surprising that those rational choice theorists who have grappled with empirical questions seriously have also distanced themselves from aggressively universalist formulations. For example, Fiorina insists that rational choice theorists share nothing more than a commitment to viewing human action as purposive. He proposes that different models be applied to different types of problem as appropriate (though he says nothing about the criteria for determining appropriateness); he embraces variants of what we describe as partial and segmented universalism in *Pathologies*, and—unlike Jon Elster and Gary Becker—he does not think there should be any presumptive preference for rational choice explanations.[127] True, at times Fiorina cannot restrain himself from such extravagant assertions as that "in terms of empirical contributions" rational choice theories "are a significant improvement on the so-called theories that have held sway in the past" without disclosing what has been learned from these contributions.[128] But most of his discussion is more circumspect.[129]

Ordeshook is even more explicit than is Fiorina in backing away both from universalism and the deductive derivation of hypotheses. "Science proceeds less coherently" than the deductive model presupposes, he argues,

> through induction and inference, informed by attempts to be practical and to manipulate real things, where those manipulations rely as much on experience, intuition, and creative insight as on theory. Out of such a process comes ideas about what is generalizable, what is best understood by existent theory, and what is an anomaly that warrants further investigation.[130]

Although, for reasons spelled out later, we disagree with Ordeshook's engineering-based conception of political science, nothing he says here is incompatible with the view we are advocating.

---

mentary Elections in Early Stuart England," in Kristin Monroe, ed., *Economic Approach to Politics* (New York: HarperCollins, 1991); Schofield, "Rational Choice and Political Economy."

[127] See Elster, "Introduction"; Gary S. Becker, "The Economic Approach to Human Behavior," in Elster, ed, *Rational Choice* (New York: New York University Press, 1986), and Fiorina, "Rational Choice, Empirical Contributions," pp. 87–89.

[128] Fiorina, "Rational Choice, Empirical Contributions," p. 91.

[129] Indeed, by embracing the family-of-theories view Fiorina goes further than we propose in backing away from universalism. Against this approach, in chapter 5 of *Pathologies* we argue for sticking to one definition of rationality in order to keep rational choice explanations analytically distinct from other accounts. See Green and Shapiro, *Pathologies*, p. 97.

[130] Ordeshook, "Engineering or Science," p. 180.

Ferejohn and Satz do not go as far as Ordeshook in distancing them-selves from universalism. However, in different places Ferejohn has em-braced both partial universalism, where rationality is assumed to ac-count for an outcome in conjunction with other independent variables, and segmented universalism, where rational choice models are assumed to apply in some types of circumstances but not in others.[131] Rechristen-ing them as two kinds of partial universalism, Ferejohn and Satz now appear to embrace both.[132] In addition, they register their endorsement of what we described in *Pathologies* as the family-of-theories view.[133] In effect this amounts to saying that some type of rationality explains some of what happens in politics some of the time. Who could possibly object to that? Certainly not us, but three points follow from adopting this stance. It is evident, first, that if defenders of the rational choice enterprise back away from universalism to the degree that Ferejohn and Satz, Ordeshook, and Fiorina do in these essays, the claim that others should be faulted for not offering an alternative universal theory of politics is not sustainable. Second, a corollary of this, is that once these moves have been made, there is nothing left of the proposition that rational choice theorists are engaged in an enterprise that is qualita-tively different from—let alone superior to—conventional empirical political science. Third, from the standpoint of these stripped-down universalisms, the merits of deductive hypothesis-generation are far from self-evident. Once it has been conceded de facto that there is no universal theory to be found, why continue to generate hypotheses as though this were not the case?

Ferejohn and Satz make heavy weather of the claim that both partial and segmented universalism are, nonetheless, forms of universalism, and that putative explanations cannot deserve the name unless they include a claim to be valid across a range of like phenomena.[134] We agree. Where we part company concerns how one goes about determin-ing the range of application of particular explanations, or of the interac-tions among independent variables in multicausal explanations. Like Shepsle, Ferejohn and Satz seem to think that it is worthwhile to go

---

[131] Partial universalism is embraced in Ferejohn, "Rationality and Interpretation," and seg-mented universalism in Satz and Ferejohn, "Rational Choice and Social Theory."

[132] See Ferejohn and Satz, "Unification, Universalism," pp. 77–78. To avoid confusion we stick to our original terms, *partial* and *segmented*, in the following discussion.

[133] *Ibid.*, pp. 81–83; Green and Shapiro, *Pathologies*, pp. 28–30, 193–94.

[134] Ferejohn and Satz, "Unification, Universalism," pp. 76–78.

about this deductively.[135] We remain skeptical. The decisions one has to make in plotting the range of application of a particular theory, determining the interactions among independent variables, and deciding which types of rationality might be germane to different types of circumstance are in part empirical decisions. Unless one goes about making these choices from a problem-driven standpoint, it is difficult to know how to think pertinently about the interactions among explanatory variables or why the domain should be restricted to one class of phenomena rather than another. It was this observation that supplied the basis for our discussion of arbitrary domain restriction in *Pathologies*.[136] None of our critics disputes it, and some, such as Fiorina, endorse it.[137]

It might be contended that our distinction between problem-driven and method-driven research is misleadingly simpleminded. For example, Ferejohn and Satz assert that the "very notion of explanatory success depends on a prior (theoretical) characterization of what exactly needs to be explained."[138] Thus, they state that before the advent of the collective action literature, nonvoting was thought by political scientists to stand in need of explanation; Olson and Downs suggested that, on the contrary, it was voting that needed to be explained. No one would dispute Ferejohn and Satz's contention that Olson and Downs had a big impact on the study of turnout, but this begs the question whether this impact was for the good. As we note in *Pathologies*, researchers had indeed studied which factors make it more or less likely that people will vote before the advent of the rational choice literature, and this comparative-statics question receded into the background after the rational choice reconceptualization of the problem.[139] The effects on turnout of perceived closeness of elections had been assessed by writers such as Gosnell and Campbell et. al, as had those of civic duty.[140] Particularly in view of the fact that, like Fiorina in his critique of us, Ferejohn and

---

[135] Shepsle, "Statistical Political Philosophy," pp. 218–19.

[136] See Green and Shapiro, *Pathologies*, pp. 44–46.

[137] Fiorina, "Rational Choice, Empirical Contributions," p. 87. It should also be said, *contra* Chong, that it is at best an open question whether the different partial and segmented universalist accounts that apply to different domains can be strung together into a general theoretical account. Chong, "Rational Choice Theory's Mysterious Rivals," pp. 47–48.

[138] Ferejohn and Satz, "Unification, Universalism," p. 72.

[139] See Green and Shapiro, *Pathologies*, pp. 67–68.

[140] Harold F. Gosnell, *Getting Out the Vote: An Experiment in the Simulation of Voting* (Chicago: University of Chicago Press, 1927), p. 3; Campbell et al., *American Voter*, pp. 99–100; Angus Campbell, Gerald Gurin, and Warren E. Miller, *The Voter Decides* (Evanston, IL: Row, Peterson, 1954), p. 199.

Satz appear to concede that rational choice models cannot account for turnout without repackaging such findings, the question arises whether Olson and Downs picked out a problem or a pseudo-problem.[141] Ferejohn and Satz point out that different theoretical frameworks can be expected to pick out different problems, but for just this reason committing oneself to a single theoretical perspective is shortsighted. In the face of *ex ante* uncertainty as to which perspective is likely to pay the best dividends, diversifying one's theoretical portfolio seems the more prudent course.

We do not deny that rational choice might be useful in generating research questions and hypotheses. Working within the rational-actor framework might be helpful, or it might send researchers on the sort of wild goose chase that the turnout literature became. By contrast, alternative means of identifying problems and generating research questions might have similar results, so that it is not clear a priori which approach will prove most fruitful. Nor do we have a difficulty with the further contention that what one perceives to be a problem will, to some degree, be a function of one's theoretical preconceptions. But there is a world of difference between agreeing with this and signing onto a method-driven research program. The manner in which one arrives at a research question is separable from the manner in which one studies it. Regardless of how one got to the question to be addressed, from a problem-driven perspective the researcher should begin with the following three questions: First, what are the existing attempts to account for the phenomenon in question, and how, if at all, are they defective? Second, if the existing accounts are defective, what alternatives are likely to account for the phenomenon, and why? Third, given that any proposed explanation might be wrong, what datum or data should persuade the researcher that this is so? It is because method-driven researchers are not guided by these questions—asking instead: How might my approach account for this or that phenomenon?—that the pathologies we described arise.

This is not to say that theorizing about the conditions under which certain types of explanations are likely to do better than others is a

[141] Ferejohn and Satz, "Rational Choice Theory and Folk Psychology" (Stanford University: Unpublished working paper, 1994). Fiorina nonetheless insists that "Every empirically based modification, generalization or even rejection of Olson is an empirical contribution stimulated by his work. . . . Even seeming counterexamples that lead people to see matters in a new light are empirical contributions." This is a bit like insisting that Robert Dahl's *Who Governs?* represents an accomplishment of elite theory. Fiorina, "Rational Choice, Empirical Contributions," p. 91. See

waste of time. It should be emphasized, however, that such theorizing should itself be tested empirically. For instance, Satz and Ferejohn conjectured that rational choice explanations are likely to do best when individual action is severely constrained.[142] Just as in economics, where rational-actor models account better for the behavior of firms than that of consumers, in politics they should be expected to do better with parties than with voters. This was a reasonable conjecture, but as we noted in *Pathologies*, rational choice models have not been shown to account for the behavior of political parties in general, suggesting that more refined constraints on the domain may be in order.[143]

Satz and Ferejohn are clearly on the right track, however. If segmented universalism is to be freed of the pathology of arbitrary domain restriction, researchers interested in the applicability of rational choice models should begin systematically to examine the conditions under which they can be expected to account for political outcomes better than the going alternatives. In this respect we applaud Kelley's attempt to specify the conditions under which rational choice explanations should be expected to apply: When goals are uncomplicated, pertinent knowledge widely available, interaction iterated, stakes high, and agents rewarded for rational behavior.[144] Likewise, Taylor's exploration of the threefold requirement that the number of options be limited, their costs and benefits clear to the agents, and the stakes high, seems to us another move in the right direction.[145] Our own conjecture builds on these suggestions. Rational choice explanations should be expected, prima facie, to perform well to the extent that the following five conditions are met: (i) the stakes are high and the players are self-conscious optimizers; (ii) preferences are well ordered and relatively fixed (which in turn may require actors to be individuals or homogeneous corporate agents); (iii) actors are presented with a clear range of options and little opportunity for strategic innovation; (iv) the strategic complexity of the situation is not overwhelmingly great for the actors, nor are there significant differences in their strategic capacities; and (v), the actors have the capacity to learn from feedback in the environment and adapt. Like those of Kelley and Taylor, our conjecture is at bottom empirical, rooted in

---

Robert A. Dahl, *Who Governs? Democracy and Power in an American City* (New Haven: Yale University Press, 1963 [1961]).

[142] Satz and Ferejohn, "Rational Choice and Social Theory."

[143] See Green and Shapiro, *Pathologies*, chap. 7.

[144] Kelley, "The Promise and Limitation," p. 101.

[145] Taylor, "Battering RAMS," pp. 225–58.

our best judgment concerning why rational choice models have failed in the literatures we have examined. As Robert Lane suggests, we might be wrong about one or more of these constraints; only the progress of empirical inquiry will tell.[146]

Some have accused us of being antitheoretical, but skepticism about rational choice theorists' claims is no more indicative of one's being against theory than is skepticism about a particular political party's claims evidence that one is against politics. We are all for the development of more rather than less general theory in the social sciences, but any theoretical proposition worth having must be empirically sustainable. Given the current condition of theoretical knowledge in political science, our sense is that the most fruitful theory-building will remain in relatively close proximity both to the data and—in the quasi-Baysean sense mentioned earlier—to the existing knowledge about the phenomenon under study. This is a pragmatic point rather than an epistemological one; it leaves as an open question whether or not there are general laws about politics to be discovered. But our view has the advantage that if there are no general laws about politics, or if valid general laws turn out to lie in some direction other than that currently being explored by rational choice theorists, it might nonetheless be possible, in the meantime, to increase the stock of empirical knowledge about politics.

It is possible that, despite its track record thus far, deductive modeling might produce empirical successes in political science. In that case the gamble will turn out to have been worth taking, despite what we have said about the odds. It might be worth pointing out, however, that—if the history of political science is anything to go by—highly ambitious attempts at theory building are likely to fail, whatever their origins. The

---

[146] Lane, "What Rational Choice Explains," p. 108. It should be added that, even when political phenomena meet our five criteria, they may nonetheless be so complex as to be intractable from the standpoint of formal modeling. For instance, in working on the impact of negotiations over the transition from authoritarianism to democracy on constitutional settlements, Jung and Shapiro noticed that this problem did seem to meet the five criteria just enumerated. When they asked several game theorists for help in modeling the process, however, the unanimous response was that the number of players, variables, constraints, and interactions made the problem too difficult to model. Courtney Jung and Ian Shapiro, "South Africa's Negotiated Transition: Democracy, Opposition, and the New Constitutional Order," *Politics and Society*, Vol. 23, No. 2 (September 1995), pp. 269–308. Problem-driven research agendas may often run into this difficulty. What differentiates the problem-driven researcher from the method-driven one is that the former will endeavor to give the most plausible possible account of the phenomenon that stands in need of explanation, whereas the method-driven researcher will study only those problems, or aspects of problems, to which his or her methods can be applied.

difference between inductive and deductive approaches comes down, then, to what one is left with in the likely event that one's hypothesis proves empirically inadequate: a rich supply of information about politics and a grasp of the going attempts to understand it, or a bunch of algebra that is unlikely to impress anyone in the math department.

COLLAPSING BRIDGES AND SELF-FULFILLING PROPHECIES

In *Pathologies*, we do not comment on the normative debates that have motivated, or arisen from, rational choice theory. Our central concern is with the extent to which rational choice models might succeed in advancing the understanding of politics, and the ways in which empirical research might be improved. Because rational choice theorists have sometimes pressed dubious or unsubstantiated empirical claims into the service of prescriptive arguments, we do note that our venture is not without normative significance.[147] Beyond this we avoid normative debates, restricting our attention to assessing the so-called positive rational choice program on its own terms. However, two normative considerations have emerged in the critical literature that seem to merit comment, the first arising out of Ordeshook's engineering-based conception of the social-scientific enterprise, the second out of Robert Abelson's survey of studies dealing with the effects of rational choice-inspired experimental work on the subjects studied.

Ordeshook calls for rational choice theorists to think about their tasks by analogy to engineers. Bridge-building engineers, he contends, generally intend to build better bridges than have been built in the past. Trying to understand why a particular bridge fell into the river motivates the enterprise of designing better bridges, and generates criteria for assessing the merits of particular efforts. Political science's failure "to connect its practical objectives to its theoretical and methodological ones results in confusion about the phenomena that warrant theoretical treatment, the distinction between theory and model, and, ultimately, the methods whereby we make scientific advances."[148] Thus, Ordeshook argues that political science should become a practical field in which we "seek not only to understand political things, but also to improve

---

[147] Green and Shapiro, *Pathologies*, pp. 11–12.
[148] Ordeshook, "Engineering or Science," pp. 181–82.

the operation of political processes and institutions."[149] Political scientists try to understand how democracy works, he insists, "so we can try to make it work better or make it work in previously authoritarian states. We study international affairs not because war amuses us, but because we want to learn how to avert conflict."[150]

Although we share Ordeshook's concerns about the quality of rational choice applications, his perspective assumes a degree of agreement on engineering objectives that cannot be taken for granted in the study of politics. People will generally agree on the purposes for which bridges should be designed, even if some in the construction business might have a pecuniary interest in bridges periodically falling into rivers. Ordeshook's account fails to come to grips with the fact that motives for studying politics vary widely. Some study war not in order to avert it but to try to ensure that their country wins the next one. Likewise, as Ordeshook asserts, some may indeed study democracy to try to make it more stable or viable. But others, including some of those whom Ordeshook praises for having advanced our understanding of it, seem to have had a different agenda: to delegitimate democracy and limit political interference with property rights and market relations.[151] Thus, although we agree with Ordeshook's preference for problem-driven research and with his skepticism that it will ever be possible "to put all the theoretical 'pieces' together into one theoretical analysis" in political science, we are doubtful that the goals can ever be self-evident in the ways the engineering analogy suggests.[152]

Ordeshook's suggestion that social scientists engage in trial-and-error engineering on unsuspecting millions may encounter difficulties from the Human Subjects Committees of most universities. These bodies may express concern about the potential social costs of such experiments in relation to the amount of reliable knowledge that can be extracted from single or small numbers of cases. These concerns are compounded by the path-dependency of experimental tinkering: Altering institutions in the real world (as opposed to under laboratory conditions) is usually irrevocable, changing the institution in question—and perhaps aspects of its environment—for all time. Attempting to

---

[149] *Ibid.*, p. 180.

[150] *Ibid.*, p. 180.

[151] See Shapiro, "Three Fallacies Concerning Majorities, Minorities, and Democratic Politics," in John Chapman and Alan Hertheimer, eds., *Nomos XXXII: Majorities and Minorities* (New York: New York University Press, 1990), pp. 79–125.

[152] Ordeshook, "Engineering or Science," p. 181.

build well-tested middle-level theory at least holds out the possibility of learning without resorting either to trial-and-error or to the unlikely-to-be-forthcoming deductive theory of everything.

In resisting Ordeshook's engineering-based approach we do not mean to suggest that the conduct of science is without normative effect. We do insist, however, that science will not make normative choices for us. This point is worth emphasizing in light of Abelson's discussion of what might usefully be described as the performative dimension of rational choice scholarship: in some circumstances rational choice theorists might actually produce the behavior in people that they believe they have discovered.[153] Studies suggesting that the propensity for strategic behavior increases with the study of economics, or that the introduction of selective incentives into children's games can make continued play dependent on those incentives where previously it was not, raise potentially worrisome possibilities. It may be that agency problems can be created, where previously they did not exist, simply by drawing people's attention to their possibility. Likewise with agenda-manipulation and free riding: researchers may help create the monster they describe by pointing out and legitimating as "rational" certain forms of strategic behavior. This is not to settle the question of whether instrumental behavior is necessarily "bad" It is to insist, however, that it is a genuine question. This can all too easily slip from view if it assumed, in advance of research and whatever its results, that strategic behavior is ubiquitous.

Concluding Remarks

Rational choice theorists are not the first to believe that the way to place the study of politics on the secure path of a science is to embrace a new paradigm, outlook, approach, or general theory. At different times, systems theorists, structural-functionalists, and Marxists, among others, have all harbored comparable theoretical ambitions. Although it is always possible that an architectonic effort of this sort will bear fruit, the history of accumulated failures leaves us skeptical. In our view, advances in political science are more likely to come at the level of the

---

[153] Robert P. Abelson, "The Secret Existence of Expressive Behavior," *Critical Review: An Interdisciplinary Journal of Politics and Society*, Vol. 9, Nos. 1–2 (Winter/Spring 1995), pp. 27–31.

hypothesis or middle-level generalization than at that of the grand theory or paradigmatic innovation, and the energy that is poured into developing new theories and paradigms, translating the existing stock of knowledge into them, and defending them against all comers, would be better spent on problem-driven research. As we have sought to establish in the preceding pages, this stance is not borne of any particular animus toward theorizing. Rather, it rests on the pragmatic judgment that empirically sustainable general theories about politics are unlikely to be formulated in any other way.

Nor does this stance place us at odds with the interdisciplinary outlook with which rational choice scholarship is often advertised. Problem-driven research pays no particular heed to existing disciplinary divisions. Whether the tools of economics, psychology, sociology or some other discipline should be brought to bear in the study of a given problem is always an open question, depending on the nature of the problem and the prior history of attempts to study it in these and other disciplines. Unlike many of our critics, we see no more reason to suppose that economic models will be successful across the board than those drawn from psychology or sociology. To assume the contrary is to clothe what is actually a parochial, not to say myopic, outlook in an interdisciplinary garb. This fact may go some way toward explaining why what rational choice theorists often take to be their open-minded and interdisciplinary spirit is seen by others as intellectual imperialism. Rational choice theorists will encounter less resistance when they supply a satisfactory answer to the question: What has been learned from rational choice theory? The present response of Diermeier and others, that its empirical accomplishments will be judged "eventually," while true, is not enough.[154]

---

[154] Diermeier, "Rational Choice and the Role of Theory," p. 59.

CHAPTER THREE

Richard Posner's Praxis

My purposes here are four. First, I reveal the internal logic of Richard Posner's microeconomic conception of judicial efficiency to be fallacious, partly for reasons indigenous to his particular formulation of it and partly for reasons that have long been known by welfare economists and political scientists to attend various compensation-based theories of allocative efficiency. Second, I show that in his writings about the federal courts and his advocacy of efficiency as a basis for common law making and statutory interpretation, Posner employs a conception of macroeconomic judicial efficiency that is not derived from his microeconomic theory and which is inconsistent with it. Third, by analyzing opinions he wrote as a federal appellate court judge on the Seventh Circuit between 1982 and 1987 in two areas—labor law and antitrust— I establish both that he fails to adhere consistently to either his microeconomic or his macroeconomic conceptions of efficiency as a judge, and that in the course of those decisions he reifies contentious and indeterminate economic theories by presenting them as uncontroversially "scientific." Last, I take note of some distributive and ideological implications of his enterprise.

Wealth Maximization as Judicial Efficiency: The Microeconomic Theory

The much celebrated and criticized "law and economics" movement has found its most lucid, prolific, and influential exponent in the person of Richard Posner. For decades he has championed the view that the common-law is best understood in terms of the theory of economic efficiency,[1] that "the basic function of law" is to "alter incentives" to maximize the efficient production of wealth.[2] Just what efficiency means will concern us shortly, but note to begin with that he advocates this theory in both descriptive and normative senses. Along with several other commentators, he has argued that the theory of economic efficiency explains the historical evolution of American common law (in directly "economic" fields such as antitrust and other regulatory law, as well as in such areas as torts, contracts, family law, products liability, and in many others), and, perhaps more contentiously, that the theory of efficiency should provide the basis for common-law adjudication in a wide variety of noneconomic fields of law.[3] Although professing agnosticism on the subject of how much of the legal terrain the economic analysis of law does and should govern, holding that this cannot be resolved a priori, that it is an empirical question to be settled as the practitioners of the law and economics movement attempt to apply it, he has suggested that economic analysis has application in torts, contracts, commercial law, property, procedure, remedies, criminal law, family law, intellectual property, and in all areas of law that have common law or "quasi common law" components, including antitrust law and constitutional law.[4] In addition he suggests that economic analysis applies in the process of statutory construction.[5]

There is an apparent tension between these descriptive and normative claims, as the descriptive claim exhibits an "invisible hand" component—that common-law judges have maximized efficiency without intending to or even knowing what they were doing, simply by applying

---

[1] Richard Posner, *Economic Analysis of Law* (Boston: Little, Brown, 1972); Richard Posner, "Some Uses and Abuses of Economics in Law," *University of Chicago Law Review*, Vol. 46, No. 2 (Winter 1979), p. 281.

[2] Richard Posner, *Economics of Justice* (Cambridge, MA: Harvard University Press, 1981).

[3] See, e.g., Gary S. Becker, "Crime and Punishment: An Economic Approach," *Journal of Political Economy*, Vol. 76, No. 2 (March/April 1968), p. 169; Paul H. Rubin, "Why is the Common Law Efficient?" *Journal of Legal Studies*, Vol. 6, No. 1 (January 1977), pp. 51–63; George L. Priest, "The Common Law process and the Selection of Efficient Rules," *Journal of Legal Studies*, Vol. 6, No. 1 (January 1977), pp. 65–82. See also Posner, "Some Uses and Abuses," pp. 281–91 (for a brief history of the "law and economics" movement with extensive citations).

[4] "[T]he limitations of economics [in legal analysis and adjudication] cannot be determined a priori, but only by the efforts of scholars to apply economics to hitherto unexplored areas of the legal system. One can reach the outer bounds of a discipline only by pushing outwards. Eventually a point will be reached where the economic theory ceases to have substantial explanatory power. Then we will know the limitations of the economic analysis of law; we do not know them yet." Posner, "Some Uses and Abuses," p. 297.

[5] *Ibid.*, p. 296; Richard Posner, *The Federal Courts: Crisis and Reform* (Cambridge, MA: Harvard University Press, 1985), pp. 261–315.

such traditional common-law notions as the negligence standard in torts and products liability.[6] And Posner has upbraided judges for trying to apply the theory of efficiency "directly," arguing that they misunderstand and misuse it. He is critical, for instance, of Judge Sneed's attempt to apply economic analysis in *Union Oil Co. v. Oppen*,[7] arguing that he misunderstood Guido Calabresi's theory of minimizing accident and avoidance costs that he was attempting to apply.[8] But Posner contends that Sneed nonetheless reached the "economically sensible" result, even though he was "unable to articulate it successfully in economic terms."[9] Likewise with Sneed's nineteenth century predecessors, in Posner's view, although it is "even less likely" that they would have wanted or been able to cast their opinions in explicit economic terms, for there was "much less awareness of the technical concepts of economics," it does not follow that their opinions did not make "implicit economic sense."[10] Taken to its logical conclusion, this reasoning would seem to suggest that the best way to promote "economically rational" adjudication would be for judges to ignore economics entirely, at least in the absence of some additional theoretical argument.

This claim is perhaps analogous to Justice Holmes's theory that once the historical evolution of the common law had been fully grasped it could be jettisoned in favor of "scientific" principles that would do the same job that the common-law adjudication had done hitherto but more efficiently because more directly.[11] Posner offers no comparable

[6] Richard Posner, "A Theory of Negligence," *Journal of Legal Studies*, Vol. 1, No. 1 (1972), p. 29. But see Guido Calabresi and Jon T. Hirschoff, "Toward a Test for Strict Liability in Torts," *Yale Law Journal*, Vol. 81, No. 1 (May 1972), p. 1055–85.

[7] 501 F.2d 558 (9th Cir. 1974).

[8] *Oppen* was a suit by a commercial fisherman whose livelihood had been harmed by the Santa Barbara oil spill of 1969. At issue was whether the defendant oil companies could be held liable for an injury to the plaintiff's loss of expected business (as opposed to harm to a vested property right). Judge Sneed held that the defendant was liable in part by reference to Calabresi's theory of strict liability, according to which losses should be allocated to the party best able to avoid the costs of accidents. Guido Calabresi, *The Costs of Accidents* (New Haven: Yale University Press, 1970), pp. 145–52. Posner's objection is not to the result reached by Judge Sneed but, rather, to the discussion of Calabresi's test and the fact that he reached the result by interpreting the defendant's stipulation as an admission of negligence, as well as the fact that he engaged in what Posner takes to be irrelevant discussion of the effects of the accident on consumption goods. Posner, "Some Uses and Abuses," pp. 298–99.

[9] Posner, "Some Uses and Abuses," pp. 300–301.

[10] *Ibid.*, pp. 297–301.

[11] Oliver Wendell Holmes, *The Common Law* (Cambridge, MA: Harvard University Press, 1963), pp. 31–33.

argument, however, and in several places he explicitly advocates efficiency as a normative basis for adjudication. He also argues that the overload crisis in the federal courts could be alleviated somewhat if both legislators and judges took better account of efficiency.[12] The implications of this tension will be considered later, after I have disentangled Posner's different notions of efficiency invoked in different contexts. The propositions I intend to examine first are the descriptive and normative versions of Posner's microeconomic thesis, the precise meaning of the claim that the common law is efficient, and the relationship between this and the claim that it ought to be.

How are we to interpret the claim that the common law is efficient? Posner tells us that "[t]he hypothesis is not that the common law does or could perfectly duplicate the results of competitive markets." Rather it is that "within the limits of administrative feasibility, the law brings the economic system closer to producing the results that effective competition—a free market operating without significant externality, monopoly, or information problems—would produce."[13] The common law promotes efficiency in the face of these various forms of market failure. And it is just for this reason that Posner needs a more complex notion of efficiency than simple Pareto-optimality, for this latter comes about, by definition, when unregulated markets are well functioning. In fact Posner's conception of microeconomic efficiency is a second cousin of the notion of compensation developed by Kaldor and Hicks in the late 1930s and early 1940s.[14] He develops it by distinguishing it from classical utilitarianism and from the neoclassical Pareto system.[15]

The difficulties with classical utilitarianism in Posner's view are three. First, there are philosophical difficulties with the notion that the only value for which people strive is pleasure. Second, there are various problems of "domain"—external effects on others of pursuing happiness—and problems in defining the class of beings whose utility is to be maximized.[16] Third, there are the well-known difficulties of measurement and

---

[12] See, for example, Posner, *The Federal Courts*, p. 294.

[13] Posner, "Some Uses and Abuses," pp. 288–89.

[14] See Ian Little, *A Critique of Welfare Economics* (Oxford: Clarendon Press, 1950), pp. 84–128; Maurice Herbert Dobb, *Welfare Economics and the Economics of Socialism: Towards a Commonsense Critique* (London: Cambridge University Press, 1969), pp. 77–118.

[15] See Anthony T. Kronman, "Wealth Maximization as a Normative Principle," *Journal of Legal Studies*, Vol. 9, No. 2 (March 1980), pp. 227, 236, for the argument that wealth-maximization is analytically equivalent to the Kaldor-Hicks test. See also Jules L. Coleman, "Efficiency, Utility and Wealth Maximization." *Hofstra Legal Review*, Vol. 8 (1980), pp. 509, 532–34.

[16] Posner, *Economics of Justice*, pp. 52–53.

administration of the utility principle—whether and how the utility of some might be sacrificed to benefit others, for "there is no reliable technique for measuring a change in the level of satisfaction of one individual relative to a change in the level of satisfaction of another."[17]

To avoid these difficulties Posner begins by defining efficiency in terms of "wealth-maximization," thereby avoiding the metaphysical questions about happiness that have been thought by many since G. E. Moore to render it hopelessly circular.[18] In fact, this was a move that even Jeremy Bentham had made implicitly, by arguing that money can function as a proxy for utility, and by holding that the redistribution of wealth should always be limited by the requirement of "abundance." Although, ceteris paribus, the principle of diminishing marginal utility requires downward redistribution of wealth, we should never redistribute beyond the point which would have negative effects on the production of abundance, because in the long run this would diminish overall utility.[19] But whereas Bentham saw preserving abundance as one necessary condition for maximizing utility, Posner's view is that efficiency should be defined as wealth-maximization, making any connection with happiness purely contingent.[20]

The other two difficulties of classical utilitarianism, concerning domain and utility measurement, are more serious from the standpoint of a theory of adjudicative efficiency. In the history of welfare economics, both were neatly resolved by the rejection of the cardinal interpersonal utility scales Bentham had worked with and their replacement with the doctrine of ordinal utility and the theory of revealed preference enshrined in the Pareto principle. Ordinal utility scales required much more easily obtainable information since they ruled out interpersonal comparisons by definition and they were concerned only with marginal changes. It was not necessary to know an agent's entire preference ranking, nor the intensity of his preferences, to predict his behavior at the

---

[17] *Ibid.*, p. 54.

[18] *Ibid.*, p. 51–52; See also Richard Posner, "Utilitarianism, Economics and Legal Theory," *Journal of Legal Studies*, Vol. 8, No. 1 (January 1979), pp. 103–40.

[19] Jeremy Bentham, "The Psychology of Economic Man," in W. Stark, ed., *Jeremy Bentham's Economic Writings* (London: Allen & Unwin, 1954), pp. 439–43. Note also that where Posner always thinks by reference to total utility, Bentham's principle was that we should maximize the greatest happiness of the greatest number, a requirement with quite different distributive implications. Depending on our reading of Bentham, this can mean maximizing the utility of a majority, or of a plurality, whereas Posner's "total utility" criterion will in some circumstances be met by maximizing the utility or wealth of a minority.

[20] Posner, *Economics of Justice*, pp. 60–65.

margins from a given status quo. The theory of revealed preference solved the problem of how to get even this limited information: the market would reveal it. Assuming that people make only those exchanges that benefit themselves, all exchanges that occur must be Pareto superior by definition, else they would not occur, and when all voluntary transactions have ceased the result must by definition be Pareto optimal. There are no further exchanges that would benefit at least one individual while harming none. It may, of course, be true that if we took some wealth from Peter and gave it to Paul, the increment in Paul's wealth would be greater than the loss to Peter (and the total amount of utility in society thereby increased) but by the Pareto principle we can never know that this is the case, since utility functions of individuals cannot be compared. On these Pareto noncomparable transactions, neoclassical welfare economics was silent.

Ronald Coase's famous theorem,[21] which did more than any other single development to get the "law and economics" movement off the ground, supplied the basis for the lawyer's analogue of the Pareto principle. It held, ceteris paribus, that in the absence of information costs, wealth effects, external effects and other blockages to exchange such as free riding, no system of liability rules is more efficient than any other, because whatever the system, people will make exchanges to produce Pareto-optimal results.

From the standpoint of a theory of adjudicative efficiency the Pareto principle has two sorts of defects. First, there is the difficulty Posner refers to as that of "domain," the problem of whose utility is to be taken into account. The Pareto principle takes it for granted that we know who the parties to a given transaction are. But in reality this is seldom unproblematic, particularly in the law, where what the economists think of as "external effects" of transactions are often what is centrally in contention. This is not quite how Posner construes the boundary problem of classical utilitarianism. He sees the problem centrally as one of what beings to take into account in the utilitarian calculus—whether to include animals and foreigners, and perhaps even alien beings—for

the logic of utilitarianism seems to favor setting as the ethical goal the maximization of the total amount of happiness in the universe. Since this goal seems attainable only by making lots of people miserable, (those of

[21] Ronald Coase, "The Problem of Social Cost," *Journal of Law and Economy*, Vol. 3, No. 1 (1960), p. 1.

us who would have to make room for all the foreigners, sheep, or whatever), utilitarians are constantly seeking ways to construct the boundary. But to do so they must go outside of utilitarianism.[22]

Posner regards his turn to wealth-maximization as a solution to this problem, for we now have a criterion for drawing the boundaries. "Animals count," he tells us, "but only insofar as they enhance wealth. The optimal population of sheep is determined not by speculation on their capacity for contentment relative to people, but by the intersection of the marginal product and marginal cost of keeping sheep."[23] Likewise, with foreigners the theory of wealth-maximization suggests that a policy of "free immigration with no public support for the immigrant will [ensure] that only wealth-maximizing immigration occurs" as "[n]o one will immigrate who anticipates an income lower than the costs of maintaining himself."[24]

Passing over the fact that Posner's theory ignores the circumstances that the immigrant is leaving, these examples indicate both that Posner fails to avoid the boundary problem that he identifies in utilitarianism, and that his own approach is deeply problematical. The examples fail to solve the boundary problem because Posner does not see that it is part of a much more general problem about action. The difficulty raised by animals is not that we no longer have to speculate about their happiness, but rather that they may have a different way, which we may not understand, of deciding what counts as wealth and wealth-maximization. With foreigners, the very definition of them as foreigners assumes what Posner has to establish, because individuals may well challenge our right to designate them as foreigners. From the standpoint of pure economic theory, we have no more business regarding them as foreigners than we do regarding the people in the next town as foreigners, or than do Native Americans have regarding us as foreigners for that matter. Indeed, in many cases the problem of boundaries will masquerade as a problem of external effects, as when an individual's property value is harmed, or when a worker loses his job as the result of a factory's relocation to another state and the owner argues that these are not relevant effects from the point of view of evaluating his action. The theory of wealth-maximization presents exactly the same difficulties as

---

[22] Posner, *Economics of Justice*, pp. 52–54.

[23] *Ibid.*, p. 76.

[24] *Ibid.*, p. 78.

utilitarianism presents in defining boundaries because, ultimately, they are unresolved problems in the philosophy of action.

Posner's discussion is illuminating, nonetheless, because it throws into sharp relief the questionable assumptions about efficiency implicit in his argument. If wealth-maximization is the key criterion of efficiency, the theory tells us to pay attention to distributive questions only to the extent that they are pertinent to maximizing wealth. As he admits, "people who lack sufficient earning power to support even a minimally decent standard of living are entitled to no say in the allocation of resources unless they are part of the utility function of someone who has wealth."[25] Posner considers and rejects the Rawlsian critique of this view—namely that it gives people an unfair advantage because of such random characteristics as intelligence and feeble-mindedness[26]—and argues instead that "[t]o treat the inventor and the idiot equally concerning their moral claim to command over valuable resources does not take seriously the differences between persons. And any policy of redistribution impairs the autonomy of those from whom redistribution is made."[27] Posner sidesteps the fact that this procedure may violate the autonomy of the poorly endowed with the quip that although this "grates on modern sensibilities," he sees "no escape from it that is consistent with any of the major ethical systems."[28] This is, of course, notably less than an argument, and it embodies distributive assumptions that have long been known to be deeply troubling to welfare economists.

It is important to remember that Posner's wealth-maximization test, like the compensation tests developed by Kaldor, Hicks, and Scitovsky, comes into play in situations of market failure, when a disinterested party, such as a judge (or a legislature in the case of welfare economics), must reallocate wealth to produce a Pareto-optimal result that, for one reason or another, is not generated in an unregulated market.[29] It is in this type of context that the various compensation tests and Posner's wealth-maximization criterion are brought into play. The logic behind

---

[25] *Ibid.*, p. 76.

[26] As Posner summarizes this view: "If [an individual] happens to be born feeble-minded and his net social product is negative, he would have no right to the means of support even though there was nothing blameworthy in his inability to support himself." *Ibid.*, p. 76.

[27] *Ibid.*, p. 76.

[28] *Ibid.*, p. 76.

[29] For two useful discussions, see Jules L. Coleman, "Efficiency, Exchange and Auction: Philosophic Aspects of the Economic Approach to Law," *California Law Review*, Vol. 68, No. 2 (March 1980), pp. 221, 509; Coleman, "Efficiency, Utility and Wealth Maximization," p. 509.

all of these is a theory of hypothetical compensation. The early compensation theorists wanted to find a way of discussing Pareto-undecidable outcomes that increased overall welfare. Intuitively, if a transfer could occur between A and B (but does not) whereby A would gain more than B would lose, it seemed plausible to say that overall social product or welfare had increased. They wanted to argue this, however, without invoking the whole Benthamite system of interpersonally comparable cardinal utilities and its radically redistributive implications. It was this need that generated the claim that if A could compensate B for B's loss and still be better off than at the status quo ante, the total product would have increased, even though no compensation occurred in fact. Now as Ian Little and others long ago observed,[30] it is a curious notion of welfare that holds that if I take your assets, provided I could in principle (but do not in practice) pay you for them and still be better off, the welfare of both of us has increased. But more to the point here, despite the formidable series of theoretical efforts from Kaldor and Hicks to Samuelson to derive a compensation theory from ordinalist premises, there is now a very wide consensus among welfare economists that this cannot be done, and that all the hypothetical compensation tests implicitly employ full-blown cardinal systems.[31]

In the context of Posner's particular application of the Kaldor-Hicks test, this means that the deciding third party must make her own evaluation, not only of who would be hurt and who would be benefited in what amounts by her forced reallocation of resources (which I discuss shortly), but she also would need a theory of economic growth to tell her what allocation of resources would maximize wealth in fact. This immediately requires that the judge depart from the realm of microeconomic logic to an empirical theory of how the economy operates, of how wealth in fact is maximized. So one might imagine that a judge who believes in neoclassical theories of investment incentives would do everything she could to minimize awards in Social Security and unemployment compensation cases before her, on the grounds that increases in transfer payments increase taxation burdens and minimize

[30] Little, *A Critique of Welfare Economics*, pp. 84–116; James S. Fishkin, *Tyranny and Legitimacy: A Critique of Political Theories* (London: Johns Hopkins University Press, 1979), pp. 91–96; Kronman, "Wealth Maximization," pp. 236–39; Ian Shapiro, *The Evolution of Rights in Liberal Theory* (Cambridge: Cambridge University Press, 1986), pp. 169–78.

[31] See Mark Blaug, *Economic Theory in Retrospect* (Cambridge and New York: Cambridge University Press, 1978), pp. 602–44. An up-to-date and accessible discussion of these issues can be found in chapter 13 on general equilibrium and welfare economics.

investment. A Keynesian judge, by contrast, might adopt the converse policy and make awards as generous as possible, as transfers from those with a low marginal propensity to consume to those with a higher one will stimulate demand, and, hence, production and overall social product or wealth. Or, by reference to Posner's example, the Keynesian theory might tell us to subsidize immigration as a means of stimulating demand and, as a result, of maximizing wealth. In other words, Posner's theory of wealth-maximization cannot be applied without the judge, or decision maker, employing a controversial and contentious empirical theory of what maximizes wealth (with major distributive implications), and it is difficult to see why one such theory should be preferred over others. What Posner in fact does, as I shall discuss, is reify one such controversial theory which generates distributive results congenial to him, and then presents it as "the" economic theory of adjudication.

Once it becomes clear that Posner's theory requires a full-blown cardinal system, it is also clear that he confronts all the measurement problems that have always attended classical utilitarianism. He needs some independent, interpersonally comparable, basis by reference to which a disinterested third party can determine whether the benefit to A does in fact exceed the detriment to B in a forced transaction, and by how much. Compensation theorists have traditionally employed money as their basic unit of account, but among the difficulties with this is that it makes it impossible to assess compensation independently of so-called wealth-effects or income-effects on demand. This is why a standard criticism of the Pareto system has always been that it implicitly ascribes moral respectability to the status quo, which in turn delimits the range of superior and optimal outcomes. This is in fact a double problem for Posner, because although the status quo could be argued to respect autonomy from Pareto's premises,[32] there is no particular reason to respect the status quo from the point of view of wealth-maximization. There is in fact no particular reason to respect property rights at all from the standpoint of this radically consequentialist ethic; if state ownership of the means of production could be shown to maximize overall wealth it should be preferred on his theory.

Now Posner has no intention of wandering anywhere near this conclusion, of course, and he avoids it by committing to the empirical

---

[32] In my view, this is not very plausible. See my, *Evolution of Rights*, pp. 165–78, in which I discuss these issues in relation to Nozick's theory of justice-in-transfer. For a more comprehensive account of the measurement problems in different variants utilitarian theory, see my *The Moral Foundations of Politics* (New Haven: Yale University Press, 2003), chaps. 2–3.

thesis that individual property rights, when allocated through markets as a by-product of "economic liberty" and then preserved by legal rules, maximize a society's wealth. "It is the almost universal opinion of economists (including Marxist economists)," he remarks with quite staggering confidence, "that free markets, whatever objections can be made to them on grounds of equity, maximize a society's wealth."[33] This means that a system of private property rights and free markets, upheld and preserved through the courts, best maximizes wealth. "The theory of property rights" he tells us (as though there was one theory) "is an important branch of modern microeconomic theory. A property right, in both law and economics, is a right to exclude everyone else from the use of some scarce resource."[34] From the point of view of economic theory, absolute property rights are desirable "when the costs of voluntary transactions are low."[35] As transactions costs increase, it makes increasing economic sense for the state to become involved in their allocation and reallocation.[36] In these latter circumstances, rights should be reallocated by the state in accordance with the theory of wealth-maximization, although again, Posner never makes clear what theory is to be employed. He simply asserts as follows:

> If transaction costs are positive . . . the wealth maximization principle requires the initial vesting of rights in those who are likely to value them most, so as to minimize transaction costs. This is the economic reason for giving a worker the right to sell his labor and the woman the right to determine her sexual partners. If assigned randomly to strangers, these rights would generally (not invariably) be repurchased by the worker and the woman; the costs of the rectifying transaction can be avoided if the right is assigned at the outset to the user who values it the most.[37]

This is doubly question-begging. First, Posner gives no indication of how to determine what the most efficient initial endowment is. Second, he pays no attention to the fact that the existing distribution of wealth at a given time will limit an individual's capacity to buy the things he values the most. In a regime which assigned the right to choice of a woman's sexual partner to someone else (such as her father), who is to

---

[33] Posner, *Economics of Justice*, p. 67 (no references to the writings of any economists, Marxist or other, are cited in support of this assertion).

[34] *Ibid.*, p. 70.

[35] *Ibid.*, p. 70.

[36] *Ibid.*, p. 70.

[37] *Ibid.*, p. 71.

say that she would have the resources to purchase that right? To assume that she would is to assume exactly what Posner has to establish if his theory is to make any sense.

As a generalized theory of the origins of property rights this notion is incomplete, since prior to the existence of property there would be nothing for which to exchange rights.[38] To posit this as a generalized theory of property endowments simply replicates and exacerbates the inequalities that prevail in a society. Posner denies this by empirical assertion:

> [T]he assignment of rights at the outset of social development is unlikely to determine the allocation of resources many generations later. Suppose at the beginning one man owned all the wealth in a society. To exploit that wealth, he would have to share it with other people—he would have to pay them to work for him. His remaining wealth would be divided among his children or other heirs at his death. Thus, over time, the goods and services produced and consumed in the society would be determined not by his preferences but by those of his employees and heirs. Probably after several generations most prices in this society, both market and shadow prices, would be similar to those in societies in which the initial distribution of wealth was more equal. If so, it means the initial distribution of wealth will eventually cease to have an important effect on the society's aggregate wealth.[39]

This is sheer fancy, and empirically implausible to boot. Wealth often concentrates in market systems over time. In any case, the initial and prevailing distribution of wealth in a society has everything to do with the production and distribution of additional wealth.

When critics like Ronald Dworkin suggest that there may be other values than wealth-maximization, such as distributive considerations, which are the law's proper concern,[40] for Posner to assert that these will all be solved "automatically" by the market once property rights have been distributed in accordance with his wealth-maximization criterion is to beg the question. Yet this is exactly what he does:

> Once these [property] rights (to one's body, labor, and so forth) are established, they will be sold, rented, or bartered to yield income to their owners. In general, the wealthier people will be those who have the higher

---

[38] Kronman, "Wealth Maximization," pp. 240–42.
[39] Posner, *Economics of Justice*, pp. 111–12.
[40] Ronald M. Dworkin, "Is Wealth a Value?" *Journal of Legal Studies*, Vol. 9, No. 2 (March 1980), pp. 191, 192–94.

marginal products, whether because they work harder, or are smarter, or for whatever reason. In a system whose goal is to maximize society's wealth, the distribution of wealth that results from paying people in rough proportion to their contribution to that goal is not arbitrary. The main point, however, is that the specific distribution of *wealth* is a mere by-product of the distribution of *rights* that is itself derived from the wealth-maximization principle. A just distribution of wealth need not be posited.[41]

Passing over the fact that Posner never even attempts to establish that such a system does reward people in proportion with their contribution—an evident problem if only because Posner endorses inherited wealth[42]—it is misleading to refer to what is being maximized as "society's" wealth. What, in fact, is being maximized is the wealth of those individuals who have the capacity to maximize wealth without reference to anyone else, except to the extent that they are instrumental in that goal. When Posner talks of wealth-maximization as producing a surplus "for the rest of us to enjoy,"[43] he is assuming a trickle-down causal theory for which he offers no evidence. Even in terms of the analytical logic behind the Pareto system, there is no necessary reason to believe that wealth-maximization by a given individual will have positive external effects on others.[44] For this reason—protestations by Posner to the contrary notwithstanding—there is no convincing sense in which wealth-maximization can be argued to respect individual autonomy.

In short, Posner dodges all distributive questions by definition and circular argument. This is why critics such as Dworkin, Anthony Kronman, and Arthur Leff[45] are justified in complaining that wealth-maximization cannot be the exclusive value guiding adjudication. To the extent that a court did follow Posner's theory, it would be invoking one particular contestable causal theory of how wealth is maximized in fact, and endorsing whatever distributive externalities turn out to be generated by it. If one of these in a system that generates Trump Tower is a bag lady

---

[41] Posner, *Economics of Justice*, p. 81.

[42] *Ibid.*, p. 82.

[43] *Ibid.*, p. 82.

[44] Strictly, all that is required is that no party be made worse off relative to his previous position, i.e., in absolute terms, relative inequalities can grow continuously in an expanding economy.

[45] Dworkin, "Is Wealth a Value?" p. 191; Kronman, "Wealth Maximization"; Arthur Leff, "Economic Analysis of Law: Some Realism about Nominalism," *Virginia Law Review*, Vol. 60 (1974), p. 451.

living out of a locker in Grand Central Station, so be it; it is a "mere by-product of the distribution of rights that is itself derived from the wealth-maximization principle."[46] Posner's defense of the market as a distributor of rights is arbitrary; it does not follow from his premises once he has admitted the existence of transaction costs and wealth effects, and it is incoherent as an account of the origins of property rights, since it presumes their existence. What Posner really wants judges to do is mimic or "shadow" the market, or what they believe would be generated by the market in a particular case where its operation is obstructed. He believes that the distributive chips must lie where they fall. This is a distributive theory that Posner never defends, and, indeed, the very need to defend it is evaded by assuming that maximizing the wealth of those who already have it somehow benefits "society"—an empirical claim not supported by his theory and which he never seeks to establish.

WEALTH-MAXIMIZATION AS JUDICIAL EFFICIENCY: THE MACROECONOMIC THEORY

Whatever the internal difficulties in the microeconomic logic of Posner's conception of efficiency as wealth-maximization, it is notable that once we move into the domains of Posner qua legal reformer and judge, the microeconomic theory is largely abandoned. This is not to say that the appeal to "law and economics" is ignored. In his prizewinning book on the crisis of overload in the federal courts, Posner contends that these courts "can improve their performance in common law adjudication by using some simple but powerful tools of economic analysis."[47] Economic analysis can, in his view, be used to improve the functioning of the federal courts in two quite different senses, the first having to do with legislative reform, and the second with an expansive interpretation of the nature of federal courts and their function as common law courts.

Economic Analysis and the Legislative Reform of the Federal Judicial System

Posner's proposals for legislative reform of the courts are conceived in terms of supply and demand. Although he does not discount entirely

---

[46] Posner, *Economics of Justice*, p. 81.
[47] Posner, *The Federal Courts*, p. 294.

the effects of such exogenous factors as demographic changes, his focus is on changes wrought by alterations in the structure of the system itself, and the effects of incentives of these changes on the behavior of litigants.[48] The explosive new demands on court time and resources in federal litigation, which he documents exhaustively,[49] are analyzed from the standpoint of supply and demand for judicial services. Viewing "federal judicial services as a product whose output, like that of other products, is governed by the laws of demand and supply,"[50] Posner sees the causes of these demands on the federal judiciary as coming from both directions. Demand has increased dramatically in diversity cases, for example, because the $10,000 minimum amount in controversy requirement has not been changed since 1958 and has been eroded by more than two thirds due to inflation.[51] Other real declines in price which have stimulated demand have been the progressive relaxation of the elements of the justifiability requirement of Article III, notably mootness and standing.[52] Another major factor in decreasing the "pricing of judicial services" has been the greatly expanded availability of lawyers for indigent claimants, notably criminal defendants, through the combined result of Supreme Court decisions expanding the right to counsel in criminal cases, and the funding of lawyers for poor people through the Legal Services Corporation and the funding of lawyers for indigent federal criminal defendants under the Criminal Justice Act of 1964. "The fall in price of that input—from prohibitive to zero—for a large class of federal litigants is the economic equivalent of a dramatic drop in the price of the services themselves."[53]

The other major factor in "shifting the demand curve for federal services outward" has been the legislative and judicial creation of new federal rights since the early 1960s.[54] Title VII of the Civil Rights Act created many new remedies for employment discrimination, but more important than any single statute has been the Warren Court and, to a slightly lesser extent, the Burger Court which have, "through broad interpretations of the Bill of Rights, the due process and equal protection clauses of the Fourteenth Amendment, the Habeas Corpus Act of

---

[48] *Ibid.*, pp. 59–60, 77.
[49] *Ibid.*, pp. 59–166.
[50] *Ibid.*, p. 77.
[51] *Ibid.*, pp. 78–79.
[52] *Ibid.*, p. 79.
[53] *Ibid.*, p. 79.
[54] *Ibid.*, p. 80.

1867, and section 1 of the Ku Klux Klan Act of 1871, and through willingness to create private rights of action under federal statutes and the Constitution itself . . . enormously enlarged the number of rights upon which a federal court suit [can] be founded."[55] Posner estimates that these factors explain 75 percent of the 250-percent increase of filings in federal district courts between 1960 and 1983.[56] Although the increase in federal appeals is more complex and difficult to explain, partly because of growing uncertainty over what is the law in a period of such massive, innovative change (which obviously stimulates appeals), the same variables have clearly had a major impact—notably in criminal appeals which increased from 25 percent in 1960 to almost 95 percent in 1982.[57]

The consequence of this large increase has been a corresponding decline in quality in the judicial process, for the conventional market mechanisms have failed to limit demand. In a private market "[i]n the short run, when (by definition) producers are unable to expand their productive capacity, price rises to ration demand to existing fixed supply" and in the longer run supply will respond by increasing. This has not happened regarding access to courts.[58] No attempt has been made to limit demand:

> [W]ithout ever clearly acknowledging their policy, the people who control the federal court system (congressmen, executive branch officials, judges, and judicial administrators) have acted consistently over this [1960–83] period as if they had an unshakable commitment to accommodating any increase in the demand for federal judicial services without raising the price of those services, directly or indirectly, in the short run or the long run.[59]

Whereas the evident political attractiveness of this approach is that it shifts the costs of dealing with the problem from vociferous interest groups to silent taxpayers and future litigants, even this policy has not been followed consistently. The number of federal district court judges has doubled while the caseload has tripled, the number of federal

[55] *Ibid.*, pp. 80–81 (citations omitted).
[56] *Ibid.*, p. 87.
[57] *Ibid.*, p. 91.
[58] *Ibid.*, p. 94.
[59] *Ibid.*, p. 95.

appeals court judges has doubled whereas appeals have increased
eightfold, and, of course, the number of Supreme Court justices has
remained fixed. The inevitable resulting strain on the system has produced much greater reliance on supporting personnel—law clerks, ref-
erees in bankruptcy, new federal magistrates operating as "kind of junior district judge[s]," "externs" (law students obtaining course credit
away from law school), and staff attorneys.[60] The political costs to legislatures of raising expenditures above certain levels (now close to having been reached), together with the relatively fixed structure of the
upper institutional echelons of the federal system, make these quality-
diminishing results more or less inevitable,[61] and the only viable direction for reform in Posner's view is to take steps to limit demand for
federal judicial services.[62] This can be done by "upping the ante," increasing filing fees, increasing the minimum amount-in-controversy in
diversity cases and reinstating it in other cases, and generally requiring
losing litigants in civil litigation to pay winners' attorneys fees to reduce the taxpayer "subsidy" of federal civil litigation.[63] Congress might
also limit or even abolish diversity jurisdiction,[64] and create new tiers
of administrative review within the executive branch.[65] These steps
would function to limit demand and to shift some of the irreducible
burden to state courts that cannot close their doors as they are constitutionally required to hear federal claims.[66]

For present purposes I will assume that the picture Posner paints of
the increase in demand for federal judicial resources is broadly accurate. Although it is useful to have the costs of the creation and enforcement of a civilized system of federal rights unambiguously pointed
out, the implicit theory of efficiency behind Posner's recommendations is undefended. What is that theory? What is the significance of
the expansion of the caseload from the standpoint of legislative reform? I will consider this first from within the terms of Posner's economic analysis, and then I will look more critically at the terms of that
analysis themselves.

[60] *Ibid.*, p. 97.
[61] *Ibid.*, pp. 130–31.
[62] *Ibid.*, pp. 95–96.
[63] *Ibid.*, pp. 131–32.
[64] *Ibid.*, pp. 139–46.
[65] *Ibid.*, pp. 160–62. Posner also considers, but is less convinced of the merits of the creation of
more specialized courts—particularly in such technical fields as antitrust, and a second tier of
Supreme Court review. *Ibid.*, pp. 147–60, 162–66.
[66] *Ibid.*, p. 133.

From the standpoint of Posner's demand/supply model, there is, of course, no particular reason for the system not to expand over time. The fact that demand for a commodity increases partly because it becomes cheaper in no way distinguishes what Posner terms "federal judicial services" from any other commodity. To assume otherwise would be to embrace a theory of "natural prices" of the sort sought after by classical economists from Petty to Ricardo—precisely the kind of theory that the neoclassical economists axiomatically rejected. The classical view was that while supply and demand might have short term effects on price, in the long run they would determine output; market prices would always fluctuate around "natural" prices that, for Petty, Smith, Ricardo, and Marx, were determined by labor or the cost of labor time.[67]

The marginalist concept of long-run equilibrium price on which neoclassical economics was founded dispensed with all notions of natural price, explaining movements in price as the sole consequence of interactions between demand and supply. From the standpoint of this theory, it makes no sense to say that demand is too great and should be limited by the state. If legal rights are the commodity, supplied by the state as a natural monopoly, which assumption is required to get the entire argument off the ground,[68] then supply of judicial services will expand in response to increased demand, even when this increase is the partial result of previous increases in supply. And the mere fact that politicians resist funding that expansion is not necessarily an indication that the objective limits to supply have been reached. This is an empirical claim that is not especially plausible given the fact that the United States has lower rates of taxation than almost all capitalist nations and that federal expenditures as a proportion of GNP are likewise comparatively low.[69] Rather, it is more likely to mean either that there is some market failure preventing supply from responding adequately to changes in demand, or perhaps more plausibly, that effective demand

---

[67] They differed greatly with one another over how these terms were to be defined and quantified. See Maurice Herbert Dobb, *Theories of Value and Distribution Since Adam Smith* (Cambridge: Cambridge University Press, 1973).

[68] Unless coercive force is regarded as a natural monopoly, perhaps in principle evolving from mutual "protection associations" or insurance companies for the protection of individual rights, the logic of efficiency cannot justify the existence of any legal system at all. See Robert Nozick, *Anarchy, State, and Utopia* (New York: Basic Books, 1974), pp. 113–19.

[69] David R. Cameron, "Does Government Cause Inflation? Taxes, Spending and Deficits," in Leon N. Lindberg and Charles S. Maier, eds., *The Politics of Inflation and Economic Stagnation: Theoretical Approaches and International Case Studies* (Washington, DC: Brookings Institution Press, 1985), pp. 224–79.

is satisfied, at least in the short term, by a greater quantity of lower quality services. If Posner's economic model is to be taken seriously, then no objective quality of services "ought" to be provided. If people demand services at a greater rate than they are prepared to tolerate increases in taxation, the result must necessarily be a decline in quality. But so what? And if, *per impossible*, Posner was able to make the case for an objective quality of service, resistance to the taxation increases necessary to finance those services at new levels of demand would still fail to show decisively that objective limits to supply had been reached. It could just as plausibly indicate the existence of free rider problems, of individuals hoping to get the benefit of better services when avoiding paying their share of the proportionate cost. In that case there would be no particular reason for preferring state action to limit demand over state action to force taxation increases to supply judicial services to meet it. Indeed, in the face of this market failure, the doctrine of consumer sovereignty would seem to dictate the latter policy.

It is clear that, on its own, Posner's economic model is fully consistent with continuous increases in demand and supply, and, indeed, if we pressed the market metaphor to its logical extreme, we might even want to regard growth in "adjudicative output" as a measure of "macrojudicial" health. This is, of course, absurd; reminiscent of the psychologist who remarked that in the best of all possible worlds everyone would always be in therapy. But the reason why it is absurd is instructive: No economic theory of efficiency can function as a substitute for policy decisions about the purposes for which a legal system exists. Once these policy decisions are determined, economic reasoning may help us decide how to realize those policies most effectively and force us to face up to the costs of the rights we decide to create. But these are quite other matters. Economic theory cannot itself tell us how many rights to create and enforce, or what quality of enforcement is desirable; for the model to make any sense within its own terms, these things must be regarded as exogenous to it.

If this is true, the central issue becomes how these questions *are* to be decided. The traditional public law answer to this question, that they are the combined result of actions in the political branches and those of a common-law-making judiciary, gets Posner's qualified endorsement. But he interprets the traditional answer in a novel way so as to reinforce his appeal to economic theory. His account of common-law-making will concern me later; for now I focus on his view of the legitimacy of the acts of the political branches.

The key question about legislative action for Posner has to be the sense in which it can be said to function in the public interest. From the standpoint of his economic theory, the existence of government is something that needs to be explained, ultimately, in terms of economies of scale and market failures. There is no room for a view of a public sector having intrinsic merit or value, or of it having an historical lineage independent of the private sector; the logic of all law is ultimately the logic of private law. Although some laws are based on appeal to "public sentiment" that "cannot easily be defended on the usual economic or utilitarian grounds,"[70] Posner thinks his economic theory can account for the two major functions of legislation having to do with market failure and the results of interest-group politics. Of the first Posner remarks that the "oldest strand" in the theory of legislation is the "public interest" conception:

> Well represented in the writings of such economists as Baumol and Pigou, and approximated by the traditional lawyer's view that legislation is designed to protect the public interest, implicitly defined in utilitarian terms, this conception asserts that both the ideal and for the most part the actual function of legislation is to increase economic welfare by correcting "market failures" such as crime and pollution.[71]

Passing over the facts that the idea that law functions in the public interest is many centuries older than either utilitarianism or welfare economics in Anglo-American jurisprudence and legal practice, and that for most of its history legislation has had very little to do with utilitarian purposes, it is clear that the "public interest" component of Posner's conception of the point of legislation has to do largely, if not exclusively, with problems of market failure: free riding and economies of scale provide the rationale. Posner is also much impressed by the interest group theory of legislation, and particularly more recent theories of log rolling and the triumph of small, powerful, single issue-oriented interest groups in legislative battles, so that this kind of legislation may be "systematically perverse from a public-interest standpoint by facilitating the redistribution of wealth from large groups to small ones."[72] Like Holmes before him, Posner does not see the redistribution

---

[70] Posner, *The Federal Courts*, p. 266.
[71] *Ibid.*, p. 262 (citations omitted).
[72] *Ibid.*, p. 264.

of wealth from large to small groups as a necessary demerit of legislation.[73] Although a complete theory of legislation would have to account for both "public interest" (in Posner's sense) and interest group legislation, from Posner's standpoint, analysis of the latter means that conventional conceptions of statutory construction in terms of legislative intent can often be highly misleading. "Courts do not have the research tools needed to uncover the motives behind legislation. Nor can they just presume the presence of an interest group somewhere behind the scenes."[74] Sometimes there will be an interest group and the courts will be dealing with special interest legislation; at others times, there will be no interest group. Only in these latter circumstances do "the actual and the ostensible purposes" of the legislation coincide.[75] But this is the relatively rare case in which legislation rectifies market failure; for Posner there is no conception of the public interest other than this.

This unclear combination of public interest legislation and the effective voice of narrow interest groups in comprising statutory law is problematic for Posner's demand/supply theory of judicial services. To the extent that statutory law really is the mere result of the battle of interest groups to get their way, and assuming that Posner is serious about his neo-Holmesian position that there is nothing wrong with this battle, Posner has no basis for his view that the rights created by such legislation as Title VII of the Civil Rights Act generate "too much" demand for judicial services. In this war of all against all, the appropriate level of demand must be defined as whatever gets generated as a by-product of the machinations of the political process. To the extent, by contrast, that law functions in the public interest, and this is understood to mean only market failure and its judicial analogues, then it is difficult to see how the demand/supply model can have any relevance at all, since we are dealing, by definition, with circumstances in which market mechanisms have broken down. In these circumstances, as I pointed

---

[73] Holmes held that "[t]he more powerful interests must be more or less reflected in legislation; which, like every other device of man or beast, must tend in the long run to aid the survival of the fittest. . . . It is no sufficient condemnation of legislation that it favors one class at the expense of another; for much or all legislation does that. . . . The fact is that legislation . . . is necessarily made by a means which a body, having the power, puts burdens which are disagreeable to them on the shoulders of somebody else." Oliver Wendell Holmes, "Herbert Spencer: Legislation and Empiricism," in Harry C. Shriver, ed., *Justice Oliver Wendell Holmes: His Book Notices and Uncollected Letters and Papers* (New York: Central Book Co., 1936), pp. 104, 107–9, quoted in *Ibid.*, p. 264.

[74] *Ibid.*, p. 267.

[75] *Ibid.*, pp. 267–68.

out earlier, there is no particular reason to believe that limiting demand is an appropriate policy response, by legislatures or courts, and, indeed, there are good reasons for thinking that it is not.

Statutory Construction and Efficient Adjudication

Posner's account of statutory construction is located in his broader theory of common law making. In its "macro-judicial" manifestations this theory rests on two premises: that there is a lot more federal common law than many of us realize and that the structure and evolution of this common law rests on and instantiates his microeconomic theory of wealth-maximization already discussed. It is through this lens that Posner perceives the realities of common law making and of statutory construction.

At least part of the first premise is not controversial today. Ever since Ronald Dworkin's seminal attack on legal positivism,[76] legal theorists have had to deal with the fact that both statute and precedent are frequently indeterminate, requiring one of several possible judicial constructions to supply determinate meaning. People differ greatly on how numerous and frequent the interpretative possibilities are, how big the gaps are, and how they are filled, but no one seriously denies that the gaps exist. What fills the gaps in Posner's view is common law, and in the federal system, federal common law. This is conceived of quite broadly:

> [not as] limited to the business of the royal courts of Westminster in the eighteenth century (the approximate sense in which "common law" is used in the Seventh Amendment and the Judiciary Act of 1789), but as encompassing all fields that have been shaped mainly by judges rather than legislators. Common law thus includes, among other fields, admiralty, equity, and modern federal civil procedure (the rules of which have been formulated under the direction of the Supreme Court justices), as well as torts, contracts, property, trusts, future interests, agency, remedies, and much of criminal law and procedure. . . . [M]any ostensibly statutory and constitutional fields really are common-law fields.[77]

Posner does not want to expand the range of common law adjudication. Indeed, he is critical of such proposals as Calabresi's argument

---

[76] Ronald Dworkin, *Taking Rights Seriously* (Cambridge, MA: Harvard University Press, 1978), pp. 14–130.

[77] Posner, *The Federal Courts*, p. 294.

that common-law courts should have the power to declare statutes ob-
solete, on the grounds that this would be a judicial usurpation of legislative authority.[78] But Posner does want to sustain the common law
within what he sees as its proper limits, to protect it from displacement
by the growth of statutory law, and to make it more robust and efficient.

In Posner's view, as soon as courts issue opinions they inevitably
begin to make law. They do this for three reasons. First, common law
arises by historical default. Until the mid-nineteenth century, English
and American legislatures concerned themselves primarily with revenue measures and local administration, so that the formulations of general rules of conduct, regulation of safety and health, trade and commerce, employment, inheritance, and internal security all came to be
regulated by judge-made law, "common law" in Posner's nontechnical
sense. This huge body of common law precedent was taken over more
or less intact after the American Revolution, and its mere existence
means that there is virtually no action a court can take without invoking, restating, and developing some aspect of it.[79]

A second reason for the inevitable survival of common law in "the
modern age of statutes" is generated by the need for specificity in judicial decisions. Legislators necessarily reason in general terms, without
knowledge of the particular fact patterns to which their rules will be
applied. "The judge has the advantage of seeing the rule in operation,
and he can deal with problems of application the legislature did not
foresee."[80] This means that where there is "play in the joints" of legislative enactments, the judge can and must "refine the rule to make it a
more apt instrument of the legislature's purposes."[81] This process of
refinement is essentially a common-law one.

The third source of enduring common law is structural and quite
Calabresian, having to do with the different compositions of courts
and legislatures. Legislatures are "large, representative bodies elected at
frequent intervals in partisan elections."[82] As such they are frequently
"handicapped in dealing effectively with technical questions, quite
apart from the inherent limitations of foresight."[83] The very "process

---

[78] Guido Calabresi, *A Common Law for the Age of Statutes* (Cambridge, MA: Harvard University Press, 1982), pp. 34, 38, cited in Posner, *The Federal Courts*, pp. 290–92.

[79] Posner, *The Federal Courts*, pp. 4–5, 298–314.

[80] *Ibid.*, p 5.

[81] *Ibid.*, p. 5.

[82] *Ibid.*, p. 5.

[83] *Ibid.*, p. 5.

of gaining agreement in a diverse, factious assembly results in compromises that are unclear and sometimes incoherent."[84] Posner highlights the differences in legislative and judicial rule-making as follows:

> [T]he built-in impediments to getting legislation passed—impediments designed to reduce the legislators' power, to weed out proposed legislation that lacks real support, and to increase the stability of legislation once enacted—make it difficult for the legislature to withdraw or revise misconceived or poorly drafted legislation. In contrast, judges operate in a less political and (until recently) less hectic atmosphere which allows them to apply a measure of relatively disinterested repair to the sometimes badly damaged products of the legislative process.[85]

In addition to this broad conception there are vast areas of the law that Posner defines as "quasi-common law" because they "require the type of balancing of utilitarian values, of benefits and costs, that makes a field of law economic at its core." Posner thus associates the term "common law" not only with "judge-created law but with law that is dominated by utilitarian, or in economic terms efficiency-maximizing, values."[86] This includes, at least, aspects of antitrust, intellectual property, choice of laws, procedure, remedies, jurisdiction, constitutional law, and the law of attorneys' fees.[87]

Given this broad conception of the common law and its operation, Posner is concerned to make the federal courts more efficient through the use of "some simple but powerful tools of economic analysis."[88] It is difficult, however, to discern a consistent economic logic underlying Posner's recommendations. On the one hand, at the outset of his discussion of common law adjudication in the federal appellate courts, Posner reaffirms his invisible-hand descriptive theory of micro-judicial efficiency—the "efficiency theory" of the common law or the idea that its evolution is "heavily influenced by a concern, more often intuitive than explicit to be sure, with promoting economic efficiency."[89] On the other hand, in several areas Posner does not affirm the kind of conservative traditionalism about the common law that this reasoning

[84] *Ibid.*, p. 5.
[85] *Ibid.*, pp. 290–92.
[86] *Ibid.*, pp. 301.
[87] *Ibid.*, p. 296; see also *ibid.*, pp. 300–314.
[88] *Ibid.*, p. 294.
[89] *Ibid.*, p. 294 (citation omitted).

would lead one to expect. The most obvious of these areas is his discussion of the rules of statutory interpretation and construction.

Posner does not characterize himself as unconditionally in favor of judicial restraint; he endorses this doctrine only to the extent that it means respecting the separation of powers.[90] Even then he holds that judicial restraint must sometimes give way to other rules of adjudication.[91] Judicial restraint cannot be "an adequate shorthand for good judging."[92] Many other things are involved: good legal research and logical analysis, "a sense of justice, a knowledge of the world, a lucid writing style, common sense, openness to colleagues' views, intelligence, fair-mindedness, realism, hard work, foresight, modesty, a gift for compromise, and a commitment to reason and relatedly to the avoidance of 'result-oriented' decisions."[93] By "result-oriented" Posner means the Tushnetian kind of approach designed to advance a particular political or ideological agenda.[94]

Although Posner thinks it inevitable "that the judge's personal policy preferences or values play a role in the judicial process,"[95] principled decisions can still be distinguished from result-oriented ones: "a decision is principled if and only if the ground of decision can be stated truthfully in a form the judge could publicly avow without inviting virtually universal condemnation by professional opinion."[96] Thus, whereas *Brown v. Board of Education*[97] was an "activist" decision, it was principled rather than result-oriented in Posner's sense.[98] There is, then, a deep conservatism to Posner's jurisprudence in that it limits the values that can inform interpretation to those which are not greatly at odds with the values prevailing in the existing judicial community. So, for instance, although Holmes's decisions were shaped by his commitment to social Darwinism, our assessment of him as a judge should not depend on whether or not we think social Darwinism good or bad, "so long as we do not think it childish, vicious, idiosyncratic, or partisan

---

[90] *Ibid.*, p. 207–20.

[91] *Ibid.*, pp. 220–22.

[92] *Ibid.*, p. 220.

[93] *Ibid.*, p. 220.

[94] Mark Tushnet, "The Dilemmas of Liberal Constitutionalism," *Ohio State Law Journal*, Vol. 42 (1981), pp. 411, 424; Posner, *The Federal Courts*, pp. 218–19.

[95] Posner, *The Federal Courts*, p. 218.

[96] *Ibid.*, p. 205.

[97] 347 U.S. 483 (1954).

[98] Posner, *The Federal Courts*, p. 220.

in the sense in which his adopting the Democratic or Republican campaign platform of 1900 as his judicial *vade mecum* would have been partisan and therefore unprincipled, result oriented."[99] Although "[t]he element of will, of personal policy preference, is inescapable in the American judicial process," the

> willful judge, the judge who makes will the dominant element of his decision making, is properly reprobated. Moreover, a preference may be too personal to be a legitimate ingredient of the judicial process. It is one thing for the judge to give expression to the big ideas of his age, and to recognize that they need not be—in our society, are unlikely to be—ideas that command universal support. But if they are idiosyncratic, the judge has no business using them to decide cases. That would make the law too quirky and unpredictable.[100]

Passing over the great difficulties of whether there is the kind of agreement on the "big ideas" that Posner postulates, there remain the further difficulties of by what criteria this alleged agreement is to be identified, by whom, and why majority values should, in any case, dominate interpretations by judges who are (at least in part) charged with preserving counter-majoritarian rights and values. All this leaves the specifics of interpretation and statutory construction untouched. It is when Posner tackles these issues that he undermines his own theory of "micro-judicial" efficiency.

Consider, for instance, Posner's analysis of canons of construction. By canons of construction he denotes the "list of ancient interpretive maxims catalogued in such works as Sutherland on *Statutory Construction* and invoked with great frequency by federal [judges] as by state judges in dealing with questions of statutory interpretation."[101] Whether or not they are technically common-law maxims, the canons of construction are certainly part of the common law in Posner's expansive sense. However, he insists that "realistic understanding of legislation," is "devastating to the canons of construction."[102] Although Posner does not go as far as Llewellyn, who held that for every canon one might bring to bear on a point there is an equal and opposite

---

[99] *Ibid.*, pp. 221–22.
[100] *Ibid.*, p. 222.
[101] *Ibid.*, p. 276 (citations omitted).
[102] *Ibid.*, p. 276.

canon,[103] Posner does argue that "with a few exceptions, they [canons] have no value even as flexible guideposts or rebuttable presumptions, even when taken one by one, because they rest on wholly unrealistic conceptions of the legislative process."[104] The plain meaning rule, for instance, which requires that interpretation should begin with the words of the relevant statute, does not adequately describe what judges typically do; they start with "some conception of its subject matter" and the case law, and they "may never return to the statutory language."[105]

A second canon, that "remedial statutes are to be construed broadly,"[106] is deficient because its rationale makes assumptions about legislative processes which we now know to be false. The idea that remedial statutes should be construed broadly rests on the notion that the legislature was trying to remedy an ill, and it would therefore want its legislation to be construed so as to make it more rather than less effective. But, Posner tells us, the scientific study of legislatures has taught us that there is rarely consensus behind legislation, that it comes about as a result of compromises and log rolling. If a remedial statute is the result of "a compromise between one group of legislators that has a simple remedial objective but lacks a majority and another group that has reservations about the objective, a court that construed the statute broadly would upset the compromise that the statute was intended to embody."[107] Nor can post-enactment legislative materials resolve this question, for "[t]o give effect to the current legislator[s'] preferences is to risk spoiling the deal cut by the earlier legislators—to risk repealing legislation, in whole or in part, without going through the constitutionally prescribed processes for repeal."[108]

A third unrealistic canon is that courts should give great weight to the interpretation of a statute by the administrative agency that enforces it. There is no reason to expect administrative agency members, appointed long after the legislation they enforce was enacted, to display special fidelity to the original intent of the legislation rather than to the current policies of the Administration and the Congress.[109]

---

[103] Karl Llewellyn, *The Common Law Tradition: Deciding Appeals* (Boston: Little, Brown, 1960), pp. 521–35; Posner, *The Federal Courts*, p. 276.

[104] Posner, *The Federal Courts*, p. 277.

[105] *Ibid.*, p. 278.

[106] *Ibid.*, p. 278.

[107] *Ibid.*, pp. 278–79.

[108] *Ibid.*, p. 279.

[109] *Ibid.*, p. 280 (citations omitted).

Other examples, such as the canons that every word in a statute must be given significance and that repeals by implication are to be disfavored, make unrealistic assumptions about the "omniscience" of Congress. In fact, Posner tells us words are often "tossed in" to statutes, or vague words are employed to cover over compromises, and legislation is often passed without knowledge of its implications for existing legislation.[110] The same is true with the canon *expressio unius est exclusio alterius* and with the canon that reenactment without a change of a statute that courts have interpreted in a particular way is evidence that Congress has adopted that construction. Often legislators will not have thought of alternative formulations and will not know of prevailing statutory interpretations in the courts.[111]

A few canons survive Posner's scientific scrutiny and have "arguable merit."[112] The canon that penal statutes should be construed narrowly is defensible on the grounds that all penal statutes over-deter to some degree, so that the "appropriate level of care" in drafting them is higher. If the legislature can be assumed to observe this higher level, "then courts that construe criminal statutes more narrowly than they construe civil statutes (as they do) do not run a serious risk of disserving the legislative will through underdeterrence."[113] The canon that statutes should be construed, where possible, to avoid raising constitutional questions can also be defended, because it avoids unnecessary constitutional decision, although the process of that avoidance generates problems of its own.[114] In short, with these few exceptions:

> [B]y making statutory interpretation seem mechanical rather than creative, the canons conceal the extent to which the judge is making new law in the guise of interpreting a statute. The judge who recognizes the degree to which he is free rather than constrained in the interpretation of statutes, and refuses to make a pretense of constraint by parading the canons of construction in his opinions, is less likely to act willfully than the judge who either mistakes freedom for constraint or has no compunctions about misrepresenting his will as that of Congress.[115]

In place of this pseudo-formalism, which supplies a misleading gloss of logical deduction to the process of statutory interpretation, Posner

---

[110] *Ibid.*, pp. 278–80.
[111] *Ibid.*, pp. 282–83.
[112] *Ibid.*, p. 283.
[113] *Ibid.*, p. 283 (citation omitted).
[114] *Ibid.*, p. 284–85.
[115] *Ibid.*, p. 285–86.

proposes that judges engage in "imaginative reconstruction" of statutes; the judge should first "put himself in the shoes of the enacting legislators and figure out how they would have wanted the statute applied to the case before him."[116] If this turns out not to be possible, as it "occasionally" will because of lack of information or because legislators failed to agree on "essential premises, then the judge must decide what attribution of meaning to the statute will yield the most reasonable result in the case at hand."[117] In this circumstance he must remember "that what seems reasonable to him may differ from the legislators' conceptions of reasonableness, and that the latter must govern as far as possible. Even with old statutes, the judge's job "is not to keep a statute up to date in the sense of making it reflect contemporary values, but to imagine as best he can how the legislators who enacted the statute would have wanted it applied to situations they did not foresee."[118]

There are four major difficulties with Posner's account that are of interest here. First, there is an ad-hoc quality to his differing evaluations of the different canons which produces internally inconsistent results. Why, for instance, should we assume that legislators do in fact draft penal statutes with a higher standard of care than other statutes? Why should we imagine that a penal statute is any less the product of compromise and log rolling which make it impossible to discern whether or not the statute over-deters or under-deters?[119] Why are all the difficulties of assuming legislative agreement and omniscience not just as severe in these circumstances as in others? If Posner's objections to the canons are to be taken seriously, it is highly implausible on its face that a certain class of statutes can be singled out and regarded as exempt from these difficulties.

Second, and more serious, the major difficulties Posner identifies with the canons of construction attend his own account of "creative reconstruction" of legislative intent. If statutes resulted from compromises that make it impossible to discern clearly what the legislators intended, how is a judge better placed to speculate on what those same

---

[116] *Ibid.*, p. 287.

[117] *Ibid.*, p. 286–87.

[118] *Ibid.*, p. 287.

[119] Indeed, there is literature in political science suggesting that the political advantages of being seen to be tough on crime often lead national legislators to stiffen criminal penalities with abandon, particularly when they have no impact on the federal government . See Stuart A. Scheingold, *The Politics of Law and Order: Street Crime and Public Policy* (New York: Longman, 1984).

compromising legislators would, collectively, have intended in the application of their statute to future fact patterns that they had not envisaged? How is he better placed to speculate about what those same legislators would, collectively, have regarded as reasonable in these unencountered circumstances? Likewise, to the extent that canons assume too much omniscience by legislators, this problem is only compounded when we add the speculative element of Posner's theory of "imaginative reconstruction." How ignorant or well informed do we decide they would have become about the collateral consequences of their legislation? Posner acknowledges that his approach "invites the criticism that judges do not have the requisite imagination and that what they will do in practice"[120] is vote their own preferences, ascribing them to legislators. Yet his reply is entirely unsatisfactory: "the irresponsible judge will twist any approach to yield the outcome that he desires, and the stupid judge will do the same thing unconsciously."[121] If this is true, Posner's approach still provides no basis for preferring his approach to the traditional one; it does not go to the problem that "imaginative reconstruction" compounds the defects he identifies in the canons of construction.

One suspects that the real motive behind the theory of imaginative reconstruction is that the theory will make it easier for judges to attribute Posner's theory of wealth-maximization to legislators' purposes when there is no evidence for this in the legislation. For instance, in interpreting the *Federal Mine Safety and Health Act in Miller v. Federal Mine Safety and Health Review Commission*,[122] Posner, writing for the court, was confronted with the problem of deciding when, if at all, an unclear part of the Act entitles a worker to walk off the job (rather than complain) if he believes there to be a safety hazard. Posner reasoned that a complaint by a worker does not disrupt the operations of the mine, so that even frivolous complaints impose few costs on the employer.[123] A work stoppage, on the other hand, is invariably a source of significant cost. "Thinking our way as best we can into the minds of the Senators and Representatives," he continued reconstructively, "we can imagine them wanting to allow miners to complain freely about the conditions of safety and health in the mine without having to worry about retaliation. . . . We are unwilling to impress on a statute that does

---

[120] Posner, *The Federal Courts*, p. 287.
[121] *Ibid.*, p. 287.
[122] 687 F.2d 194 (7th Cir. 1982).
[123] *Ibid.*, p. 196.

not explicitly entitle miners to stop work a construction that would make it impossible to maintain discipline in the mines."[124] Of course, Posner has no way of knowing that maintaining "discipline" in the mines had anything to do with the legislators' purposes, but if they are imagined to be wealth maximizers in his sense, then this goal can "imaginatively" be attributed to them.

The third difficulty is more serious still: if Posner's discussion of the defects of the canons is accepted, it seriously undermines his theory of "micro-judicial" efficiency, and particularly the claim that the common law (as he broadly conceives it) is efficient. If the canons are part of the common law in his sense, which they must be, then the mere fact that they have evolved entails, presumably, that they serve some efficient purpose, else they would not have evolved. And for Posner to hold that they should be jettisoned, lock, stock, and barrel, in favor of his new approach based on "imaginative reconstruction" violates the whole gradualist ideal of common-law-making. Indeed, protestations to the contrary notwithstanding, the major premise behind Posner's account smacks much more of old-fashioned legal realism than of any attempt to revivify the common-law tradition. How else are we to interpret the claim that the canons make "unrealistic" assumptions about how legislatures operate, and the argument that political scientists' theories of legislatures tell us that there is no unambiguous thing called legislative intent? These, as well as Posner's prescriptions, assume that if common-law rules can be shown by "realistic" policy sciences to be based on muddles, they should be jettisoned for more "scientific" principles of statutory construction. Whatever the merits of this view, it is obviously inconsistent with the claim that the common law is naturally efficient.

In what may be an attempt to undermine the force of this criticism, Posner intimates in a footnote that his concept of "imaginative reconstruction" is not new, and is in fact traceable at least to Blackstone's *Commentaries*.[125] But if this line of argument was to be developed into a claim to the effect that this theory of imaginative reconstruction has long been a part of the common law, this would raise the further difficulty that two conflicting modes of statutory interpretation are both part of the common law, which in turn further undermines the claim that the theory generates determinate and "efficient" results.

---

[124] *Ibid.*, p. 196.
[125] Posner, *The Federal Courts*, p. 287.

This also raises another and yet more serious difficulty, which is that if the common law is conceived of as broadly as Posner conceives it, it is hard to see how economic efficiency can have much to do with its reform. Quite apart from the analytical point that if the thesis were true the common law would not be in need of reform, Posner's discussion of the merits of economic reasoning in substantive areas of federal common law bears no obvious relationship to the "micro" theory and does not begin to generate determinate results. He reifies controversial empirical economic theories by writing always in universalist terms, referring to *the* theory of efficiency when there are many conflicting theories, to "economic analysis" when there are invariably many economic analyses, by comparing the enterprise of "law and economics" to astronomy "[w]ithout meaning to wrap myself in the prestige of the physical sciences"[126]—thus supplying pseudoscientific garb to what are in fact empirically contentious and invariably controversial assertions.

I argued earlier that this evaluation was true even of his micro-judicial theory; it is far more obviously true once economic theories are applied to macro legal processes. For instance, when Posner describes "quasi common law" fields as those which require "balancing of utilitarian values,"[127] he fails to note that this does not itself tell us what the weights should be. Consider some of his own examples. As one instance of "virtually an explicit economic test" in the quasi common law field of procedural due process, he refers (without discussion) to the Supreme Court's "balancing test" announced in *Mathews v. Eldridge*,[128] to determine how many procedural safeguards must be provided before a person can be deprived of a property right by the government. But what is the *Mathews v. Eldridge* test? It states that in deciding how much process is due in these circumstances it is necessary to take the following factors into account:

> First, the private interest that will be affected by the official action; second, the risk of an erroneous deprivation of such interest through the procedures used, and the probable value, if any, of additional or substitute procedural safeguards; and finally, the Government's interest, including the function involved and the fiscal and administrative burdens that the additional or substitute procedural requirement would entail.[129]

---

[126] Posner, "Some Uses and Abuses," p. 294.
[127] Posner, *The Federal Courts*, p. 300.
[128] 424 U.S. 319 (1976), cited in Posner, *The Federal Courts*, p. 311.
[129] 424 U.S. 319, 335 (1976).

In *Matthews*, the Supreme Court employed the test and reached the conclusion that disability benefits could be terminated by an administrative agency without holding an evidentiary hearing. In a subsequent decision, the Court followed the test to the conclusion that an indigent mother could have her maternal rights terminated without the assistance of court-appointed counsel to assist her at the termination hearing.[130] Yet it is difficult to see how the "economic" component of this test bears decisively on the result in either case. What is critical is the value assigned to the initial rights to begin with, and the weight attributed to the state interest—whether it is "compelling" or merely "legitimate." These are constitutional questions, not economic ones, and as Justice Blackmun's dissent in *Lassiter v. Department of Social Services*[131] made plain, if they are weighted differently the test will produce different results.[132] The test itself does not resolve the difficult constitutional decision about those weights; in fact it really does no more than make explicit that some weighting of costs and benefits of enforcing rights is unavoidable in constitutional adjudication. It tells a judge neither which rights are fundamental nor which should be. To say that this is an instance of the quasi common law of procedural due process "dominated by economic issues"[133] is to make an awful lot of theoretical hullabaloo about very little. Moreover, it is misleading when placed in the context of a discussion of how a few "simple but powerful tools of economic analysis"[134] can improve the functioning of the federal courts because it creates the impression that economic analysis can resolve questions that it cannot.

The same is true of Posner's discussion of the "marketplace of ideas" metaphor in terms of which the Supreme Court deals with First Amendment questions. This "can be analyzed by the same tools that economists use to analyze conventional markets."[135] The "economic character" of the First Amendment can be brought out when we restate it by saying that the government "may not limit competition in ideas."[136] Whether or not it was true, as Holmes claimed in *Abrams v. United States*,[137] that it is "the theory of our Constitution" that "the best test

[130] *Lassiter v. Department of Social Servs.*, 452 U.S. 18 (1981).

[131] 452 U.S. 18 (1981).

[132] *Ibid.*, pp. 35–59.

[133] Posner, *The Federal Courts*, p. 310.

[134] *Ibid.*, p. 294.

[135] *Ibid.*, p. 311.

[136] Posner, *Economic Analysis*, p. 541.

[137] 250 U.S. 616 (1919).

of truth is the power of the thought to get itself accepted in the competition of the market,"[138] Posner is certainly right that this interpretation has since dominated Supreme Court analysis of the First Amendment in many areas, ranging from incitement, defamation and obscenity through the regulation of the media, commercial speech, political speech, and the relationship between money and speech. But it is quite wrong to think that "economic analysis" can resolve the major differences that dominate discussion in these areas, as can be seen by taking a closer look at the recent history of the Court's view of the relationship between money and speech.

The Supreme Court is sharply divided on the capacity of the government's ability legitimately to regulate the expenditure of money which is instrumental in propagating speech, but in a long *per curiam* decision in *Buckley v. Valeo* in 1976 the Court held that the only legitimate state interest in regulating the use of money to expound political ideas was to prevent corruption or the appearance of it, and the Court narrowly interpreted corruption to mean bribery.[139] This reasoning led the Court to distinguish campaign contributions from expenditures by individuals, corporations and political action committees, and to hold that only the former may legitimately be regulated by Congress. The Court and several concurring opinions explicitly rejected as "wholly foreign to the First Amendment" the argument that government has any interest in or responsibility for equalizing access in public debate or in equalizing the volume of political speech, and insisted affirmatively that the First Amendment is best served when the quantity and sources of political speech are wholly unregulated by government:

> A restriction on the amount of money a person or group can spend on political communication during a campaign necessarily reduces the quantity of expression by restricting the number of issues discussed, the depth of their exploration, and the size of the audience reached. This is because virtually every means of communicating ideas in today's mass society requires the expenditure of money.[140]

Although some Justices rejected the majority's distinction between contributions and expenditures as without constitutional significance,[141] all accepted the appropriate terms of analysis as fixed by the

[138] *Ibid.*

[139] 424 U.S. 1 (1976).

[140] *Ibid.*, p. 19 (citations omitted).

[141] Burger and Blackmun held that neither may be regulated and White, later joined by Marshall in dissent in *Federal Election Comm'n v. National Conservative Political Action Comm.*, 470 U.S. 480 (1985), held that both may be regulated.

metaphor of the marketplace of ideas. And when the Court came to extend this holding to corporate expenditures in referenda three years later in *First National Bank of Boston v. Bellotti*,[142] by holding that a corporation is a person for purposes of the first amendment, the same terms of discussion formed the common ground between adherents of the Opinion of the Court and the dissenters.

The disagreements focused not on the desirability of the marketplace analysis, but rather on competing causal theories of how that marketplace actually operates. Thus, Justice Powell, writing for the majority, rejected the argument that a Massachusetts statute limiting corporate expenditures should be upheld on the grounds that "corporations are wealthy and powerful and their views may drown out other points of view" because no such explicit finding had been made in the courts below.[143] The Court, thus, implicitly endorsed the laissez-faire view it had taken in *Buckley*, that absent a specific showing of reasons to the contrary, it should be assumed that this market is naturally well-functioning and works to the benefit of all, or at least to the detriment of none, by improving the "quantity of expression" on public issues and the "depth of their exploration."[144] Of course, this is just one theory of how such markets operate; it could be argued on the basis of the British experience that highly regulated forums of public discussion during election campaigns result in a considerably higher quality of discussion, and "exploration" of considerably greater "depth." Yet by reifying the neoclassical theory and placing the burden of proof in particular cases on those who would question it, the Court rationalizes striking down all restrictions on corporate expenditures to influence referenda in the name of laissez-faire. Because corruption of the political process was narrowly construed as bribery of public officials or the appearance of it in *Buckley*, the *Bellotti* Court never had to confront the question of corruption, as referenda do not directly involve public officials. The question whether vast expenditures of wealth can themselves corrupt the democratic process in this context could, therefore, not arise.

The dissenters in *Bellotti* adopted a competing market theory. Justice White, writing also for Justices Brennan and Marshall, acknowledged that *Buckley* had foreclosed the argument that the state has an interest in equalizing access to the forum of political speech, but adopted a

---

[142] 435 U.S. 765 (1978).
[143] *Ibid.*, p. 789.
[144] 424 U.S. 1, 19 (1976).

different and more minimalist antitrust theory. "It has long been recognized," he argued, "that the special status of corporations has placed them in a position to control vast amounts of economic power which may, if not regulated, dominate not only the economy but also the very heart of our democracy, the electoral process."[145] For this reason the state of Massachusetts did have a legitimate interest in "preventing institutions which have been permitted to amass wealth as a result of special advantages extended by the State for certain economic purposes from using that wealth to acquire an unfair advantage in the political process."[146]

The Court's disagreements about the regulation of contributions and expenditures during elections since *Bellotti* have revolved around these competing theories of the workings of the market in political speech. A majority continues to stand behind the laissez-faire theory, which was reinforced in *Federal Election Commission v. NCPAC* in 1985.[147] There the Court held it an unconstitutional limitation on political speech for Congress to limit expenditures of political action committees on behalf of candidates as a condition for those candidates to receive public funds during election campaigns.[148] The Court explicitly invoked the neoclassical reasoning of *Buckley* and reaffirmed its narrow definition of corruption.[149] The dissenters continue to emphasize that money is not itself speech and to affirm some version of the antitrust theory, although they may have different (more or less egalitarian) views of what the implicit "distributive" standard should be. Although the equality of access, neoclassical, and various antitrust models have figured most prominently in the Court's discussions of money and political speech, there are other theories invoked implicitly at times. For instance, it might be argued that the exception in *Buckley* from disclosure requirements for minor and unpopular parties (reaffirmed in *Brown v. Socialist Workers '74 Campaign Committee*)[150] presupposes a kind of "infant industry" theory of the marketplace in political speech.[151]

In sum, even in areas where courts explicitly invoke economic terminology and modes of analysis, it is quite misleading to suggest as Posner

---

[145] 435 U.S. 765, 809 (1978).

[146] *Ibid.*

[147] 470 U.S. 480 (1985).

[148] *Ibid.*, 493–94.

[149] *Ibid.*, 496–97.

[150] 459 U.S. 87 (1982).

[151] 424 U.S. 1, 58–74 (1976). See also Rehnquist, dissenting in part, at 424 U.S. at 290–94, rejecting this view.

does that this in itself resolves constitutional and other normative disagreements. It merely generates a vocabulary in terms of which those
disagreements are cast and sets some wide limits to discussion. For
every economic theory there is a competing one, embodying different
normative premises and purposes, and it is typically the premises and
purposes which are in contention. No amount of "economic analysis"
should be permitted to obscure this.

Economic Theory and Posner's Adjudication

I turn next to Posner the judge, to see how he makes use of economic
reasoning in his activities on the federal bench. What are the principles
of efficient adjudication that we should expect to find Posner attempting to put into practice as an appellate court judge? Some of these,
at least, are spelled out explicitly in his account of the crisis of the
federal courts. He argues that there should be "a rededication by federal
judges to the principles of judicial self-restraint and institutional responsibility, the latter implying such specific reforms as greater brevity
in opinions, a greater willingness to impose sanctions on parties (and
their lawyers) who abuse federal judicial processes, a modest shift from
loose, multifactored standards to precise rules, a reduction in the number of concurring opinions, and rules of intercircuit deference."[152]
There also should be an "expansion of appellate capacity within federal
administrative agencies such as the National Labor Relations Board
(NLRB) and the Social Security Administration," among other reforms.[153] Leaving aside, for now, the issue of how much "economic
analysis" is really behind these proposals how consistently does Posner
try to advance them as a judge?

I examine Posner's decisions in two areas, labor and antitrust law.
These are both fields that have substantial common law components (in
Posner's sense) and they are both fields that Posner regards as traditionally economic. They are at the core, therefore, of the domain in which
he alleges economic analysis to be most obviously helpful. If the theory
is discredited here in its own castle, we can forget the periphery of out-
buildings and other dependencies beyond the moat; the theory of efficiency, as a basis for adjudication, will decisively have been laid to rest.

---

[152] Posner, *The Federal Courts*, p. 319.
[153] *Ibid.*, p. 319.

Labor Law Opinions

Labor law is one of Posner's federal common law areas. It is interesting from our standpoint for procedural and substantive reasons. Procedurally, the existence of federal legislation and administrative agencies for at least part of its implementation allows us to test Posner's claims about judicial deference, to see how serious he is about husbanding judicial resources, judicial self-restraint, and deferring to cheaper, nonjudicial forms of dispute resolution such as those practiced by the NLRB. Even under existing law, Posner notes, the decisions of administrative law judges in labor cases as reviewed by the NLRB are due "as much and maybe more deference" than decisions of district courts, and he argues that this cheaper form of dispute resolution should be enhanced.[154] Substantively, labor law is illuminating because it is an area where allegedly scientific principles of economic analysis can be manipulated in the service of particular interests, so we can see clearly what use of substantive economic theories by judges in labor disputes amounts to in practice.

Despite Posner's emphasis on encouraging arbitration, deference to administrative agencies, and avoiding wasteful appeals, he has not adhered consistently to his "noninterventionist" view. When it suits him, he is quite prepared to engage in *post hoc* de novo reevaluation of the factual record from a court, arbitrator, or administrative agency below, in violation of both traditional principles of judicial review and Posner's conception of "macro-judicial" efficiency.

Here are some examples. In *Continental Web Press, Inc. v. NLRB*,[155] Posner rejected the Board's certification of the pressmen in a company as a union, rather than part of a larger union, despite his acknowledgment that the NLRB need only choose an appropriate bargaining unit (not the most appropriate one), that the union wanted to be thus designated, and that the reviewing court's power is restricted to ensuring that the Board apply its own procedures with reasonable consistency. "The greatest conflicts of interest among workers are over wages, fringe benefits and working conditions," he argued, "[b]ut there do not seem to be any significant differences between the preparatory employees [constituting the existing union] and the pressmen in *Continental Web's* plant along any of these dimensions."[156] Yet whether these claims are

---

[154] Posner, *The Federal Courts*, p. 161.
[155] 742 F.2d 1087 (7th Cir. 1984).
[156] *Ibid.*, 1091.

true are surely questions of fact that the NLRB is better equipped to decide on the basis of testimony before it than a reviewing court that has only the written record.

In *NLRB v. Acme Die Casting Corp.*,[157] although he enforced the Board's order on other grounds, Posner found that an administrative law judge had been wrong in finding that questions to a worker by his supervisor concerning the union amounted to coercive interrogation within the meaning of the NLRA. Posner noted that

> the courts . . . have identified a number of factors as relevant to deciding whether a particular inquiry is coercive, though we and other courts have made clear that these factors provide general guidelines rather than a formula for decision. The factors are the tone, duration and purpose of the questioning, whether it is repeated, how many workers are involved, the setting, the interrogator's authority, the ambience of the questioning (has the company created an atmosphere of hostility to the union?), and, more doubtfully, whether the worker answers truthfully.[158]

But just because these factors go to the factual makeup of the situation, great deference is supposed to be due to the hearing officer or tribunal that hears the witnesses, rather than to a reviewing judge's post hoc speculations as to whether or not the worker understood the question the employer asked.[159]

In *NLRB v. Village IX, Inc.*,[160] this post-hoc re-deciding of factual questions is perhaps most blatant. In that case a company had petitioned for review of an NLRB bargaining order imposed as a remedy for alleged unfair labor practices during a union organizing campaign. Although some of the Board's findings were affirmed, the Board's remedy was considered an excessive sanction on the grounds that questioning a retarded employee about the union was not an unfair labor practice and that a speech made by the employer to the employees about the union was not coercive within the meaning of the Act. Among other things this speech included the following:

> Unions do not work in restaurants. . . . The balance is not here. . . . If the Union exists at Shenanigans, Shenanigans will fail. That is it in a nutshell. . . . I won't be here if there is a Union within this particular

---

[157] 728 F.2d 959 (7th Cir. 1984).
[158] *Ibid.*, 962 (citations omitted).
[159] *Ibid.*, 962.
[160] 723 F.2d 1360 (7th Cir. 1983).

restaurant. I am not making a threat. I am making a statement of fact. . . . I respect anyone who wants to join the union if that in essence is a workable place and can afford to pay Union wages. We can't in the restaurant business. . . . Shenanigans can possibly exist with labor problems for a period of time. But in the long run we won't make it. The cancer will eat us up, and we will fall by the wayside. And if you walk into this place five years down the road, if there is a Union in here, then I guarantee you it won't be a restaurant. . . . I am not making a threat. I am stating a fact. When you are dealing with the Union you had better consider the pros and cons. I haven't looked into them a great deal because this is my first experience with them. I only know from my mind, from my heart and from my pocketbook how I stand on this. And I don't like the idea of looking at a Union as far as my employees are concerned.[161]

The NLRB held that this speech was coercive, but Posner reversed this finding, holding that the employer offered a "competent if extremely informal analysis of likely economic consequences of unionization in a highly competitive market."[162] He acknowledged that "[s]ince the only effective way of arguing against the union is for the company to point out to the workers the adverse consequences of unionization, one of which may be closure, it is often difficult in practice to distinguish between lawful advocacy and threats of retaliation."[163] Yet Posner offered no reasons for thinking that a reviewing court was in this instance better placed than the Board to make this determination, noting only that the Board did not question the factual accuracy of the employer's speech.[164] If an employer's description of a union as "cancer" is not sufficient in this connection to substantiate the Board's findings that it was threatening to the workers, it is difficult to imagine what could be.

On the issue of coercion, the record was replete with evidence that the speech was coercive, apart from its very terms. The following Board findings were upheld: that the discharge of a union organizer and an assault on another organizer were unfair labor practices within the meaning of the Act; that the company's "no-distribution" rule, adopted the day the organizer was reinstated, was an unfair labor practice; that preventing the organizer from distributing leaflets in the restaurant parking lot was an unfair labor practice, and that delaying the mailing

---

[161] *Ibid.*, 1364.
[162] *Ibid.*, 1367.
[163] *Ibid.*, 1367.
[164] *Ibid.*, 1367.

of the employee-organizer's invitations to the company's anniversary party was an unfair labor practice.[165] For Posner to suggest that "[n]othing in the circumstances . . . suggests that the question [to a retarded employee about whether he had been visited by the union] had a natural tendency to discourage him from voting for the union"[166] is less than credible. Perhaps a case might be made that a court or tribunal hearing the evidence might have reached the result that Posner would have preferred (although it is difficult to imagine how), but that is not the standard for appellate review.

These examples are sufficient to establish that, in labor cases at least, Posner the judge does not consistently adhere to traditional principles of deference to appropriate lower bodies on questions of fact. He thereby violates at least one component of his theory of "macro-judicial" efficiency, namely a "rededication by federal judges to the principles of judicial self-restraint."[167]

Antitrust Opinions

Antitrust is a "quasi-" common-law field in Posner's terms, one that is largely governed by statute but involving utilitarian balancing in its application. Because antitrust litigation invariably involves complex factual argument and also involves economic reasoning on a subject in which Posner has considerable expertise,[168] it provides a useful test of his fidelity to traditional notions of deference to lower courts on questions of fact and of the role of economic reasoning in his own utilitarian balancing in practice.

On the procedural question Posner does not adhere consistently to his own traditional view, sometimes to the point of provoking dissents from various of his colleagues on the grounds that an appellate court was without the authority to engage in de novo review of factual questions decided in the court below. In *Roland Machinery Co. v. Dresser Industries*,[169] Posner reversed a district court decision granting a preliminary injunction in a claim against a domestic equipment manufacturer

---

[165] *Ibid.*, 1360.

[166] *Ibid.*, 1369 (citations omitted).

[167] Posner, *The Federal Courts*, p. 319.

[168] Richard Posner, *Antitrust Law: An Economic Perspective* (Chicago: University of Chicago Press, 1976).

[169] 749 F.2d 380 (7th Cir. 1984).

which had cancelled an exclusive distributorship with the dealer when it signed a similar agreement with a foreign manufacturer. Posner held that the evidence supporting the foreign manufacturer being harmed by an exclusive dealership was tenuous. Judge Swygert objected to Posner's opinion on the grounds that the discretion that inheres in the decision whether to grant a preliminary injunction cannot rest with the reviewing court, but must lie in the district court and should only be reversed if that discretion is abused.[170]

In *Illinois v. F. E. Moran, Inc.,*[171] Posner, writing for the Seventh Circuit, reversed a district court order for disclosure of grand jury testimony by defendants in an antitrust suit on the grounds that the plaintiff had failed to make the required showing of particularized harm.[172] Judge Cudahy dissented on the grounds that it was wholly unprecedented to find, as a matter of law, that the particularized harm need did not exist, and that at most the case should be remanded for a determination of the plaintiff's particularized harm.[173] The Supreme Court has prescribed a balancing test for determining when the interest in maintaining secrecy of grand jury testimony outweighs the interest of those seeking disclosure and emphasized that the district court judge has considerable discretion in evaluating those interests. In Judge Cudahy's view "[w]e should not undertake to usurp the discretion vested in the district court judge nor should we substitute our view for that of the district judge who, once the correct legal standard is applied, is in the better position to make the factual determination."[174]

In *Marrese v. American Academy of Orthopedic Surgeons,*[175] Posner authored an opinion vacating a district judge's finding of contempt after the defendant in an antitrust action refused to produce its files in conformity with his discovery order.[176] The controversy concerned whether the defendant (the American Academy of Orthopedic Surgeons) had an interest in not divulging its records, which contained information material in an antitrust suit, so as to preserve its clients'

---

[170] *Ibid.*, 398–99.

[171] 740 F.2d 533 (7th Cir. 1984).

[172] *Ibid.*, 539.

[173] *Ibid.*, 541.

[174] *Ibid.*, 541.

[175] 726 F.2d 1150 (7th Cir. 1984).

[176] This was in fact an opinion on a petition for rehearing after *Maresse v. American Academy of Orthopedic Surgeons* had resulted in a reversal of the district court's discovery order (also authored by Posner). 706 F.2d 1488 (7th Cir. 1982).

confidentiality and, thus, bar discovery. The district court judge resolved this by ordering discovery pursuant to a restrictive protective
order. In a prior appellate review Judge Stewart had dissented from
Posner's opinion on the ground that the district judge has discretion
to order discovery in an antitrust violation and should be reversed on
appeal only if there is "clear error," or if the district judge had abused
his discretion.[177] Judge Stewart insisted that there was no evidence of
such abuse of discretion.[178] After the original opinion had been vacated,
Posner authored a second opinion holding that the suit was barred
under the doctrine of *res judicata* because the plaintiff had previously
failed in a state action against the defendant.[179] Judge Harlington Wood
Jr., writing also for Judges Cummings and Cudahy, dissented on the
grounds that the prior opinion had "created the impression that this
court was trying the case on its antitrust merits before it had much of
a chance to get started in the trial court," and that this "prejudgment
pall still hangs heavy over Judge Posner's latest opinion."[180] The dissenters argued, *inter alia,* that there was no basis for the reversal since Posner's majority opinion itself had demonstrated no abuse of discretion
by the district judge,[181] so that the court was illicitly usurping the trial
judge's authority. No doubt Posner would dispute these assertions, but
it is notable that four different judges reached the conclusion that this
was illicit interference with the discretionary authority of the district
court judge in an antitrust case.[182]

Even when Posner affirms a lower court decision, he can provoke his
colleagues to write separate opinions dissociating themselves from his
unnecessary theorizing about the lego-economic dicta. For example, in
Brunswick Corp. v. Riegel Textile,[183] Judge Harlington Wood dissociated
himself from a long and irrelevant discussion of the relationship between antitrust and patent law, which Posner engaged in the course of
affirming a district judge's dismissal of an action barred by the statute

---

[177] *Ibid.,* 1493–94.

[178] *Ibid.,* 1498.

[179] 726 F.2d 1150, 1152–56 (7th Cir. 1983).

[180] *Ibid.,* 1167.

[181] *Ibid.,* 1171–72.

[182] I do not suggest that Posner never defers to the lower court or administrative findings in an
antitrust case to the benefit of plaintiffs, only that generally he does not. For a notable exception,
arguably the exception that proves the rule, see *Hospital Corp. of Am. v. FTC,* 807 F.2d 1381 (7th
Cir. 1986).

[183] 752 F.2d 261 (7th Cir. 1984).

of limitations.[184] Again, in *Jack Walters & Sons Corp. v. Morion Building*,[185] Judge Swygert filed a separate opinion concurring in the result, an affirmance of a district judge's summary judgment for the defendant in an antitrust suit, but dissociating himself from Posner's long majority opinion discussing the nature of, and limits to, antitrust law and standing in antitrust cases. "I cannot concur in much of the discussion contained in the majority opinion," he wrote, "not because that discussion may not state correct principles of law, but because I believe it is dicta—dicta that might tend to influence and prejudice decisions in cases yet un-born."[186] These various concurrences and dissents make it clear that in the antitrust field Posner does not heed his own principles of macro-judicial efficiency, which include encouraging judges to write shorter opinions and to observe traditional roles of deference and self-restraint.[187] When Posner believes he is right on the merits he seems to find a way to review and reverse a district judge.

And of course in antitrust law, as in all areas of law that involve economic theory, various theories contend with one another. Posner has long been and advocate of a minimalist view of antitrust law aimed only at preventing collusive pricing. In his view the existence of too much "redundant" antitrust legislation has led to "an uncritical and unwise expansion in the prohibitory scope of antitrust."[188] He believes that the entire Clayton Act, all the antitrust provisions of the Federal Trade Commission Acts, and all but Section 1 of the Sherman Act should be repealed. It is not surprising that he fills the Dworkinian gaps in the law with restrictive interpretations of antitrust legislation, placing heavy burdens on plaintiffs in antitrust suits, and to declining to permit preliminary injunctions to issue in circumstances where he believes that the plaintiff should have no chance of success on the merits.

If Posner was a district court judge this might be unobjectionable. A district judge is often required to use discretion in the early stages of antitrust litigation, relating to restraining orders, injunctions, and discovery, and it seems likely that these decisions cannot be made without some implicit theory of the proper scope of antitrust. But as an appellate judge, whose task is to determine whether or not a district judge has abused his discretion, Posner has a quite different responsibility,

---

[184] *Ibid.*, 272.
[185] 737 F.2d 698 (7th Cir. 1984).
[186] *Ibid.*, 713.
[187] Posner, *The Federal Courts*, p. 319.
[188] Posner, *Antitrust Law: An Economic Perspective*, pp. 212–17.

and it is in this context that advancing one particular substantive economic theory as somehow the objective truth is pernicious.

Consider, for example, *Roland Machinery Co. v. Dresser Industries*,[189] in which Posner, writing for the majority, reversed a district judge's order granting an injunction to a construction equipment dealer against a domestic equipment manufacturer. The manufacturer had cancelled its exclusive retail agreement with the dealer when the dealer signed a similar agreement with a Japanese manufacturer.[190] At issue were both the appropriate standard for appellate review of preliminary injunctions and the substantive merits of the antitrust claim under the Clayton Act. On the first issue, Posner undertook a lengthy discussion of the different standards prevailing in different circuits and concluded that in this area more than perfunctory review was appropriate, because the power to issue preliminary injunctions is far-reaching and because Congress would not have made an exception to the finality requirement for appealability of preliminary injunctions if it had intended appellate review of them to be mere rubber stamping of district judge decisions.[191] This means that the term "abuse of discretion" cannot in the injunction context mean merely that the lower judge must be said to have acted "irrationally or fancifully" as is the case in other areas. Yet Posner nonetheless acknowledged that "considering the imponderable character of the balancing process and the judge's superior feel for the issues which a cold transcript may not fully communicate to the reviewing court," reviewing courts should not substitute their own judgment for the district judge's. "The question for us is whether the judge exceeded the bounds of permissible choice in the circumstances, not what we would have done if we had been in his shoes."[192] This means that unless the judge made a clear error of fact or an error of law in issuing a preliminary injunction, he should not be reversed.

Yet applying this more stringent than usual standard of review, Posner was not justified in reversing the district judge in this case. For a preliminary injunction to issue, the plaintiff must establish that "irreparable harm" will result for him if the injunction does not issue. This means that he will have "no adequate remedy at law" to repair the harm done, and that he has "some likelihood of succeeding on the

---

[189] 749 F.2d 380 (7th Cir. 1984).
[190] *Ibid.*, 381–82.
[191] *Ibid.*, 389.
[192] *Ibid.*, 390.

merits" when the case goes to trial.[193] In this case the district judge found that the plaintiff would probably go out of business if the preliminary injunction did not issue, which would certainly meet the irreparable harm test. Posner disputed this finding as a "clear error of fact," on the principal ground that although half of the plaintiff's revenues were derived from selling the equipment it had been guaranteed by the agreement the defendant was terminating, the judge was mistaken in estimating that its sales from the foreign manufacturer would not increase in the future.[194] "This is unrealistic," Posner claimed. "Surely Roland [the plaintiff] expects to do better in its second and subsequent years [of the agreement with the foreign manufacturer]. In sum, the loss of the distributorship will be painful, but it will not be fatal."[195] Yet this is pure speculation by an appellate judge; if this is a "clear error of fact," it is difficult to see what could not be argued to be.

Posner also found that the district judge erred in trying to fashion the remedy that would avoid harming the defendant. The defendant anticipated harm in the absence of an injunction, worrying that that the plaintiff would start to phase its equipment out of the plaintiff's business while the defendant's hands were tied by the injunction. The judge addressed this concern by requiring that the plaintiff maintain, "within normal economic fluctuations, the approximate market share which it now has obtained for Dresser products."[196] Posner held that this condition involved an error of law because the district judge "failed to consider the possible impact on competition of the injunction that freezes Dresser's market share until the end of the lawsuit."[197] Yet, as Judge Swygert noted in dissent, Posner simply ignored the component of the district judge's decree that permitted the defendant to obtain additional distributors in the plaintiff's territory, as well as the explicit finding of fact below "that there was no evidence to support Dresser's contention that Roland would cease or had ceased vigorously to market Dresser Products."[198] "The alleged error of law concerning the anticompetitive effects of the preliminary injunction," he continued, "goes only to the question of the appropriate scope of the decree, not whether or not it should issue." In short, Posner simply substituted his judgment

---

[193] *Ibid.*, 386–87.
[194] *Ibid.*, 391–92.
[195] *Ibid.*, 391.
[196] *Ibid.*, 382.
[197] *Ibid.*, 392.
[198] *Ibid.*, 401–12.

for the district court's.[199] In fact, even if Posner was correct that the judge had failed to consider the anticompetitive effects of his decree, the injunction should not have been vacated; it should have been remanded for a determination of those effects (a question of fact) and, if appropriate, modification of the decree.

Posner took the position, additionally, that the plaintiff had not made sufficient showing of likelihood of succeeding on the merits, in opposition to the district judge and to dissenting Judge Swygert. To prevail in a claim under Section 3 of the Clayton Act[200] a plaintiff has to show both that there was an agreement (which may not have been explicit) and that the agreement was likely to have a substantial (though not necessarily immediate) anticompetitive effect. Despite the fact that the Clayton Act specifically provides that the agreement need not be explicit, Posner held that there was no agreement because there was no "meeting of the minds" (a fiction which is not observed in many areas of contract law), and which has explicitly been repudiated by the Supreme Court in the antitrust context. In *Standard Oil Co. v. United States*[201] the Court construed the broad language of Section 1 of the Sherman Act as intended to protect commerce from all constraints, "old or new." In *Copperweld Corp. v. Independence Tube Corp.*, Justice Stevens, writing in dissent, noted that this broad interpretation has justified the Court's refusal, over time, "to limit the statute to actual agreements. Even mere acquiescence in an anticompetitive scheme has been held sufficient to satisfy the statutory language."[202] Posner's "meeting of the minds" requirement has no basis in the statute and is in direct contradiction to the prevailing interpretation of it by the Supreme Court.

More importantly, Posner held in *Roland Machinery* that the exclusive dealership arrangement did not necessarily have anticompetitive effects. Here we see Posner's restrictive antitrust theory at work in practice. He begins by noting that the exclusion of one or several competitors is not ipso facto unreasonable because, although the "welfare" of the particular competitor may be damaged, this is not the concern of the federal antitrust laws which are concerned with the health of competitive process itself. The Supreme Court opinion in *Copperveld Corp.*

[199] *Ibid.*, 402.
[200] 15 U.S.C. §14 (1914).
[201] 221 U.S. 1, 59–60 (1910).
[202] 467 U.S. 752 (1984) (citations omitted).

v. Independence Tube Corp. is cited as authority in this regard.[203] It is true that the Court there affirmed its view that the "antitrust laws . . . were enacted for the protection *of competition,* not *competitors*"[204] but this evades the issue in at least two different ways. First, the court below had heard evidence on the question of anticompetitive effect, and found that there was sufficient likelihood of it for the injunction to issue. Second, the way in which the antitrust laws protect competition is by protecting competitors; if protecting the competitive process was their *exclusive* purpose it is hard to see why damages would be retained as the appropriate remedy in antitrust cases, rather than fines, for example. No doubt the "economic" justification for this is that it is more efficient to enforce this law in a private law context, but if *that* is the case Posner cannot simultaneously argue that market power that harms individual competitors does not harm competition.

This aside, Posner gives his dictum operational focus by claiming that the plaintiff in such an action must prove at least two things: first, that it is likely to keep at least one significant competitor of the defendant from doing business in the relevant market, and, second, that the probable effect of the exclusion will be to raise prices above (and therefore reduce output below) the competitive level, or otherwise injure competition. "[H]e must show in other words that the anticompetitive effects (if any) of the exclusion outweigh any benefits to competition from it."[205]

This reflects, again, the neoclassical theory of monopoly, which Posner has elsewhere explicitly embraced and reified as "the" theory of monopoly,[206] by reference to which high concentration indices and even monopolies in some industries can be argued to be efficient. But there are of course alternative theories.[207] For Posner to claim that a version of his theory is now embraced by a majority on the Supreme

---

[203] *Roland Mach. Co. v. Dresser Indus.,* 749 F.2d 380, 394. (7th Cir. 1984).

[204] *Copperweld Corp. v. Independence Tube Corp.,* 467 U.S. 752, 767 (1984).

[205] 749 F.2d at 394.

[206] Posner, *Antitrust Law: An Economic Perspective,* p. 237–55.

[207] For accounts of the findings of many different empirical studies on the effects of concentration on competition, see *Concentration and Competition Policy,* Report of the Committee of Experts on Restrictive Business Practices, Organization for Economic Cooperation and Development (1979); for theories of administered pricing that are alternatives to the neoclassical theory (and some discussion of evidence), see Gardiner Means, "Simultaneous Inflation and Unemployment: A Challenge to Theory and Policy," *Challenge* (September–October 1975), pp. 6–20; Antonio Carlo, "Inflation," *Theory and Society,* Vol. 7, No. 3 (May 1979), p. 398; Howard J. Sherman, *Stagflation: A Radical Theory of Unemployment and Inflation* (New York: Harper and Row Publishers, 1976).

Court does not in itself establish that it is economically rational. In fact, in the very Supreme Court decision that Posner cites, in which the Court broke with precedent and endorsed vertical integration by holding that a parent corporation and a wholly owned subsidiary are legally incapable of conspiring with one another within the meaning of Section 1 of the Sherman Act, three dissenting justices explicitly embraced the administered pricing theory of monopoly, in terms of which the key variable is not collusion, but market power. "As an economic matter," wrote Justice Stevens (with Brennan and Marshall concurring) "what is critical [for violation of the Act] is the presence of market power, rather than plurality of actors. From a competitive standpoint, a decision of a single firm possessing power to reduce output and raise prices above competitive levels has the same consequence as a decision by two firms who have acquired the equivalent amount of market power through an agreement not to compete."[208] These conflicting arguments turn on different theories of the price mechanisms in monopolistic markets. The neoclassical theory might currently be endorsed by a majority on the Supreme Court, but this in no way entails either that it embodies the purpose of the Sherman Act (which is difficult to believe, given its sweeping language), or that it is the self-evident economic truth.

In *Roland Machinery* Posner exploited the heavy burden that the neo-classical theory places on the plaintiff by finding that he had not met either component of his two-part test. Posner was unconvinced by the record that the Japanese manufacturer would in fact be kept out of the market,[209] although, as Judge Swygert noted in dissent, Posner entirely ignored the evidence before and findings of the district judge on this question.[210] Indeed, Posner did not even claim that there was error of any kind, on this point, and since the criterion is supposed (by Posner's own account) to exclude substitution of its own judgment by the appellate court for the district judge's finding, this is indefensible. This is exactly what Posner did here. How else can we interpret Posner's speculations that "[t]he likeliest consequence of our dissolving the preliminary injunction would be to accelerate Komatsu's [the Japanese manufacturer's] efforts to promote its brand through the Roland dealership"?[211] Even Posner was forced to admit here that "this

---

[208] *Copperweld Corp. v. Independence Tube Corp.*, 467 U.S. 752, 789–90 (1984).
[209] *Roland Mach. v. Dresser Indus.*, 749 F.2d 380, 394 (7th Cir. 1984).
[210] *Ibid.*, 400.
[211] *Ibid.*, 394.

analysis may exaggerate the smoothness with which the competitive process operates."[212]

Enough has by now been said to show that Posner employs a contentious and restrictive theory of monopoly to overturn district court decisions. He seems unable to distinguish neoclassical models from reality, and this enables him to ignore evidence or arguments that are at variance with his beliefs. In this connection Leff was right to point out that there is an irreducible nominalist component to Posner's view.[213] On the procedural questions, too, we have seen that Posner does not adhere consistently to the traditional principles of deference which his microeconomic and macroeconomic theories of judicial efficiency require him, for different reasons, to do. As a judge he has violated these principles too often, with results that are too one-sided, to make credible the claim that he adheres consistently to his theory in practice, or that he is not "result-oriented" as a judge in just the sense in which he objects to this in the writings of Professor Mark Tushnet.[214]

IDEOLOGICAL IMPLICATIONS OF POSNER'S VIEW

One of Holmes's most frequently repeated aphorisms is his remark, in dissent in *Lochner v. New York*,[215] that "[t]he Fourteenth Amendment does not enact Mr. Herbert Spencer's *Social Statics*."[216] The antipathy for substantive due process it reflected revealed what is often held up as an admirable evenhandedness, particularly in the economic areas of private law.[217] It can and has been shown that Holmes was not entirely consistent in this regard; that in some of his Commerce Clause decisions, for instance, he appealed to substantive economic theories;[218] that his refusal to employ antitrust legislation against trade unions was at least made easier for him by his belief that as forms of economic organization they would be bound to fail;[219] and that when Congress enacted

---

[212] *Ibid.*, 394.

[213] Leff, "Some Realism about Nominalism," pp. 451, 456.

[214] Posner, *The Federal Courts*, pp. 218–19.

[215] 198 U.S. 45 (1905).

[216] *Ibid.*, 74 (1905).

[217] For examples of Holmes's dissents in labor cases, see *Vegelahn v. Guntner*, 167 Mass. 92, 104, 44 N.E. 1077, 1079–80 (1896); *Plant v. Woods*, 176 Mass. 492, 504, 57 N.E. 1011, 1015–16 (1900); *Adair v. United States*, 208 U.S. 161, 190 (1908); *Coppage v. Kansas*, 236 U.S. 1, 28 (1915).

[218] Max Lerner, ed., *The Mind and Faith of Justice Holmes: His Speeches, Essays, Letters, and Judicial Opinions* (Boston: Little Brown, 1943), pp. 135, 148, 241.

[219] *Ibid.*, p. 119.

legislation comfortable to his prejudices, at times he rushed to judgment with evident rhetorical glee.[220] Indeed, establishing that the common law evolved, increasingly, during the nineteenth century, to facilitate the consolidation of American capitalism has been something of a research agenda for critical legal historians; they have sought to show that the neutral language of the law adapted and developed itself to the changing needs of capitalism. And their critics have sought to dispute these claims, at least in part.[221]

What is as ironic as it is astonishing about Posner's theory of wealth-maximization is that he turns this highly controversial thesis into an axiom. He grants what the critical legal historians have been slaving to establish for decades, and then naively proceeds to try to reify it as a timeless "scientific" truth. This is done in many different ways as I have shown, in his writings on the microeconomics of wealth-maximization, in his analysis of the overload problems of the federal courts, in his theory of adjudication and in his practice as a judge. In all these areas, at every turn Posner presents controversial and contentious empirical economic theories as part of "the" theory of wealth-maximization. In his microeconomic discussion, he employs this procedure to legitimate an arbitrary commitment to "shadowing" the market in the allocation of property rights and their externalities so as to promote wealth-maximization, without reference to distributive consequences, and by simply asserting the truth of a trickle-down causal theory by reference to which this could be alleged to function in "society's" interest. In his analysis of the overload in the federal courts, Posner employs the demand/supply model when it suits him, but he quite arbitrarily switches it off (without acknowledging this) and asserts without argument that the level of demand for federal judicial resources is too high, so that they should be made more expensive for litigants. On examining Posner's trumpeted assertions that economic analysis plays an important role in such areas as the *Mathews v. Eldridge* test and the first amendment, I explained that this is much ado about precious little, since most of the difficult issues that divide courts in both these areas

---

[220] See Mary Dudziak, "Oliver Wendell Holmes as a Eugenic Reformer: Rhetoric in the Writing of Constitutional Law," *Iowa Law Review,* Vol. 71 (1986), pp. 833 for an analysis of the rhetorical structure of Holmes's decision in *Buck v. Bell,* in the context of his commitment to the policies of the eugenics movement.

[221] Harry N. Scheiber, "Law and the Imperatives of Progress: Private Rights and Public Values in American Legal History," in J. Roland Pennock and John W. Chapman, eds., *Nomos XXIV: Ethics, Economics, and the Law* (New York: New York University Press, 1982), pp. 303–20.

could not be resolved by economic analysis because there are competing solutions, consistent with different and competing economic theories. After surveying Posner's policy recommendations for judges and legislatures for making the courts function more effectively, we found a list of ad-hoc suggestions for husbanding judicial resources which are not derived from his economic theory and are inconsistent with it. And when I looked at his activities as a judge, I showed that he fails to adhere to his ad-hoc policy recommendations for various kinds of judicial restraint, or to traditional principles of judicial restraint that might have been thought to be entailed by his "micro-" theory of judicial efficiency.

Instead, Posner adheres to principles of judicial restraint as and when it suits him, and he happily violates these to advance his own particular neoclassical conceptions of the economics of labor and antitrust law. All along, Posner presents these economic theories as uncontroversial when in fact they are anything but that, and he hides from their inegalitarian distributive implications by pretending that they are mere "by-products" of his scientific theory of allocation. But once it is shown that the theory of allocation is no less controversial than is the assertion that if you take my assets and could pay me for them but do not we would both be better off, the extent to which "law and economics" is, in this context, nothing more than thinly veiled ideology to legitimate the inequalities wrought by market systems is undeniable. The amazing thing is that these arguments can have so much influence among lawyers when they were thoroughly discredited by welfare economists over thirty years ago. That, one supposes, is eloquent testimony to the staying power of an intellectually bankrupt but dominant ideology.

Gross Concepts in Political Argument

POLITICAL THEORISTS often fail to appreciate that arguments about how politics ought to be organized typically depend on relational claims involving agents, actions, legitimacy, and ends. If they did, they would see that to defend the standard contending views in many of the controversies that occupy them is silly. In what follows I work through a number of debates about the nature of right, law, autonomy, utility, freedom, virtue, and justice, showing this to be true. I argue, further, that political theorists frequently think in terms of *gross concepts*: They reduce what are actually relational claims to claims about one or another of the components of the relation. This not only obscures the phenomena they wish to analyze; it also generates debates that can never be resolved because the alternatives that are opposed to one another are vulnerable within their own terms. Finally I offer a pair of explanations for why gross concepts persist in political theory, and suggest a way for avoiding their trap.

ARGUMENTS FOR THE SUPREMACY OF AUTONOMY

John Stuart Mill's harm principle, Isaiah Berlin's defense of "negative" over "positive" freedom, Robert Paul Wolff's defense of anarchism, John Rawls's bid for the "priority of liberty" and Robert Nozick's rejection of "patterned" theories of justice all embrace variants of the thesis that individual autonomy is the primary political end, that other ends can be justified only to the extent that they are compatible with it. These views are often called antiteleological, anticonsequentialist, deontological, or neo-Kantian, in virtue of this primacy they ascribe to individual autonomy. Yet autonomy is a value *to* people *for* purposes, it is not sitting out there waiting to be apportioned. Nor is it something, like teeth, that people have and that should not gratuitously be extracted. As Gerald MacCallum Jr. showed long ago, any assertion about freedom or autonomy minimally involves reference to agents, restraining (or enabling) conditions, and action. It always makes sense to ask of any use of the term: *who* is free, *from* what restraint (or *because of* what enabling condition) *to* perform which action? I endorse MacCallum's account but modify it in two ways. First, when we talk about political freedom a fourth term enters, having to do with legitimacy; it may be thought of in terms of the question *why,* in virtue of what justification, is the agent free? Second, what MacCallum had to say about freedom is true of a much larger class of political terms. At least the ideas of right, justice, virtue, and community exhibit analogous relational structures.

Now there is scarcely a mention of freedom, liberty, or autonomy in the journals without a genuflecting reference to MacCallum's argument. Yet what he had to say has penetrated little. William Parent, for example, makes the point that conformity to MacCallum's schema is necessary but insufficient for an assertion's being about freedom.[1] MacCallum never denied this. His aim was to shift discussion away from conceptual debates about the meaning of the term "freedom," by showing that most debates that seem to be about it are really about the substantive variables in his triad. The triad itself is empty. Theorists of freedom would do better to get involved in first-order arguments about the terms in the relation, and avoid the meta-analyses of "kinds" of freedom that take this debate in endless circles.[2]

Another misreading of MacCallum's point informs a discussion by Quentin Skinner, who seeks to show that Machiavelli's republican view of freedom is superior to modem doctrines of negative liberty. Skinner argues that MacCallum's view is really a version of the doctrine of negative liberty, that "insofar as MacCallum's analysis suggests a negative understanding of freedom as the absence of constraints upon an agent's options (which it does), this ["that the only coherent account that can

---

[1] William A. Parent, "Some Recent Work on the Concept of Liberty," *American Philosophical Quarterly,* Vol. 11, No. 3 (July 1974), pp. 149–67.

[2] Gerald C. MacCallum, Jr., "Negative and Positive Freedom," in Peter Laslett, W. G. Runciman, and Quentin Skinner, ed., *Philosophy, Politics, and Society,* Fourth Series (Oxford: Blackwell, 1972), p. 174.

possibly be given of liberty is a negative one"] is also the implication of his account and of those that depend on it."[3] Yet it was just MacCallum's point that *all* accounts of liberty have both negative and positive elements, some of which are usually implicit; that negative libertarians focus mainly on the second component of his triadic relation ("from what?"), while positive libertarians attend to the third ("to what?"). To be sure, he acknowledged that all intelligible concepts of freedom or liberty involve some notion of constraints or their absence, but just because *this* element could never amount to *an account of freedom*, talk of freedom from constraint or restraint did not make an account "negative." The opposition should be eschewed, for constraints and enabling conditions can easily be redescribed as one another. Is a prisoner unfree because of the presence of a locked door or the absence of a key? It is thus misleading to think of negative or positive language as indicative of a logical difference.[4] Some hermeneutists would resist this claim entirely, holding that the term means nothing more nor less than users of it understand it to mean,[5] but it is doubtful that Skinner is still one of these, and certainly MacCallum was not writing for them. His point was that ordinary and academic debate in this area is confused. This is admittedly a whiggish view, and later I will outline a more complex account of the relationship between the structure of political grammar and people's beliefs about that structure.

A last example of the failure of MacCallum's analysis to penetrate comes from Rawls.[6] In his discussion of liberty in *A Theory of Justice* he embraces MacCallum's account, stating that "I shall simply assume that liberty can always be explained by reference to three items: the agents who are free, the restrictions or limitations they are free from, and what it is that they are free to do or not do."[7] But almost everything Rawls has ever said about liberty is at variance with this. His view that the first of his two principles protects liberties while the second deals

[3] Quentin Skinner, "The Idea of Negative Liberty: Philosophical and Historical Perspectives," in Richard Rorty, J. B. Schneewind, and Quentin Skinner, ed., *Philosophy in History* (Cambridge, UK: Cambridge University Press, 1984), p. 196.

[4] MacCallum, "Negative and Positive Freedom," p. 182 n. 9.

[5] See my "Realism in the Study of the History of Ideas," *History of Political Thought*, Vol. 3, No. 3 (November 1982), pp. 568–69.

[6] This discussion of Rawls is partly based on a more extended analysis that can be found in Ian Shapiro, *The Evolution of Rights in Liberal Theory* (Cambridge, UK: Cambridge University Press, 1986), pp. 218–25.

[7] John Rawls, *A Theory of Justice* (Cambridge, MA: Harvard University Press, 1971), p. 202.

with social and economic inequalities obviously violates it.[8] Taking MacCallum's analysis seriously, Rawls would have to see that the first principle cannot be reasoned about independently of, and given lexical priority to, the second. Issues about economic inequality affect peoples' capacities to perform actions, which is a large part of what the concept of liberty, on that analysis, means.[9] It is hard to see why the liberties Rawls enumerates, "liberties of the person and liberty of conscience and freedom of thought,"[10] are given priority over other liberties, or how even they can be secured without reference to economic matters dealt with under his second principle. Rawls's attempt to sidestep these difficulties compounds them:

> The inability to take advantage of one's rights and opportunities as a result of poverty and ignorance, and a lack of means generally, is sometimes counted among the constraints definitive of liberty. I shall not, however, say this, but rather I shall think of these things as affecting the worth of liberty, the value to individuals of the rights that the first principle defines . . . liberty is represented by the complete system of the liberties of equal citizenship, while the worth of liberties to persons and groups is proportional to their capacity to advance their ends within the framework the system defines.[11]

Inequalities in the *worth* of liberty are governed by the difference principle. They are secondary to, and can never dictate changes in, the definition of the liberties themselves. Rawls, then, defines "freedom" independently both of people's capacities to exercise that freedom, and of the uses to which it is put. The whole point of MacCallum's analysis was to show that this makes no sense. Rawls openly embraces the standard negative libertarian view, the Nozickian idea of the right to autonomy as a "sphere in moral space" that can never be violated without the "owner's" consent.[12] The continual references throughout *A Theory*

[8] *Ibid.*, pp. 61, 119.

[9] This is all the more obviously so given Rawls's "grave risks" assumption, that under moderate scarcity the worst-off in society may be extremely precarious, so that considering society from their standpoint, utilitarianism must be rejected. *Ibid.*, pp. 167–73.

[10] *Ibid.*, p. 61.

[11] *Ibid.*, p. 204.

[12] Rawls explicitly likened his position on this point to Nozick's, claiming that his "basic liberties" protected by the first principle are inalienable "and therefore can neither be waived nor limited by any agreements made by citizens, nor overridden by shared collective preferences." John Rawls, "Social Unity and Primary Goods," in Amartya Sen and Bernard Williams, ed., *Utilitarianism and Beyond* (Cambridge, UK: Cambridge University Press), pp. 159–85. This is a stronger

of Justice and elsewhere to "the standpoint of liberty itself," "the priority of liberty," and "the principle of equal liberty"[13] show that he never came to grips with the relational character of freedom.

This failure infects Rawls's broader "deontological" enterprise. He contrasts this to "teleological" theories such as utilitarianism. But this distinction confronts difficulties analogous to the negative/positive dichotomy. What is objectionable about utilitarianism for Rawls is that it defines the right "as that which maximizes the good," so that "there is no reason in principle why the greater gains of some should not compensate for the lesser losses of others."[14] Rawls's principles are intended, by contrast, to be "procedural expressions of the categorical imperative," in the same way as Nozick's rights as "side-constraints" allegedly preserve Kantian autonomy.[15] That Rawls and Nozick both defend their deontological conceptions by reference to what they take to be the unhappy *consequences* of utilitarianism make it clear that consequentialist reasoning is decisive in the arguments they advance in support of their own principles. In Rawls's case, both his principles are in their bones consequentialist. The claim that we should all receive the most extensive system of basic liberties compatible with a like liberty for all requires an empirical theory (however deeply implicit) of what system is thus compatible, as soon as Rawls begins to enumerate specific institutional liberties that allegedly meet this criterion. The difference principle is appealed to precisely because it allegedly rules out certain distributive consequences.

Nozick also rests his thesis that rights-as-side-constraints can be respected only via the Pareto principle on the misleading claim that this is somehow not a teleological or "end-state" principle. This is false not only for the specific reason that once he invokes the consequentialist notion of externality to justify forcible inclusion, with compensation, of those anarchists who refuse to join his minimal state, he has obviously embraced interpersonal comparisons of utility with all its teleological consequences.[16] Nozick must also embrace the more general conse-

---

version of the negative libertarian claim than even Nozick's (for whom rights can be traded by agreement or even violated with compensation in some circumstances). For more evidence on these points, see Rawls, "Social Unity and Primary Goods," pp. 171ff.

[13] Rawls, *A Theory of Justice*, pp. 207, 211.

[14] *Ibid.*, pp. 24, 26.

[15] Robert Nozick, *Anarchy, State and Utopia* (Oxford: Blackwell, 1974), pp. 28–30; Rawls, *A Theory of Justice*, p. 171 n.

[16] In the absence of an "end-state" preference for the minimal state, there would be no reason to hold that the externality of the independent's refusal to join Nozick's dominant protective

quentialist claim that market-based appropriation will never run afoul of Locke's second proviso, which requires as a condition of exclusive appropriation that as much and as good be left for others in common.[17] Both writers use consequentialist argument not out of lack of philosophical acumen, but because it is impossible otherwise to defend any substantive principle of right or justice, impossible not to incorporate considerations Kant dubbed "anthropological." This was obvious to Kant,[18] but is obscured from these writers in their tendency to think of liberty in terms of spheres surrounding individuals—"hyperplanes" in moral space, to use Nozick's phrase. If the claim that there are rights is partly a claim about what they are rights *to*, it cannot be surprising that rights theorists presuppose empirical theories of how the objects of value to which people attach rights are created and distributed. Rawls's hope that political theory can be "strictly deductive," conducted as a kind of "moral geometry," misses this.[19]

The same confusion attends Ronald Dworkin's attempts to distinguish questions of "principle" from those of "policy," holding that the former—the preserve of courts—have to do with rights and the latter—the preserve of legislature and executive—with consequences. His most recent formulation of this has already drawn heavy critical fire.[20] Just as it should be obvious to Dworkin that something is amiss when the value of rights is demonstrated by appealing to the allegedly awful consequences of utilitarianism,[21] making evident nonsense of the claim that rights are unconcerned with consequences, so it should be obvious that the more general distinction obscures more than it reveals: all normative claims about politics involve reference to both principle and consequence, however deeply implicit either might be. Legislators can no

---

association—the fear of members at the threat he would continue to pose—justified his forcible inclusion. The independents could, alternatively, be forced to compensate the members for their fear.

[17] Nozick, *Anarchy, State and Utopia*, pp. 175–82.

[18] In "The contest of the faculties," in the context of discussing state welfare provision, Kant argued that "welfare does not have any ruling principle, either for the recipient or for the one who provides it, for each individual will define it differently. It depends, in fact, on the will's material aspect, which is empirical and thus incapable of becoming a universal rule." Immanuel Kant, *Kant's Political Writings*, Hans Reiss, ed. and H. B. Nisbet, trans. (Cambridge, UK: Cambridge University Press, 1970), pp. 183–84 n.

[19] Rawls, *A Theory of Justice*, p. 121.

[20] See, for instance, the reviews of *A Matter of Principle* by Brian Barry in the *Times Literary Supplement* (October 25, 1985) and by Bernard Williams in the *London Review of Books* (17 April 1986), pp. 7–8.

[21] Ronald Dworkin, *A Matter of Principle* (Cambridge, MA: Harvard University Press, 1985), pp. 81–89ff.

more ignore principles than can judges articulate them without reference to consequences.

Perhaps the starkest illustration of the types of the muddles that get
generated when the consequentialist/anticonsequentialist dichotomy is
assumed can be found in Robert Paul Wolff's argument that unanimous direct democracy is the only system that would not, in principle,
violate the categorical imperative. Wolff does not explicitly discuss the
dichotomy, but he assumes that decision rules can be critically evaluated without reference to consequences, which is fatal to his argument.
All variants of majority rule are objectionable for Wolff on the (implicitly consequentialist) ground that problems of voting cycles and agenda
control inevitably violate the autonomy of some. Unanimity need not
in principle have this result, since nothing could be done unless everyone agreed. The problems with unanimity are merely practical for
Wolff, even if practically insurmountable.[22] Yet this ignores the consequences of unanimity *as a decision rule*. If a direct democracy committed to unanimity rule voted on any proposed change in the status quo
and revealed itself to be divided (in any way), the rule would require
retaining the status quo. But that, of course, would violate the autonomy of those who had just revealed themselves to be opposed to it.
Only if the status quo itself had always been the product of unanimous
decisions could this difficulty be obviated (assuming people may not
change their minds—but why should we assume that?), but this would
be impossible. The mere fact that people are born and die means that
some (and, after a couple of generations, all) would find themselves
governed by a status quo that they did not choose.

Wolff's analysis is quite fanciful, but not without significant ideological implications. For the alleged difficulties with majority rule have
been argued by many public choice theorists since Buchanan and Tullock to undermine all activities by states that rest on variants of it, to
make the idea of state minimalism seem comparatively attractive on
the grounds that it most closely approaches the (admittedly unattainable) ideal of unanimity.[23] Departures from unanimity can be justified
"not because they will produce 'better' collective decisions (they will

---

[22] Robert Paul Wolff, *In Defense of Anarchism* (New York: Harper & Row, 1970), pp. 22–27.

[23] For further discussion of the difficulties with unanimity as a decision rule, see Douglas W.
Rae, "Decision-rules and Individual Values in Constitutional Choice," *American Political Science
Review*, Vol. 58, No. 1 (March 1969), pp. 40–56 and "The Limits of Consensual Decision," *Ameri-
can Political Science Review*, Vol. 69, No. 4 (December 1975), pp. 1270–94. Generally, see Brian
Barry, *Political Argument* (Hertfordshire: Harvester Wheatsheaf, 1990), pp. 242–85, 312–16.

not), but rather because, on balance, the sheer weight of the costs involved in reaching decisions unanimously dictates some departure from the 'ideal' rule."[24] Once we look at unanimity *as a decision rule*, it becomes clear that this is simply false. It is just because libertarian writers think of liberty and autonomy as spheres surrounding individuals, without ever attending to its relational nature, that they miss this.

The confusions behind the negative libertarian view can be traced at least to Locke's theory of natural law.[25] Natural law, he argued, "ought to be distinguished from natural right: for right is grounded in the fact that we have the free use of a thing, whereas law enjoins or forbids the doing of a thing."[26] Right, then, differs qualitatively from law, the former indicating a capacity for autonomous action, and the latter externally imposed obligatory constraints. Yet it has been clear at least since Kant that my right to x *is* your obligation to respect that right, even if this is understood in the minimal sense of a Hohfeldian duty to respect my negatively defined liberty.[27] Unless employed in the purely descriptive sense of Hobbes's natural rights, which Locke clearly does not intend, an account of rights entails a view of law and obligation. Locke's model requires natural right to be basic and prior to natural law. Although he equivocates a good deal, it is clear from the *Essay,* the *Second Treatise,* and the *Reasonableness of Christianity,* as well as the early natural law writings, that Locke conceived of natural laws as God's natural rights. There is thus no tension between recognizing the analytic priority of right in Locke's account and the interpretive scholarship of recent decades that emphasizes the centrality of his theology to his politics.[28]

Locke was never entirely comfortable with this view.[29] If natural law was tied to the will of God, it was presumably alterable with that will.

---

[24] James M. Buchanan and Gordon Tullock, *The Calculus of Consent: Logical Foundations of Constitutional Democracy* (Ann Arbor: University of Michigan Press), p. 96.

[25] The following discussion of Locke is partly drawn from, and partly elaborates on, my discussion in *Evolution of Rights,* pp. 100–18.

[26] John Locke, *Essays on the Law of Nature,* W. von Leyden, ed. (Oxford: Clarendon, 1958), p. 111.

[27] In Hohfeldian terms, although the juridical "opposite" of a right is a "no-right," its juridical "correlate" is a "duty" attaching to some third person to respect that right. Wesley N. Hohfeld, *Fundamental Legal Conceptions as Applied to Juridical Reasoning* (New Haven: Yale University Press, 1923), pp. 65ff.

[28] See John Dunn, *The Political Thought of John Locke* (Cambridge, UK: Cambridge University Press, 1969); James Tully, *A Discourse on Property: John Locke and His Adversaries* (Cambridge, UK: Cambridge University Press, 1980), pp. 35–79; and Richard Ashcraft, *Locke's Two Treatises of Government* (London: Allen & Unwin, 1987), pp. 35–80.

[29] For elaboration, see Anthony Kenny, *The God of the Philosophers* (New York: Oxford University Press, 1979), pp. 16–22.

But if natural law was a body of rules in conformity with the rational nature of things, this could be argued to imply that God did not have the power to alter natural law by command, that natural law is binding even on God, or that it would be valid, as Hugo Grotius had argued, even if God did not exist.[30] Locke wanted to hold both his celebrated view that morality, like mathematics, is open to conclusive demonstration, and his doctrine of theological voluntarism that made the will of God, and hence *His* natural right, basic and prior to natural law. This generated a tension in his view of natural law between his voluntarist theology and theory of action, on the one hand, and his conviction that natural law was part of an immutable natural order, on the other.[31] His confusing and sometimes contradictory utterances on the nature, content, and accessibility of natural law continue to be debated,[32] but it is beyond question that whatever else it is, natural law is God's will for Locke. His frequent appeals, so ably portrayed by James Tully, to metaphors of workmanship and watchmaking in the *Two Treatises* and elsewhere,[33] make men obliged to God because of his purposes in making them.[34]

Locke was thus opening the way for modern doctrines of the priority of right, even if he himself only held this view in an unqualified form as it applied to God's actions—men's actions being free only within the limits imposed by the law of nature or God's natural right.[35] Where natural law is silent we cannot be bound. Just because God has created

[30] For further discussion, see von Leyden's introduction to Locke's *Essays on the Law of Nature,* pp. 52ff.

[31] For textual evidence see Shapiro, *Evolution of Rights,* pp. 100–12. For a fuller discussion of Locke's theological voluntarism, see Patrick Riley, *Will and Political Legitimacy: A Critical Exposition of Social Contract Theory in Hobbes, Locke, Rousseau, Kant, and Hegel* (Cambridge, MA: Harvard University Press, 1982), pp. 87ff.

[32] For one useful account, see von Leyden's introduction to Locke's *Essays on the Law of Nature,* especially pp. 43–60.

[33] Tully, *A Discourse on Property,* pp. 35–36ff.

[34] Men are "the Workmanship of one Omnipotent, and infinitely wise Maker. They are His Property, whose Workmanship they are, made to last during His, not one anothers Pleasure." John Locke, *Two Treatises of Government,* Peter Laslett, ed. (Cambridge, UK: Cambridge University Press, 1988), p. 311. Like Newton, Locke rejects the Aristotelian view that the world is uncreated, that matter must be eternal, on the grounds that it "denies one and the first great piece of His [God's] workmanship, the creation." John Locke, *An Essay Concerning Human Understanding* (New York: Dover, 1959), vol. 2, p. 320. For further discussion see Tully, *A Discourse on Property,* p. 37, and Dunn, *Political Thought of John Locke,* p. 95.

[35] Although these were conceived of as quite broad constraints. Provided they do not violate natural law men can act as they please, and indeed create obligations to themselves by their own autonomous actions, ". . . for we are not bound to anything except what a law-maker in some way has made known and proclaimed as his will." Locke, *Essays on the Law of Nature,* p. 187.

man with free will and the capacity for autonomous action, men can create laws and obligations to themselves. "Every man is put under a necessity, by his constitution as an intelligent being, to be determined in willing by his own thought and judgment what is best for him to do: else he would be under the determination of some other than himself, which is want of liberty."[36] Within the limits set by the law of nature men can act, as Tully notes, in a God-like fashion: "man as maker . . . [has] analogous maker's knowledge of, and a natural right in his intentional actions."[37] Once God is removed from the picture, this asymmetrical model of right and law entails that there are no constraints on us besides our own wills, bequeathing to Locke's inheritors the impossible task of deriving a set of determinate political institutions from the idea of an autonomous individual will and nothing else.

The difficulty of executing this task has been a core liberal concern since Locke's time. It is at the heart of Sidgwick's dispute with Kant.[38] It frames the disputes among classical and neoclassical utilitarians over ordinal versus cardinal utility,[39] and the tension, in Mill's writings, between his early acceptance of utilitarianism and his later commitment to the harm principle. The hope that respect for the autonomy of individual wills can, alone, generate an argument for determinate political institutions has set many of the terms of contemporary debate, and if the myriad of specific solutions to this puzzle fail, it is because there are no institutions that can simultaneously protect the autonomy of all in some general unspecified sense. Different institutions benefit different people differently. This is why the various autonomy-preserving institutions that dominate contemporary political theory are inevitably vulnerable to counterexample. The idea of autonomy typically invoked by liberal theorists is unadministerable; it lacks relational specification in my sense. Its defenders resist such specification just because engaging in it undermines the deontological spirit that motivates them.

Nowhere is this more clear than in *On Liberty*. At the outset Mill offers his famous formulation that the "sole end for which mankind are warranted, individually or collectively, in interfering with the liberty of action of any their number is self-protection."[40] The only justification for such interference is to "prevent harm to others. His own good,

---

[36] Locke, *Essay Concerning Human Understanding*, vol. 1, p. 346.
[37] Tully, *A Discourse on Property*, pp. 109–10, 121.
[38] On which see Rawls, *Theory of Justice*, pp. 254–57.
[39] On which see Shapiro, *Evolution of Rights*, pp. 169, 214–18, 260–62, 285–87.
[40] John Stuart Mill, *On Liberty* (London: Macmillan, 1985), p. 13.

either physical or moral, is not a sufficient warrant." This is not, strictly,
an argument for the priority of right, for it is essential to Mill's case
that the consequence of harming others may warrant state action.
But for "private-regarding" actions that do not fall into this class, no
third party is ever warranted in interfering with the actions of an individual. The right is prior to the good. In Rawlsian terms we might
call this a teleologically constrained deontological system, or in terms
more congenial to public choice theorists, it is a cardinally constrained
ordinal system.

As has often been noted, Mill's argument assumes some account of
what harm is, of where the limits to "private-regarding" actions are to
be drawn, and by whom. The difficulties this raises in the philosophy
of action are massive.[41] Now we need only note that as soon as Mill
reaches the problem of administering his principle, he is forced to allow
considerations of purpose and contestable judgments about the public
good to intrude into his evaluation of harm. Thus, in his chapter on
"Applications" he notes that whoever succeeds in an overcrowded profession or in a competitive examination "reaps benefit from the loss of
others, from their wasted exertion and disappointment." Yet this is not
a harm that should concern us because "it is, by common admission,
better for the general interest of mankind that persons should pursue
their objects undeterred by this sort of consequences." Likewise, free
trade is supported over various systems of regulated pricing (even
though some might correctly believe themselves to be harmed by it) on
the consensualist grounds that "it is now recognized, though not till
after a long struggle, that both the cheapness and the good quality of
commodities are most effectually provided for by leaving the producers
and sellers perfectly free."[42] Mill explicitly invokes consensus about the
common good, and particular and contested theories about its efficient
provision. This at least supplements, and arguably even overrides, the
requirements of the harm principle. In its pure form the harm principle
is unadministerable, just because in a whole host of areas of social life
some policy has to be followed, and it will harm some people.

---

[41] The most serious of these have to do with the unintended consequences of actions, and with
acts of omission. There are also serious issues raised by the possibility of multiple descriptions of
the same action. These issues are usefully taken up in G.E.M. Anscombe, "Modern Moral Philosophy," in W. D. Hudson, ed., *The Is-Ought Question: A Collection of Papers on the Central Problems
in Moral Philosophy* (London: Macmillan), pp. 175–95.

[42] Mill, *On Liberty*, p. 115.

Mill's only attempt to deal with this is his distinction between speech and action: Mere speech will never be interpreted to inflict harm, whereas action, in some (theoretically unspecified) circumstances will be. Thus

> an opinion that corn-dealers are starvers of the poor, or that private property is robbery, ought to be unmolested when simply circulated through the press, but may justly incur punishment when delivered orally to an excited mob assembled before the house of a corn dealer, or when handed about among the same mob in the form of a placard.[43]

This assumes just what Mill cannot, that some principle anterior to the harm principle tells us when it should be invoked. Just as the Pareto principle reinforces the distributive status quo by permitting only voluntary transactions, Mill's harm principle has a structurally identical bias.[44] To pursue his own example, if the corn-dealer *is* a starver of the poor, or if private property *is* robbery, it is sheer fancy to suppose that printing this in the press will convince corn-dealers and other property-owners to give up their ill-gotten gains, facts that reflect the serious limits of a theory of politics lacking any explicit theory of power. For Mill in *On Liberty*, the anterior commitment that regulates the administration of the harm principle is the belief (which he questioned elsewhere) that unregulated markets promote utilitarian efficiency. Like all principles of right or autonomy, the harm principle cannot be evaluated without reference to its content and purposes in particular cases, without reference, that is, to the components of its relational structure.

On Liberty, then, is an important document in the history of liberal ideology not because it challenged the classical utilitarian theory of value (this had been done many times before), but because Mill tried to redefine utilitarianism to entail a doctrine of individual rights palatable to the liberal consciousness. The tendency of liberals since has been either to defend a deontological theory of individual rights, while working implicitly with a utilitarian theory of value and purpose, or to do the converse, to defend a version of utilitarianism alleged to preserve individual autonomy as a by-product of maximizing efficiency. The explicit dialectic of liberal theoretical argument is to lurch back and forth among variants of autonomy and utility; the implicit dialectic is

[43] *Ibid.*, pp. 67–68.
[44] I am indebted to Douglas Rae for pointing out this parallel.

to fuse these Kantian and Benthamite concerns either through unarticulated causal assumptions about how markets operate, or through political principles that, if not analogous to those on which the market rests, are at least congenial to them. This explains the subliminal attractiveness of the Millian project to those predisposed to the market system, and its perceived irrelevance by those otherwise disposed. The real argument is never whether "autonomy" is "important." Rather, it should be seen for what it is: an argument over which feasible principles of political and economic organization create and preserve which liberties for whom to perform what actions, and at what cost to whom. The simple question of whether freedom or autonomy is the ultimate value, we can now see, is silly.

Arguments for the Supremacy of Purpose

Now we can also see how beside the point much of the communitarian reaction against arguments for the supremacy of autonomy really is. Some critics of the neo-Kantians take them at their word when they claim either to have no conception of the good, or to be neutral among competing "rational" conceptions,[45] and object to *that*. Most, however, go the route of Sandel in discerning that the Rawlsian-style "thin" theories may be thicker than their proponents admit, but in not liking the particular density they discern. For Sandel, liberalism's commitment to the primacy of justice, and to the priority of right it brings with it, make it fundamentally unsatisfying.[46] Divorcing public from private lives, it recognizes only in the latter the constituting roles of cultural attachments. The deontological liberal holds that "while we may be thickly-constituted selves in private, we must be wholly unencumbered in public, and it is there that the primacy of justice prevails" so that we become "submerged in a circumstance that ceases to be ours." By placing the cultural self beyond the reach of politics, liberalism "makes human agency an article of faith rather than an object of continuing attention and concern, a premise of politics rather than its precarious

---

[45] See, for instance, Allan Bloom, "Justice: John Rawls vs. the Tradition of Political Philosophy," *American Political Science Review,* Vol. 69 No. 2 (June 1975), pp. 648–62.

[46] Michael J. Sandel, *Liberalism and the Limits of Justice* (Cambridge, UK: Cambridge University Press, 1982), pp. 11–14.

achievement."[47] Sandel claims that extending the intimacies of our cultural commitments into an explicit theory of the political good would provide a more satisfying public community than the impoverished deontological vision. But doing this does not begin to free us of the need to give some account of the right; a comprehensive theory of politics must range over persons, actions, and criteria for legitimacy as well as purposes, and these former cannot be deduced from such a commitment alone. Although Hobbes's view of the plurality of human passions does not generate a state that is neutral among them as some have thought (he never believed it did, as I have shown elsewhere),[48] he was surely right to argue that goods must always be understood relationally, in terms of the persons of whom they are predicated.[49] To say that all morality is teleological does not begin to establish that there may not be different and conflicting goods for different persons in the same, different, and overlapping communities.

Sandel's view that justice belongs characteristically to the world of "strangers" reified in the deontological vision he rejects both misdescribes the private communities we live in, and evokes expectations for a theory of politics that cannot withstand analysis from our relational standpoint. First, it is simply untrue that the idea of justice does not operate in our private communal lives. In the family, that paradigm of the private community, held together in the ideal by bonds of intimacy and affection, justice and the sense of it play indispensable roles. The pertinent currency of family life is not voting rights or economic well-being, but caring and affection. While these are not properly distributed on the basis of merit, desert, efficiency, or Rawls's difference principle, they have their own system of equities that, when violated, generate powerful felt injustice and sometimes conflict. The child who knows herself to be loved or respected less, or the abused wife, will certainly bring to bear notions of injustice because they will feel the pertinent economy of love and affection has been violated.[50] The idea that existing

---

[47] Sandel, *Liberalism*, p. 183.

[48] Shapiro, *Evolution of Rights*, pp. 55–59, 275, 282–84.

[49] So Aristotle was held to be wrong in defining "good" simply as "that which all men desire since different men desire and shun different things, there must needs be many things that are good to some and evil to others . . . one cannot speak of something as being simply good since whatsoever is good, is good for someone or other." Thomas Hobbes, "De homine," in Charles T. Wood, T.S.K. Scott-Craig, and Bernard Gert, eds. and trans., *Man and Citizen: Thomas Hobbe's De homine* (Garden City, NY: Anchor, 1972), p. 47.

[50] I assume here, with Walzer, MacIntyre, and others that all social goods are not reducible to a single index. I differ from both, however, in holding that the most politically interesting prob-

private communities provide a yardstick for a kind of post-political politics assumes a benign view of those communities that Sandel nowhere defends. And just as there are some happy and stable families, blessed by abundance, good health and fortune, many are not this lucky. The language of justice comes into play whenever there is scarcity of, and conflict over, the goods internal to the relevant community.

More romantic still is the attempt by other communitarians to base the post-political community not on some existing private community, but instead on a community yet to be created. In these formulations the need for a system of justice can be abolished only when the causes of present conflict and scarcity go with it. This was the young Marx's view—that a communist society would differ from all its predecessors in that a superabundance of wealth would obviate the conflict generated by scarcity. Goods would be distributed on the basis of need, and government displaced by mere administration. It is often thought that such a view could be persuasive if a theory of needs could be developed that distinguished them from wants. Wants may be infinite, as the bourgeois economists argued, and scarcity with respect to them inevitable therefore, but needs are not. A well-developed theory of needs could provide an Archimedean point for limiting the induced wants of the market, making an economy of needs not subject to the limitations of scarcity at least a possibility.

These formulations assume a static and unrealistic view of human needs.[51] Such lifesaving technologies as dialysis machines and artificial hearts satisfy needs, not wants, on any credible definition, yet clearly the potential for such innovation is limitless. Once technological change is taken into account, human needs are infinite, scarcity and concomitant conflict inevitable, and the languages of politics and distributive justice inescapable. Political conflict is endemic to the human social condition. It is absurd to suppose that by modeling politics on present or past private communities, or on imagined communities of the past or future, the need for a system of justice will evaporate.[52]

---

lems of distributive conflict occur not between "spheres" or "practices," but within them, as people struggle over what the definition of the good within a particular sphere should be. Michael Walzer, *Spheres of Justice: A Defense of Pluralism and Equality* (New York: Basic Books, 1983); Alisdair MacIntyre, *After Virtue* (Notre Dame, IN: University of Notre Dame Press, 1984).

[51] At times Marx embraced a more dynamic view of needs, as in the argument in *Capital* that what counts as subsistence is socially and historically conditioned. But he never came to terms with the difficulties this raised for his account of communism as a permanent state of superabundance.

[52] Many contemporary Marxists have eschewed the Utopian ambitions of Marx's politics. See, for example, Carmen Sirianni, "Production and Power in a Classless Society: A Critical Analysis

This is why writers such as Pocock obscure more than they reveal when they contrast liberalism's "law-centered paradigm," in which the individual "is looked on as inhabiting a cosmos regulated by rational and moral principles," in which even God "is looked on as a *lex loquens*, and even His role as the author of inscrutable grace does not much detract from this image," with an alternative "virtue-centered" civic humanist "mode" of "discoursing" about politics, one which is not "philosophical and juristic," but is rather cast in an alternative, "markedly discontinuous" vocabulary, which "encounter[s] different problems, and employ[s] different strategies of speech and argument."[53]

Unsurprisingly, Pocock characterizes these paradigms in terms of negative and positive liberty. Liberal autonomy is paradigmatically freedom from politics, a negative constraint on the power of others (principally, if not exclusively, the state). By contrast,

> republican vocabulary employed by the *dictatores*, rhetoricians and humanists articulated the positive conception of liberty: it contended that *homo*, the animate *politician*, was so constituted that his nature was completed only in a *vita activa* practiced in a *vivere civile*, and that *libertas* consisted in freedom from restraints upon the practice of such a life.[54]

Although liberal jurisprudence tends to "lower the level of participation and deny the premise that man is by nature political," preoccupied as it is with what "can be distributed, with things and rights," classical republican positive liberty elevates participation through the Aristotelian affirmation that we are naturally political animals.

> The republic or *politeia* solved the problem of authority and liberty by making *quisque* [everyone] participant in the authority by which he was ruled; this entailed relations of equality which made in fact extremely stern demands upon him, but by premising that he was *kata phūsin* formed to participate in such a citizenship it could be said that it was his

---

of the Utopian Dimensions of Marxist Theory," *Socialist Review*, Vol. 59 (1981), pp. 33–82; Ernesto Laclau and Chantal Mouffe, *Hegemony and Socialist Strategy: Toward a Radical Democratic Politics* (New York: Verso, 1985); and Jeffrey Isaac, *Power and Marxist Theory: A Realist View* (Ithaca, NY: Cornell University Press, 1987), chap. 6. The question for these authors has to be whether there is anything distinctively Marxist about their politics once the classical Marxian telos is abandoned.

[53] J. G. A. Pocock, *Virtue, Commerce and History: Essays on Political Thought and History, Chiefly in the Eighteenth Century* (Cambridge, UK: Cambridge University Press, 1985), p. 39.

[54] J.G.A. Pocock, "Virtues, Rights, and Manners: A Model for Historians of Political Thought," *Political Theory*, Vol. 9, No. 3 (August 1981), p. 357.

"nature," "essence," or "virtue" to do so. But [*sic*] nature may be developed, but cannot be distributed; you cannot distribute a *telos*, only the means to it; virtue cannot therefore be reduced to matter of right."[55]

The laws of the republic, then "the *lois* obeyed by Montesquieu's *vertu politique*—were therefore far less *regulae juris* or modes of conflict resolution than they were *ordini* or 'orders'; they were the formal structure within which political nature developed to its inherent end."[56]

As Pocock is forced to concede, there have always been ideas of distribution and legitimacy inherent in the republican tradition. "If the citizens were to practice a common good, they must distribute its components among themselves, and must even distribute the various modes of participating in its distribution." Indeed, Aristotelian, Polybian, and Ciceronian analysis within the republican tradition had shown "that these modes were highly various and capable of being combined in a diversity of complex patterns; political science in the sense of the science of *politeia* took this as its subject matter." Yet Pocock continues to maintain that since the virtues which it was the business of these different distributions of means to realize could not be reduced to those means, "the republican or political conception of virtue exceeded the limits of jurisprudence and therefore of justice as a jurist conceived it."[57] Even this formulation should suggest to Pocock that his dichotomous classification is misleading. It is only because he operates with the implausible assumption that the liberal view reduces politics to an account of law and right that he can entertain the notion of an alternative and "discontinuous" republican vocabulary that reduces it to an account of the social good.

From our relational standpoint it cannot be surprising that the whole historiographic debate spawned by Pocock's casting of republicanism as an alternative paradigm (even if he equivocates about the periods in which it is said to have been distinct)[58] has created more fog than illumination. On the one hand, numerous commentators have been quick to point out that liberalism has always rested on conceptions of virtue.[59] On the other, it has been noted that writers like Harrington,

---

[55] *Ibid.*, pp. 358, 359.

[56] *Ibid.*, p. 359.

[57] *Ibid.*, p. 358.

[58] For a recent statement, see *Ibid.*, pp. 353–68.

[59] See, for instance, William A. Galston, "Defending Liberalism," *American Political Science Review*, Vol. 76, No. 3 (September 1982), pp. 621–29; Rogers M. Smith, *Liberalism and American Constitutional Law* (Cambridge, MA: Harvard University Press, 1985), pp. 13–59; and James T. Kloppenberg, "The Virtues of Liberalism: Christianity, Republicanism, and Ethics in Early American Political Discourse," *Journal of American History*, Vol. 74, No. 1 (June 1987), pp. 9–33.

whom Pocock deemed paradigmatically republican, employed much of the liberal vocabulary of law and value.[60] And as with all historiographical fads, the endless contortions engaged in to save the thesis dilute its explanatory power. An increasingly diverse collection of theorists is deemed somehow to have been republican, including writers such as Adam Smith who explicitly rejected standard republican arguments.[61] Even Locke now teeters on the verge of incorporation into the new civic humanist rewriting of early modern political thought.[62] How ironic in light of Pocock's original motivation, his dissatisfaction with the tendency of Marxists and Straussians alike to give too much attention to Lockean liberalism, and to discover everywhere they looked after about the time of Machiavelli either the rise of bourgeois modes of thought or the decline of Western civilization.[63] My point is not that a more scrupulous depiction of the paradigm would resolve these difficulties, but rather that just as liberalism has always taken conceptions of the good and of virtue for granted, so republican writers have been concerned with law and legitimacy, however implicitly, because any plausible theory of politics has to be concerned with both.[64] Although Pocock has acknowledged this critique, he has never dealt with it.[65]

[60] On Harrington, see Jeffrey Isaac, "Republicanism vs. Liberalism: A Reinterpretation," *History of Political Thought*, Vol. 9, No. 2 (Summer 1988), pp. 349–77; and Shelley Burtt, "Private Interest, Public Passion and Patriot Virtue: Comments on a Classical Republican Ideal in English Political Thought," paper delivered at Folger Institute of Renaissance and Eighteenth Century Studies (October 23–24, 1986). For a critical assessment of republicanism as an alternative paradigm in America, see J. David Greenstone, "Political Culture and American Political Development: Liberty, Union and the Liberal Bipolarity," in Karen Orren and Stephen Skowronek, eds., *Studies in American Political Development*, Vol. 1 (New Haven: Yale University Press), pp. 1–49.

[61] See Donald Winch, *Adam Smith's Politics: An Essay in Historiographic Revision* (Cambridge, UK: Cambridge University Press, 1980). For a good critique, see Edward J. Harpham, "Liberalism, Civic Humanism and the Case of Adam Smith," *American Political Science Review*, Vol. 78, No. 3 (September 1984), pp. 764–74.

[62] Although Ruth Grant does not call Locke a civic humanist, she argues that his doctrine "is perfectly compatible with community in many forms and with strong communal institutions." Ruth Grant, "Locke's Political Anthropology and Lockean Individualism," *Journal of Politics*, Vol. 50, No. 1 (February 1988), pp. 42–63.

[63] For an illustration of his ringing denunciation of "the paradigm of liberalism," see Pocock, *Virtue, Commerce and History*, pp. 59–62.

[64] Riesenberg criticized an earlier version of the civic humanist "alternative paradigm" view as formulated by Hans Baron (1966), by arguing that citizenship in the Italian republics was mainly defined in jurisprudential terms, not those arising from the humanist vocabulary of vita active and vivere civile. Hans Baron, *The Crisis of the Early Italian Renaissance*, 2nd ed. (Princeton: Princeton University Press, 1966); Peter N. Riesenberg, "Civism and Roman Law in Fourteenth-century Italian Society," *Explorations in Economic History*, Vol. 7, No. 1–2 (Fall/Winter 1969), pp. 237–54.

[65] J. G. A. Pocock, *The Machiavellian Moment: Florentine Political Thought and the Atlantic Republican Tradition* (Princeton: Princeton University Press, 1975), p. 83; Pocock, "Virtues, Rights and Manners," p. 355. Note also that historians such as Gordon Wood and Bernard Bailyn, who first pointed to the importance of republican ideals with European roots in shaping American revolu-

Some writers have understood themselves as embracing a civic humanist ideal as an alternative to some other, but we make a great error simply to take them at their word. The very facts that civic humanist writers employ so many different and conflicting concepts of virtue,[66] that the idea of liberty plays so central a role in both alleged "paradigms," and that the American republican revolutionaries were obsessed with questions of law and legitimacy should make us suspicious. There is no exclusive political "language of the virtues" (or of "law"). All views of politics embody conceptions of virtue and of legality, and can be reduced to neither. The interesting questions are about which, and this is obscured by the mindless opposition of gross concepts. No doubt an argument can be made by Pocock and other "new historians" that their interest, in keeping with their hermeneutic procedures,[67] is simply to recover the terms of debate as protagonists understood them.[68] But my analysis reveals real limits to their methods: If a set of assumptions about purposes, or about legitimacy, is implicit in an argument—perhaps not even evident to its author—this may be one of the more interesting things about it, and exclusive preoccupation with authorial intention will miss it. If political argument often does proceed via the surface opposition of gross concepts, law *versus* virtue, negative *versus* positive, right *versus* good, but these oppositions systematically misdescribe, then that is something to be explained. Whether or not the new historians can give a description of their enterprise that makes these issues exogenous, contemporary communitarians such as MacIntyre and Sandel, who invoke the revival of interest in republicanism as the normative basis for an allegedly alternate theory of politics, cannot legitimately avoid them.

---

tionary ideology and subsequent politics, never suggested for a minute that this was an alternative "paradigm" to liberalism. On the contrary, both books are testimonies to their coexistence, and even their mutual reinforcement. See Bernard Bailyn, *The Ideological Origins of the American Revolution* (Cambridge, MA: Harvard University Press, 1967), pp. vii–viii, and Gordon S. Wood, *The Creation of the American Republic* (New York: W. W. Norton, 1969), pp. 73, 91–96, 100, 137ff. These writers were engaged in the different enterprise of rejecting Progressive explanations of the causes of the American revolution. See Gordon S. Wood, "Rhetoric & Reality in the American Revolution," *William and Mary Quarterly,* Third Series, Vol. 23, No. 1 (January 1966), pp. 3–32.

[66] Three of which have usefully been separated by Burtt, "Private Interest, Public Passion."

[67] For analysis of these, see my "Realism in the Study of the History of Ideas," *History of Political Thought,* Vol. 3, No. 3. (November 1982), pp. 535–78.

[68] For instance, Tuck makes excellent use of the distinction of "active" from "passive" rights as an exegetical tool in his analysis of medieval natural rights theories. How much more illuminating it might have been had he recognized this as an early version of the negative/positive liberty dichotomy, and gone on to ask questions about the internal coherence of these theories. Richard

What Sandel understands to be the limits of justice are really the limits to the politicization of communities. By declaring a community to be beyond politics, part of the private sphere, we are rendering it immune from political criticism. So when Nozick suggests, for instance, that sexual leering may "use" women in ways that violate the categorical imperative, but insists that this is not a political form of using, he assumes a relatively narrow definition of politics.[69] Yet the accepted boundaries to politics are constantly shifting as the result of political struggles. When the law changes from denying the possibility of marital rape by conclusive presumption to creating such a crime by statute, an important movement of this kind has occurred. The public / private dichotomy in this and other prevalent formulations misses such poignant complexities.[70] Those who invoke the idea of justice in traditionally private communities such as the family are generally those on the short end of power or distributive relationships in them. The general rule (to which there are doubtless exceptions) is that the dominated try to politicize to delegitimize while the dominators try to depoliticize to legitimize. It is little more than romantic assertion to suppose that the relations of scarcity, power, and domination that render battles over politicization unavoidable either do not exist in the private sphere of the present or would not exist if we could return to some idyllic public sphere—or create some such sphere in the future. This is not to imply, with Foucault, that just because all social structures, historical, actual, and possible, involve relations of power, domination, and scarcity, that they are all alike. It may be that some are to be preferred to others on various grounds; I hold that arguments about those grounds should be among our central concerns. But such arguments cannot even be engaged in, there is no linguistic space for them, so long as the terms of debate are allowed to be a variant of "whether-or-not-community." We need to know how different communities affect different agents in the pursuit of different goods differently, and a second-order commitment to "community" can no more tell us this than can a second-order commitment to "autonomy."

Tuck, *Natural Rights Theories: Their Origin and Development* (Cambridge, UK: Cambridge University Press, 1979), pp. 5ff.

[69] Nozick, *Anarchy, State and Utopia*, p. 32.

[70] On the changing law of marital rape, see "To Have and to Hold: The Marital Rape Exemption and the Fourteenth Amendment." Note, *Harvard Law Review*, Vol. 99, No. 6 (April 1986), pp. 1255–73. Problems relating to changing conceptions of political reality are usefully taken up in

POSSIBLE EXPLANATIONS

Why are political theorists so often blind to the relational structure of the core concepts of politics, so that even those who doff a genuflecting cap to it typically ignore it in their substantive analyses? Two elements of a plausible—though incomplete—answer have to do with the division of labor and structure of incentives in the academy, and with the nature of our expectations from politics and political theory.

Acknowledging the relational character of politics brings with it a theoretical holism that threatens our jobs in the intellectual division of labor, for it implies a need for substantive interdisciplinary knowledge. If a comprehensive theory of rights, for instance, requires an account of what there are rights *to*, this in turn requires an account of how those things are created and distributed—a political economy. If a theory of freedom is partly a theory of enabling and restraining conditions, many, if not most, of the most pressing and politically charged questions will be empirical ones about their operation. Likewise with virtue, if theorists could agree on its meaning, they would then need to devote serious attention to causal arguments over which institutions foster which virtues at what cost and to whom—which requires knowledge of the dynamics of institutions. This is most obviously true with writers such as MacIntyre, who invoke notions of virtue that, if they have ever been successfully embodied in political institutions (which I dispute), they were institutions so different from ours in scale and organization that there is little reason to suppose them viable, even in principle, today. Faced with this claim, a communitarian might dispute it, but my point is that we are not even having that argument. With the defenders of "the" virtues, so with those of "the" higher or natural law reading of the Constitution. The fact that their opponents reject their terms of discussion by invoking an alternative gross concept enables them to get away with supposing that employing the language of the virtues, or of natural law, will actually resolve problems. It will not. There are theories of natural law and of virtue to be invoked in behalf of every substantive political position. We should be arguing about the feasibility and desirability of those positions.

This is not a Humean claim that if all factual questions were resolved no moral questions would remain. The empirical questions that drive

William E. Connolly, *Appearance and Reality in Politics* (Cambridge, UK: Cambridge University Press, 1981), pp. 63–89.

much normative political argument—whether market-based appropriation *does* work to the benefit of all, whether deficit spending causes or cures recessions—are so loaded ideologically that we must doubt that they will ever be definitively resolved.[71] Rather, I want to deny that moral questions can be bracketed from empirical ones. The terms in the relations over which political claims range are parts of the meanings of those claims while being partly empirical. My account, then, is incompatible with a view of political theory either as the queen of the disciplines or as an isolated subdiscipline within political science or philosophy. Political theory is best thought of as principled social criticism.[72] Necessarily prescriptive in that it engages willy-nilly with theoretical explanations of our circumstances and the possibility and desirability of altering them, it is also irreducibly descriptive because it is *about* a concrete set of particulars—the changing relations of scarcity, power, and finitude that set the terms of human social interaction. It is not that the purely conceptual components can never be extracted for analytical discussion, but that discussion of them will never get anywhere, because it is discussion of parts of complex concepts as if they were whole simple ones.

When political theorists argue by reference to gross concepts, they engage in a double reduction. First, they reduce complex relational ideas to one or another of the terms in the relation over which they range, dealing with the other terms implicitly while seeming not to deal with them at all. Second, they reduce what are often substantive disagreements about one or another of the terms in a relational argument to disagreements that are alleged to be about the meanings of the terms themselves—making a self-fulfilling prophecy out of the "essential contestability" thesis.[73] My claim is not that there are no essentially contestable concepts (almost certainly there are some), only that there is no reason to assume that all the normative concepts of politics are

---

[71] There are also philosophical reasons, having to do with counterfactuals and multiple descriptions, which reinforce the idea that definitive resolution of such questions is not on the cards. See Shapiro, *Evolution of Rights*, pp. 291–95.

[72] This is not to be confused with Walzer's idea of "connected criticism," depending centrally on the emotional bonds between critic and those criticized. Michael Walzer, "Commitment and Social Criticism: Camus's Algerian War," *Dissent*, Vol. 31, No. 4 (Fall 1984), pp. 424–32. See also Walzer, *Interpretation and Social Criticism* (Cambridge, MA: Harvard University Press, 1987), pp. 35–66. For reasons on which I elaborate elsewhere, Walzer's view confronts serious difficulties. See *Political Criticism* (Berkeley and Los Angeles: University of California Press, 1990), chap. 3.

[73] This is the term popularized by W. Bernard Gallie, "Essentially Contested Concepts," *Proceedings of the Aristotelian Society* (1956), Vol. 56, pp. 167–98.

in fact contested when protagonists seem to disagree. Defenders of the essential contestability thesis leap much too rapidly from surface disagreements to their conclusion. A paradigm case of this, we saw, is the negative / positive liberty debate. If an argument over which laws empower agents to act in certain ways most effectively is presented as a disagreement over what the protagonists mean by the term "freedom," possibilities that they might argue their disagreement to a conclusion are foreclosed or at least diminished.

The endless oppositions of gross concepts might not be *designed* to serve academic careers, but we may say without overstatement that it is in our collective professional interest that there be the relatively autonomous discourse of political theory which endures mainly by feeding off its own controversies because we depend on it for our livelihood. And the beauty of it is that there is always a level at which the debates are genuine. Just because political theorists set up gross concepts and defend them as the core organizing ideas of politics, they are invariably vulnerable to critical attack and the dissecting intelligence of sharp minds. Worse than this, there are positive rewards. Articulating gross but flawed concepts that fail to explain what they purport to attracts the often less imaginative but perhaps more diligent attention of scholars who criticize, defend, modify, buttress, recast, and thereby canonize the original formulator. Pocock's virtue, Nozick's side-constraints, Sandel's community, Wolff's autonomy, Mill's harm-principle, Bentham's utility (to pick a few), all share this in common: Their originators contributed a phrase that embodies a gross concept and so invites such fuss and attention. So it is never that the communitarian critics of deontological liberalism are not right, or that liberal writers who worry about the potentially tyrannous effects of communitarian alternatives are not right. The defenders of autonomy and of community are right about the defects of one another's arguments. As a result, their debates can go on forever: Law, right, utility, autonomy, teleology, deontology, community.

These debates are reinforced by our expectations from political theory. We have a tremendously powerful need to reduce complexity to simplicity, to come up with elegant explanations that make life intelligible, meaningful and predictable. We want to be able to derive our moral injunctions from a small number of indubitable premises, if not a single one. That is what makes gross concepts attractive. In recent years there has been a tendency pejoratively to identify all such projects as preoccupations with "foundationalism," to see them as forlorn attempts to complete the Cartesian and Kantian projects of placing philosophy on the secure path of a science, modeled on Euclidean geometry. The new contextualists want us to abandon all such projects as hopeless. Since my argument here may appear to put me in this camp, I want in conclusion to indicate why I think that abandoning "foundationalism" is itself a hopeless prescription resting on a misdiagnosis of the problem; indeed, that the opposition between "foundationalism" and "contextualism" is simply one more misleading dichotomy.

We should immediately be suspicious of the claim that "contextualism" is a meaningful alternative to "foundationalism" when we find one of its most lucid defenders arguing that he wants to "clear the ground" to defend the antifoundationalist view.[74] The difficulties with this position are many, but two concern us.[75] First, none of the contextualist writers supplies convincing causal accounts of our felt need for certainty. Rorty and MacIntyre both argue that it is the result of errors made by philosophers in the past and that consequently we can decide to give it up, perhaps after a period of historical reeducation—the philosophical equivalent of therapeutic liberation.[76] Aside from the manifest irony of invoking this extreme voluntarism as a basis for rejecting the Cartesian project, this greatly misleads. The need for certainty is much older than something called the Enlightenment Project, obviously implicated, for example, in all religions. It is a mechanism of psychological denial as the young Sartre argued. It emanates from our terror at the transience of all things, including ourselves. We can no more abandon it than can we cease to be intelligent creatures. Ignoring

[74] Don Herzog, *Without Foundations: Justification in Political Theory* (Ithaca, NY: Cornell University Press, 1985), p. 27.

[75] The sense of *foundationalism* employed here includes the neo-Kantian theorists. Note, however, that some, like Timmons, argue that Rawlsian argument is antifoundationalist because it is ultimately a coherence view of ethical justification based on "wide reflective equilibrium." Mark Timmons, "Foundationalism and the Structure of Ethical Justification," *Ethics*, Vol. 97, No. 3 (April 1987), p. 595. A comparable argument might be developed concerning Bruce Ackerman's reliance on dialogue in *Social Justice in the Liberal State* (New Haven: Yale University Press, 1980). These issues are too intricate to take up here, but I have argued elsewhere that Rawls's argument from reflective equilibrium fails to establish his conclusions, and in fact presupposes them. The argument for the principles must stand or fall on the so-called "Kantian interpretation." Shapiro, *Evolution of Rights*, pp. 234–46. Generally the neo-Kantians are hostile to contextual argument. See Ronald Dworkin, "To Each His Own," *New York Review of Books* (14 April 1983), pp. 4–6, and "Spheres of Justice: An Exchange," *New York Review of Books* (21 July 1983), pp. 43–46.

[76] Richard Rorty, *Philosophy and the Mirror of Nature* (Princeton: Princeton University Press, 1979), pp. 33, 136; MacIntyre, *After Virtue*, p. 36. I have taken up some of these difficulties in *Political Criticism* (Berkeley and Los Angeles: University of California Press, 1990), especially chaps. 2 and 5.

this will blind theorists to why people continue to construct foundational theories, however rickety they turn out to be and whatever they fail to explain.

More important, such theorists run the risk of failing to grasp the ideological power of simplifying architectonic assumptions that speak to the need to deny inexplicable complexity and uncertainty. "Too many notes!" as a devastated young Mozart discovered to his cost in *Amadeus*, can be sufficient to ensure the disdain of those who wield public power. Or consider the political mileage Ronald Reagan was able to extract, in 1980, from the claim that the Democrats were wrong to tell us about the complexities of our problems and the limits to our legitimacy; that there *are* simple solutions, that the republic *is* on a solid foundation. A political theorist who underestimates the sociological and psychological cravings to which such ideologies speak runs the risk of being bypassed by politics entirely. Thus Lyotard's unsubstantiated assertion that in "postmodern" culture "[t]he grand narrative has lost its credibility, regardless of . . . whether it is a speculative narrative or a narrative of emancipation."[77] But what is the crusading conservatism of the New Right if not grand narrative? It is just because people have powerful needs for unifying, simplifying, comforting, omni-explanatory foundational concepts, concepts over which flags can fly, that they cling to gross concepts, and the relational structure of their moral and political grammar is so often opaque to them. Grand narratives frequently just *are* gross concepts embodied in political ideologies.

No doubt there is in this the strategic lesson that those who would have influence in the world should articulate and defend gross concepts, even if they know these to be flawed. That is a choice that a theorist can make, but it seems to me to involve substantial abdication. There is no ultimate proof of this; I would only ask he who seriously disputes it if he would sooner be Salieri than Mozart. If political theory is to advance it cannot do so by replicating public ideological exchange in the perhaps more subtle and rarefied discourse of the academy, finding intellectually respectable ways of telling people what they want to hear. Whether it *can* advance in fact is another matter. But at a minimum this requires resistance to the opposition of misleading alternatives to one another in ways that perpetuate the process of that opposition,

[77] Jean-François Lyotard, *The Postmodern Condition: A Report on Knowledge*, Geoff Bennington and Brian Massumi, trans. (Minneapolis: University of Minnesota Press, 1984), p. 37.

ensuring that debates about substantive questions are never straightforwardly presented—let alone resolved. It may be naive to think that such resistance can be influential, but I see no reason to rule out this possibility a priori.

At bottom there is, anyhow, no alternative to this aspiration, since what makes principled social criticism principled is a basic commitment to the pursuit of accuracy and authentic understanding.[78] Unprincipled criticism is mere rhetoric, and if a theorist's goals are fundamentally rhetorical, they will be neither interesting nor particularly well served by being pursued within the language and constraints of an academic discipline.

As a theoretical matter the contextualists commit the fallacy of identifying one type of bad foundationalist argument with all attempts to provide the foundations needed for our beliefs. Since we cannot find a secure basis for all knowledge in deductive introspection, so the argument goes, we should abandon the enterprise. This makes no more sense than saying that just because there is no single type of foundation on which all buildings, whatever their size, function, and location, can be built such that they will last forever, we should henceforth build all houses without any foundations at all. Then they would fall over. In the fullness of time perhaps all our cultural artifacts and social structures will disappear as will we, but this cannot concern us much. We must live in the here and now, building our no doubt corrigible foundations as best we can with the materials ready to hand. That these foundations will be incomplete and largely empirical seems obvious to me, and I would argue that writers such as Hume (whom the new contextualists now claim for their own) were concerned with contingent naturalist foundations in just this sense. But that is a subject for a different essay.

---

[78] Anyone who finds this unacceptably whiggish might ponder Foucault's claim that "[t]he intellectual no longer has to play the role of an advisor. The project, tactics and goals to be adopted are a matter for those who do the fighting. What the intellectual can do is provide the instruments of analysis." Michel Foucault, *Power/Knowledge: Selected Interviews and Other Writings 1972–1977* (New York: Pantheon, 1980), p. 62.

CHAPTER FIVE

Problems, Methods, and Theories in the Study of Politics: Or, What's Wrong With Political Science and What to Do about It

OUR MANDATE is to engage in navel-gazing about the condition of political theory.[1] I confess that I find myself uncomfortable with this charge because I think political theorists have become altogether too narcissistic over the past half-century. Increasingly, they have come to see themselves as engaged in a specialized activity distinct from the rest of political science—either a bounded subdiscipline within it or an alternative to it. Political theorists are scarcely unusual in this regard; advancing specialization has been a hallmark of most academic disciplines in recent decades. When warranted, it facilitates the accumulation of knowledge in ways that would not otherwise occur. In many physical, biomedical, and informational sciences, the benefits are visible in expanding bodies of knowledge that were scarcely conceivable a generation ago. Specialization also has proceeded apace in the human sciences, seen in the proliferation of dedicated journals, professional organizations and sub-organizations, and esoteric discourses notable for their high entry costs to the uninitiated. Here tangible advances in knowledge are less easily identified, however. In political science, even when the new subfields fly interdisciplinary banners (as with the new political economy in much American and comparative politics, the turn to social theory in international relations, or to approaches from moral philosophy in theorizing about justice), those who have not paid the entry costs would be hard-pressed to understand—let alone evaluate—the alleged contributions of the new specialized fields.

---

[1] Originally written for the thirtieth anniversary issue of *Political Theory* in which all contributors were asked to address the question: "What Is Political Theory?" Vol. 30, No. 4 (August 2002), pp. 596–619.

The specialization that has divided political philosophy from the rest of political science has been aided and abetted by the separation of normative from empirical political theory, with political philosophers declaring a monopoly over the former while abandoning the enterprise of "positive" political theory to other political scientists. This seems to me to have been bad for both ventures. It has produced normative theory that is no longer informed, in the ways that the great theorists of the tradition took it for granted that political theory should be informed, by the state of empirical knowledge of politics. A result is that normative theorists spend too much time commenting on one another, as if they were themselves the appropriate objects of study. This separation has also fed the tendency for empirical political theory to become banal and method driven—detached from the great questions of the day and focused instead on what seems methodologically most tractable. Both types of theory have evolved close to the point where they are of scant interest to anyone other than their practitioners. This might bump up citation indexes and bamboozle tenure committees, but it scarcely does much for the advancement of knowledge about what is or ought to be the case in politics.

My discomfort extends to commenting at length on this state of affairs, which replicates the disorder under discussion even more than Descartes's *cogito* established his existence. Rather, my plan here is to illustrate what I take to be one of the central challenges for political theorists: serving as roving ombudsmen for the truth and the right by stepping back from political science as practiced, to see what is wrong with what is currently being done and say something about how it might be improved. Holding the discipline's feet to the fire might be an appropriate slogan. Let me hasten to add that I have no interest in declaring this is the only important task for political theorists or indeed that it is the most important task; only that it is *an* indispensable task. If political theorists do not do it, then it seems to me to be unlikely that it will be done at all.

Donald Green and I have previously criticized contemporary political science for being too method-driven, not sufficiently problem-driven.[2] In various ways, many have responded that our critique fails to take full account of how inevitably theory-laden empirical research is. Here I agree with many of these basic claims, but I argue that they

---

[2] See Donald Green and Ian Shapiro, *Pathologies of Rational Choice Theory: A Critique of Applications in Political Science* (New Haven: Yale University Press, 1994) and chapter 2 in this volume.

do not weaken the contention that empirical research and explanatory theories should be problem-driven. Rather, they suggest that one central task for political theorists should be to identify, criticize, and suggest plausible alternatives to the theoretical assumptions, interpretations of political conditions, and above all the specifications of problems that underlie prevailing empirical accounts and research programs—and to do it in ways that can spark novel and promising problem-driven research agendas.

My procedure will be to develop and extend our arguments for problem-driven over method-driven approaches to the study of politics. Green and I made the case for starting with a problem in the world, next coming to grips with previous attempts that have been made to study it, and then defining the research task by reference to the value added. We argued that method-driven research leads to self-serving construction of problems, misuse of data in various ways, and related pathologies summed up in the old adage that if the only tool you have is a hammer everything around you starts to look like a nail. Examples include collective action problems such as free riding that appear mysteriously to have been "solved" when perhaps it never occurred to anyone to free ride to begin with in many circumstances, or the concoction of elaborate explanations for why people "irrationally" vote, when perhaps it never occurred to most of them to think by reference to the individual costs and benefits of the voting act. The nub of our argument was that more attention to the problem and less to vindicating some pet approach would be less likely to send people on esoteric goose chases that contribute little to the advancement of knowledge.

What we dubbed "method-driven" work in fact conflated theory-driven and method-driven work. These can be quite different things, though in the literature they often morph into one another—as when rational choice is said to be an "approach" rather than a theory. From the point of view elaborated here, the critical fact is that neither is problem-driven, where this is understood to require specification of the problem under study in ways that are not mere artifacts of the theories and methods that are deployed to study it. Theory-drivenness and method-drivenness undermine problem-driven scholarship in different ways that are attended to below, necessitating different responses. This is not to say that problem-selection is, or should be, uninfluenced by theories and methods, but I will contend that there are more ways than one of bringing theory to bear on the selection of problems, and that some are better than others.

Some resisted our earlier argument on the grounds that refinement of theoretical models and methodological tools is a good gamble in the advancement of science as part of a division of labor. It is sometimes noted, for instance, that when John Nash came up with his equilibrium concept (an equilibrium from which no one has an incentive to defect) he could not think of an application, yet it has since become widely used in political science.[3] We registered skepticism at this approach in our book, partly because the ratio of success to failure is so low, and partly because our instinct is that better models are likely to be developed in applied contexts, in closer proximity to the data. I do not want to rehearse those arguments here. Rather, my goal is to take up some weaknesses in our previous discussion of the contrast between problem-drivenness and method- and theory-drivenness, and explore their implications for the study of politics.

Our original formulation was open to two related objections: that the distinction we were attempting to draw is a distinction without a difference, and that there is no theory-independent way of characterizing problems. These are important objections, necessitating more elaborate responses than Green and I offered. My response to them leads to a discussion of the fact that there are always multiple true descriptions of any given piece of social reality, where I argue against the reductionist impulse always to select one type of description as apt. This leaves us with the difficulty of selecting among potential competing descriptions of what is to be accounted for in politics, taken up in the second half of the chapter. There I explore the notion that the capacity to generate successful predictions is the appropriate criterion. In some circumstances this is the right answer, but it runs the risk of atrophying into a kind of method-drivenness that traps researchers into forlorn attempts to refine predictive instruments. Moreover, insisting on the capacity to generate predictions as the criterion for problem-selection risks predisposing political scientists to study trivial, if tractable, problems. In light of prediction's limitations, I turn to a discussion of other ways in which the aptness of competing accounts can be assessed. There I argue that political theorists have an important role to play in scrutinizing accepted accounts of political reality: exhibiting their presuppositions, both empirical and normative, and posing alternatives. Just because observation is inescapably theory-laden, this is bound to be an

[3] John F. Nash Jr., "The Bargaining Problem," *Econometrica*, Vol. 18, No. 2 (April 1950), pp. 155–62. For explication, see John Harsanyi, "Advances in Understanding Rational Behavior," in Jon Elster, ed., *Rational Choice* (New York: New York University Press, 1986), pp. 92–94.

ongoing task. Political theorists have a particular responsibility to take it on when accepted depictions of political reality are both faulty and widely influential outside the academy.

A DISTINCTION WITHOUT A DIFFERENCE?

The claim that the distinction between problem- and theory-driven research is a distinction without a difference turns on the observation that even the kind of work that Green and I characterized as theory-driven in fact posits a problem to study. This can be seen by reflecting on some manifestly theory-driven accounts.

Consider, for instance, a paper sent to me for review by the *American Political Science Review* on the probability of successful negotiated transitions to democracy in South Africa and elsewhere. It contended, inter alia, that as the relative size of the dispossessed majority grows the probability of a settlement decreases for the following reason: members of the dispossessed majority, as individual utility maximizers, confront a choice between working and fomenting revolution. Each one realizes that, as their numbers grow, the individual returns from revolution will decline, assuming that the expropriated proceeds of revolution will be equally divided among the expropriators. Accordingly, as their relative numbers grow they will be more likely to devote their energy to work than to fomenting revolution, and, because the wealthy minority realizes this, its members will be less inclined to negotiate a settlement as their numbers diminish since the threat of revolution is receding.

One only has to describe the model for its absurdity to be plain. Even if one thought dwindling minorities are likely to become increasingly recalcitrant, it is hard to imagine anyone coming up with this reasoning as part of the explanation. In any event, the model seems so obtuse with respect to what drives the dispossessed to revolt and fails so completely to take manifestly relevant factors into account (such as the changing likelihood of revolutionary success as the relative numbers change), that it is impossible to take seriously. In all likelihood it is a model that was designed for some other purpose, and this person is trying to adapt it to the study of democratic transitions. One can concede that even such manifestly theory-driven work specifies problems, yet nonetheless insist that the specification is contrived. It is an artifact of the theoretical model in question.

Or consider the neo-Malthusian theory put forward by Charles Murray to the effect that poor women have children in response to the perverse incentives created by Aid to Families with Dependent Children (AFDC) and related benefits.[4] Critics such as Katz pointed out that on this theory it is difficult to account for the steady increase in the numbers of children born into poverty since the early 1970s, when the real value of such benefits has been stagnant or declining.[5] Murray's response (in support of which he cited no evidence) is hard to read with a straight face: "In the late 1970s, social scientists knew that the real value of the welfare benefit was declining, but the young woman in the street probably did not."[6] This is manifestly self-serving for the neo-Malthusian account, even if in a palpably implausible way. Again, the point to stress here is not that no problem is specified; Murray is interested in explaining why poor women have children. But the fact that he holds on to his construction of it as an attempt by poor women to maximize their income from the government even in the face of confounding evidence suggests that he is more interested in vindicating his theory than in understanding the problem.

Notice that this is not an objection to modeling. To see this, compare these examples to John Roemer's account of the relative dearth of redistributive policies advocated by either political party in two-party democracies with substantial ex-ante inequality.[7] He develops a model which shows that if voters' preferences are arrayed along more than one dimension—such as "values" as well as "distributive" dimensions—then the median voter will not necessarily vote for downward redistribution as he would if there were only a single distributive dimension. Roemer's model seems to me worth taking seriously (leaving aside for present purposes how well it might do in systematic empirical testing), because the characterization of the problem that motivates it is not forced as in the earlier examples. Trying to develop the kind of model he proposes in order to account for the dearth of redistributive platforms seems therefore to be worthwhile.[8]

[4] See Charles Murray, *Losing Ground: American Social Policy, 1950–1980* (New York: Basic Books, 1984).

[5] Michael B. Katz, *The Undeserving Poor: From the War on Poverty to the War on Welfare* (New York: Pantheon, 1989), pp. 151–56.

[6] Charles Murray, "Does Welfare Bring More Babies?" *The Public Interest* (Spring 1994), p. 25.

[7] John Roemer, "Does Democracy Engender Justice?" in Ian Shapiro and Casiano Hacker-Cordón, ed., *Democracy's Value* (Cambridge, UK: Cambridge University Press, 1999), pp. 56–68.

[8] It should be noted, however, that the median voter theorem is eminently debatable empirically. For discussion, see Green and Shapiro, *Pathologies*, pp. 146–78.

In light of these examples we can say that the objection that theory-driven research in fact posits problems is telling in a trivial sense only. If the problems posited are idiosyncratic artifacts of the researcher's theoretical priors, then they will seem tendentious, if not downright misleading, to everyone except those who are wedded to her priors. Put differently, if a phenomenon is characterized as it is so as to vindicate a particular theory rather than to illuminate a problem that has been independently specified, then it is unlikely to gain much purchase on what is actually going on. Rather, it will be a strained and unconvincing specification driven by the impulse to save the pet theory. It makes better sense to start with the problem, perhaps asking what the conditions are that make transitions to democracy more or less likely, or what influences the fertility rates of poor women. Next, see what previous attempts to account for the phenomenon have turned up, and only then look to the possibility of whether a different theory will do better. To be sure, one's perception of what problems should be studied might be influenced by prevailing theories, as when the theory of evolution leads generations of researchers to study different forms of speciation. But the theory should not blind the researcher to the independent existence of the phenomenon under study. When that happens appropriate theoretical influence has atrophied into theory-drivenness.

All Observation Is Theory-Laden?

It might be objected that the preceding discussion fails to come to grips with the reality that there is no theory-independent way to specify a problem. This claim is sometimes summed up with the epithet that "all observation is theory-laden." Even when problems are thought to be specified independently of the theories that are deployed to account for them, in fact they always make implicit reference to some theory. From this perspective, the objection would be reformulated as the claim that the contrast between problem-driven and theory-driven research assumes there is some pre-theoretical way of demarcating the problem. But we have known at least since the later Wittgenstein, J. L. Austin, and Thomas Kuhn that there is not. After all, in the example just mentioned, Roemer's specification of problem is an artifact of the median voter theorem and a number of assumptions about voter preferences. The relative dearth of redistributive political platforms is in tension with that specification, and it is this tension that seems to call for an explanation. Such considerations buttress the insistence that there simply is no pre-theoretical account of "the facts" to be given.

A possible response at this juncture would be to grant that all description is theory-laden but retort that some descriptions are more theory-laden than others. Going back to my initial examples of democratic transitions and welfare mothers, we might say that tendentious or contrived theory-laden descriptions fail on their own terms: there is no need to challenge the theory that leads to them to challenge them. Indeed, the only point of referring to the theory at all is to explain how anyone might come to believe them. The failure stems from the fact that, taken on its own terms, the depiction of the problem does not compute. We have no good reason to suppose that revolutionaries will become less militant as their relative numbers increase or that poor woman have increasing numbers of babies in order to get decreasingly valuable welfare checks. Convincing as this might be as response to the examples given, it does not quite come to grips with what is at stake for social research in the claim that all description is theory-laden.

Consider theory-laden descriptions of institutions and practices that are problematic even though they do not fail on their own terms, such as Kathleen Bawn's claim that an ideology is a blueprint around which a group maintains a coalition[9] or Russell Hardin's claim that constitutions exist to solve coordination problems.[10] Here the difficulty is that, although it is arguable that ideologies and constitutions serve the designated purposes, they serve many other purposes as well. Moreover, it is far from clear that any serious investigation of how particular ideologies and constitutions came to be created or are subsequently sustained would reveal that the theorist's stipulated purpose has much to do with either. They are "just so" stories, debatably plausible conjectures about the creation and or operation of these phenomena.[11]

---

[9] Kathleen Bawn, "Constructing 'Us': Ideology, Coalition Politics and False Consciousness," *American Journal of Political Science*, Vol. 43, No. 2 (April 1999), pp. 303–34.

[10] Russell Hardin, *Liberalism, Constitutionalism, and Democracy* (Oxford and New York: Oxford University Press, 2000), pp. 35, 86–88, 106, 114, 144, 285.

[11] I leave aside, for present purposes, how convincing the debatable conjectures are. Consider the great difficulties Republican candidates face in forging winning coalitions in American politics that keep both social and libertarian conservatives on board. If one were to set out to define a blueprint to put together a winning coalition, trying to fashion it out of these conflicting elements scarcely seems like a logical place to start. Likewise with constitutions viewed as coordinating devices, the many veto points in the American constitutional system could just as arguably be said

The difficulty here is not that Bawn's and Hardin's are functional explanations. Difficult as functional explanations are to test empirically, they may sometimes be true. Rather, the worry is that these descriptions might be of the form: Trees exist in order for dogs to pee on. Even when a sufficient account is not manifestly at odds with the facts, there is no reason to suppose that it will ever get us closer to reality unless it is put up against other plausible conjectures in such a way that there can be decisive adjudication among them. Otherwise we have "Well, in that case what are lampposts for?" Ideologies may be blueprints for maintaining coalitions, but they also give meaning and purpose to people's lives, mobilize masses, reduce information costs, contribute to social solidarity, and facilitate the demonization of "out-groups"—to name some common candidates. Constitutions might help solve coordination problems, but they are often charters to protect minority rights, legitimating statements of collective purpose, instruments to distinguish the rules of the game from the conflicts of the day, compromise agreements to end or avoid civil wars, and so on. Nor are these characterizations necessarily competing: ideologies and constitutions might well perform several such functions simultaneously. Selecting any one over others implies a theoretical commitment. This is one thing people may have in mind when asserting that all observation is theory-laden.

One can concede the point without abandoning the problem-driven/ theory-driven distinction, however. The theory-driven scholar commits to a sufficient account of a phenomenon, developing a "just so" story that might seem convincing to partisans of her theoretical priors. Others will see no more reason to believe it than a host of other "just so" stories that might have been developed, vindicating different theoretical priors. By contrast, the problem-driven scholar asks, "Why are constitutions enacted?" or "Why do they survive?" and "Why do ideologies develop?" or "Why do people adhere to them?" She then looks to previous theories that have been put forward to account for these phenomena, tries to see how they are lacking, and whether some alternative

---

to be obstacles to coordination. See George Tsebelis, *Veto Players: How Political Institutions Work* (Princeton: Princeton University Press, 2002). This might not seem problematic if one takes the view, as Hardin does, that the central purpose of the U.S. constitution is to facilitate commerce. On such a view institutional sclerosis might arguably be an advantage, limiting government's capacity to interfere with the economy. The difficulty with going that route is that we then have a theory for all seasons: constitutions lacking multiple veto points facilitate political coordination, while those containing them facilitate coordination in realms that might otherwise be interfered with by politicians. Certainly nothing in Hardin's argument accounts for why some constitutions facilitate more coordination of a particular kind than do others.

might do better. She need not deny that embracing one account rather than another implies different theoretical commitments, and she may even hope that one theoretical outcome will prevail. But she recognizes that she should be more concerned to discover which explanation works best than to vindicate any priors she may happen to have. As with the distinction-without-a-difference objection, then, this version of the theory-ladenness objection turns out on inspection at best to be trivially true.

MULTIPLE TRUE DESCRIPTIONS AND APTNESS

There is a subtler sense in which observation is theory-laden, untouched by the preceding discussion though implicit in it. The claim that all observation is theory-laden scratches the surface of a larger set of issues having to do with the reality that all phenomena admit of multiple true descriptions. Consider possible descriptions of a woman who says "I do" in a conventional marriage ceremony. She could be:

- Expressing authentic love
- Doing (failing to do) what her father has told her to do
- Playing her expected part in a social ritual
- Unconsciously reproducing the patriarchal family
- Landing the richest husband that she can
- Maximizing the chances of reproducing her genes

Each description is theory-laden in the sense that it leads to the search for a different type of explanation. This can be seen if in each case we ask the question *why?*, and see what type of explanation is called forth.

- Why does she love him? predisposes us to look for an explanation in terms of her personal biography
- *Why does she obey (disobey) her father?* predisposes us to look for a psychological explanation
- *Why does she play her part in the social ritual?* predisposes us to look for an anthropological explanation
- *Why does she unconsciously reproduce patriarchy?* predisposes us to look for an explanation in terms of ideology and power-relations
- *Why does she do as well as she can in the marriage market?* predisposes us to look for an interest-based rational choice explanation
- *Why does she maximize the odds of reproducing her genes?* predisposes us to look for a sociobiological explanation

The claim that all description is theory-laden illustrated here is a claim that there is no "raw" description of "the facts" or "the data." There are always multiple possible true descriptions of a given action or phenomenon, and the challenge is to decide which is most apt.

From this perspective theory-driven work is part of a reductionist program. It dictates always opting for the description that calls for the explanation that flows from the preferred model or theory. So the narrative historian who believes every event to be unique will reach for personal biography; the psychological reductionist will turn to the psychological determinants of her choice; the anthropologist will see the constitutive role of the social ritual as the relevant description; the feminist will focus on the action as reproducing patriarchy; the rational choice theorist will reach for the explanation in terms of maximizing success in the marriage market; and for the socio-biologist it will be evolutionary selection at the level of gene reproduction.

Why do this? Why plump for any reductionist program that is invariably going to load the dice in favor of one type of description? I hesitate to say "level" here, since that prejudges the question I want to highlight: whether some descriptions are invariably more basic that others. Perhaps one is, but to presume this to be the case is to make the theory-driven move. Why do it?

The common answer rests, I think, on the belief that it is necessary for the program of social science. In many minds this enterprise is concerned with the search for general explanations. How is one going to come up with general explanations if one cannot characterize the classes of phenomena one studies in similar terms? This worry misunderstands the enterprise of science, provoking three responses, one skeptical, one ontological, and one occupational.

The skeptical response is that whether there are general explanations for groups of phenomena is a question for social-scientific inquiry, not one to be prejudged before conducting that inquiry. At stake here is a variant of the debate between deductivists and inductivists. The deductivist starts from the preferred theory or model and then opts for the type of description that will vindicate the general claims implied by the model, whereas the inductivist begins by trying to account for particular phenomena or groups of phenomena, and then sees under what conditions, if any, such accounts might apply more generally. This enterprise, might, often, be theory-influenced for the reasons discussed earlier, but is less likely to be theory-driven than the pure deductivist's one because the inductivist is not determined to arrive at any particular theoretical destination. The inductivist looks for general accounts, but she regards it as an open question whether they are out there waiting to be discovered.

The ontological response is that although science is in the second instance concerned with developing general knowledge claims, it must in the first instance be concerned with developing valid knowledge claims. It seems to be an endemic obsession of political scientists to believe that there must be general explanations of all political phenomena, indeed to subsume them into a single theoretical program. Theory-drivenness kicks in when the pursuit of generality comes at the expense of the pursuit of empirical validity. "Positive" theorists sometimes assert that it is an appropriate division of labor for them to pursue generality while others worry about validity. This leads to the various pathologies Green and I wrote about. One we did not mention that I emphasize here is that it invites tendentious characterizations of the phenomena under study because the selection of one description rather than another is driven by the impulse to vindicate a particular theoretical outlook.

The occupational response is that political scientists are pushed in the direction of theory-driven work as a result of their perceived need to differentiate themselves from others, such as journalists, who also write about political phenomena for a living—but without the job security and prestige of the professoriate. This aspiration to do better than journalists is laudable, but it should be unpacked in a Lakatosian fashion. When tackling a problem we should come to grips with the previous attempts to study it, by journalists as well as scholars in all disciplines who have grappled with it, and then try to come up with an account that explains what was known before—and then some. Too often the aspiration to do better than journalists is cashed out as manufacturing esoteric discourses with high entry costs for outsiders. All the better if they involve inside-the-cranium exercises that never require one to leave one's computer screen.

PREDICTION AS A SORTING CRITERION?

A possible response to what has been said thus far is that prediction should be the arbiter. Perhaps my skepticism is misplaced, and some reductionist program is right. If so, it will lead to correct predictions, whereas those operating with explanations that focus on other types of description will fail. Theory-driven or not, the predictive account should triumph if it is the one that shows that interest-maximization, or gene-preservation, or the oppression of women, or the domination of the father-figure, and so on, is "really going on." On this instrumentalist view we would say, with Friedman: deploy whatever theory-laden description you like, but lay it on the line and see how it does in predicting outcomes. If you can predict from your preferred cut, you win.[12]

This instrumental response is adequate up to a point. Part of what is wrong with many theory-driven enterprises, after all, is that their predictions can never be decisively falsified. From Bentham through Marx, Freud, functionalism, and much modern rational choice theory, too often the difficulty is that the theory is articulated in such a capacious manner that some version of it is consistent with every conceivable outcome. In effect the theory predicts everything, so that it can never be shown to be false. This is why people say that a theory that predicts everything explains nothing. If a theory can never be put to a potentially disconfirming test, there seems little reason to take it seriously.

Theories of everything to one side, venturing down this path raises the difficulty that prediction is a tough test that is seldom met in political science. This difficulty calls to mind the job applicant who said on an interview that he would begin a course on comparative political institutions with a summary of the field's well-tested empirical findings, but then had nothing to say when asked what he would teach for the remaining twelve weeks of the semester. Requiring the capacity to predict is in many cases a matter of requiring more than can be delivered, so that if political science is held to this standard there would have to be a proliferation of exceedingly short courses. Does this reality suggest that we should give up on prediction as our sorting criterion?

Some, such as MacIntyre, have objected to prediction as inherently unattainable in the study of human affairs because of the existence of free will.[13] Such claims are not convincing, however. Whether or not human beings have free will is an empirical question. Even if we do, probabilistic generalizations might still be developed about the conditions under which we are more likely to behave in one way rather than another. To be sure, this assumes that people are likely to behave in similar ways in similar circumstances which may or may not be true, but the possibility of its being true does not depend on denying the existence of free will. To say that someone will probably make choice x

---

[12] Milton Friedman, "The Methodology of Positive Economics," in *Essays in Positive Economics* (Oxford, UK: Oxford University Press, 1953).

[13] Alasdair MacIntyre, *After Virtue* (Notre Dame, IN: University of Notre Dame Press, 1984), pp. 88–108.

in circumstance q does not mean that they cannot choose not-x in that circumstance or, that, if do they choose not-x, it was not nonetheless more likely ex-ante that they would have chosen x. In any event, most successful science does not proceed by making point predictions. It predicts patterns of outcomes. There will always be outliers and error terms. The best theory minimizes them vis-à-vis the going alternatives.

A more general version of this objection is to insist that prediction is unlikely to be possible in politics because of the decisive role played by contingent events in most political outcomes. This, too, seems overstated unless one assumes in advance—with the narrative historian—that social life consists of one damn thing after another. A more epistemologically open approach is to assume that some things are contingent, others not, and try to develop predictive generalizations about the latter. For instance, Courtney Jung and I have developed an account of the conditions that make negotiated settlements to civil wars possible. It depends on such factors as whether government reformers and opposition moderates can combine to marginalize reactionaries and revolutionary militants on their flanks. We have also developed an account of the conditions that are more and less likely to make reformers and moderates conclude that trying to do this is better for them than the going alternatives.[14] Assuming we are right, contingent triggers will nonetheless be critical in whether such agreements are successfully concluded, as can be seen by reflecting on how things might have developed differently in South Africa and the Middle East had F. W. DeKlerk been assassinated in 1992 or Yitzhak Rabin had not been assassinated in 1995. The decisive role of contingent events rules out ex-ante prediction of success, but the theory might correctly predict failure—as when a moderate IRA leader such as Gerry Adams emerged in the mid-1990s but the other necessary pieces were not in place, or when Yasir Arafat was offered a deal by Ehud Barak at a time when he was too weak to outflank Hamas and Islamic Jihad. Successful prediction of failure over a range of such cases would suggest that we have indeed taken the right descriptive cut at the problem.[15]

---

[14] See Courtney Jung and Ian Shapiro, "South Africa's Negotiated Transition: Democracy, Opposition, and the New Constitutional Order," *Politics and Society*, Vol. 23, No. 2 (September 1995), pp. 269–308.

[15] What is necessary in the context of one problem may, of course, be contingent in another. When we postulate that it was necessary that Arafat be strong enough to marginalize the radicals on his flank if he was to make an agreement with Barak in 2000, we do not mean to deny that his relative strength in this regard was dependent on many contingent factors. For further discussion,

There are other types of circumstance in which capacity to predict will support one descriptive cut at a problem over others. For instance, Przeworski et al. have shown that although level of economic development does not predict the installation of democracy, there is a strong relationship between level of per capita income and the survival of democratic regimes. Democracies appear never to die in wealthy countries, whereas poor democracies are fragile, exceedingly so when per capita incomes fall below $2,000 (in 1975 dollars). When per capita incomes fall below this threshold, democracies have a one in ten chance of collapsing within a year. Between per capita incomes of $2,001 and $5,000 this ratio falls to one in sixteen. Above $6,055 annual per capita income, democracies, once established, appear to last indefinitely. Moreover, poor democracies are more likely to survive when governments succeed in generating development and avoiding economic crises.[16] If Przeworski et al. are right, as it seems presently that they are, then level of economic development is more important than institutional arrangements, cultural beliefs, presence or absence of a certain religion, or other variables for predicting democratic stability. For this problem the political economist's cut seems to be the right sorting criterion.[17]

These examples suggest that prediction can sometimes help, but we should nonetheless be wary of making it the criterion for problem selection in political science. For one thing, this can divert us from the study of important political phenomena where knowledge can advance even though prediction turns out not to be possible. For instance, generations of scholars have theorized about the conditions that give rise to democracy (as distinct from the conditions that make it more or less likely to survive once instituted, just discussed). Alexis de Tocqueville alleged it to be the product of egalitarian mores.[18] For Seymour Martin

---

see Courtney Jung, Ellen Lust-Okar, and Ian Shapiro, "Problems and Prospects for Democratic Transitions: South Africa as a Model for the Middle East and Northern Ireland?" *Politics and Society*, Vol. 33, no. 2 (July 2005). In some ultimate—if uninteresting—sense, everything social scientists study is contingent on factors such as that the possibility of life on earth not be destroyed because of a collision with a giant meteor. To be intelligible, the search for lawlike generalizations must be couched in "if . . . then" statements that make reference, however implicitly, to the problem under study.

[16] Adam Przeworski, Michael Alvarez, José Cheibub, and Fernando Limongi, *Democracy and Development: Political Institutions and Well-Being in the World, 1950–1990* (Cambridge, UK: Cambridge University Press, 2000), pp. 106–17.

[17] For Przeworski et al.'s discussion of other explanatory variables, see *ibid.*, pp. 122–37.

[18] Alexis de Tocqueville, *Democracy in America*, J. P. Mayer, ed., and George Lawrence, trans. (New York: Harper Perennial, 1966 [1832]).

Lipset, it was a byproduct of modernization.[19] Barrington Moore identified the emergence of a bourgeoisie as critical, whereas Rueschemeyer, Stephens, and Stephens held the presence of an organized working class to be decisive.[20] We now know that there is no single path to democracy and, therefore, no generalization to be had about which conditions give rise to democratic transitions. Democracy can result from decades of gradual evolution (Britain and the United States), imitation (India), cascades (much of Eastern Europe in 1989), collapses (Russia after 1991), imposition from above (Spain and Brazil), revolutions (Portugal and Argentina), negotiated settlements (Bolivia, Nicaragua and South Africa), or external imposition (Japan and West Germany).[21]

In retrospect this is not surprising. Once someone invents a toaster, there is no good reason to suppose that others must go through the same invention processes. Perhaps some will, but some may copy it, some may buy it, some may receive it as a gift, and so on. Perhaps there is no cut at this problem that yields a serviceable generalization, and, as a result, no possibility of successful prediction. Political scientists tend to think they must have general theories of everything as we have seen, but looking for a general theory of what gives rise to democracy may be like looking for a general theory of holes.[22] Yet we would surely be making an error if our inability to predict in this area inclined us not to study it. It would prevent our discovering a great deal about democracy that is important to know, not least that there is no general theory of what gives rise to it to be had. Such knowledge would also be important for evaluating claims by defenders of authoritarianism who contend that democracy cannot be instituted in their countries because they have not gone through the requisite path-dependent evolution.

[19] Seymour Martin Lipset, "Some Social Requisites of Democracy: Economic Development and Political Legitimacy," *American Political Science Review*, Vol. 53, No. 1 (March 1959), pp. 69–105.

[20] Barrington Moore, *The Social Origins of Dictatorship and Democracy: Lord and Peasant in the Making of the Modern World* (Boston: Beacon Press, 1966), pp. 413–32; and Dietrich Rueschemeyer, Evelyne Huber Stephens, and John D. Stephens, *Capitalist Development and Democracy* (Oxford, UK: Polity Press, 1992).

[21] See Adam Przeworski, *Democracy and the Market* (Cambridge, UK: Cambridge University Press, 1991), pp. ix–xii, 1–9, 51–99; Przeworski et al., *Democracy and Development*, pp. 78–106; Samuel P. Huntington, *The Third Wave: Democratization in the Late Twentieth Century* (Norman: University of Oklahoma Press, 1991), pp. 3–18; and Ian Shapiro, *Democracy's Place* (Ithaca, NY: Cornell University Press, 1996), pp. 79–108.

[22] Perhaps one could develop such a theory, but only of an exceedingly general kind such as: "holes are created when something takes material content out of something else." This would not be of much help in understanding or predicting anything worth knowing about holes.

Reflecting on this example raises the possibility I want to consider next: that making a fetish of prediction can undermine problem-driven research via wag-the-dog scenarios in which we elect to study phenomena because they seem to admit the possibility of prediction rather than because we have independent reasons for thinking it worthwhile to study them. This is what I mean by method-drivenness, as distinct from theory-drivenness. It gains impetus from a number of sources, perhaps the most important being the lack of uncontroversial data concerning many political phenomena. Predictions about whether or not constitutional courts protect civil rights run into disagreements over which rights are to count and how to measure their protection. Predictions about the incidence of war run into objections about how to measure and count the relevant conflicts. In principle it sounds right to say let's test the model against the data. In reality there are few uncontroversial datasets in political science.

A related difficulty is that it is usually impossible to disentangle the complex interacting causal processes that operate in the actual world. We will always find political economists on both sides of the question whether cutting taxes leads to increases or decreases in government revenue, and predictive tests will not settle their disagreements. Isolating the effects of tax cuts from the other changing factors that influence government revenues is just too difficult to do in ways that are likely to convince a skeptic. Likewise, political economists have been arguing at least since Bentham's time over whether trickle-down policies benefit the poor more than do government transfers, and it seems unlikely that the key variables will ever be isolated in ways that can settle this question decisively.

An understandable response to this is to suggest that we should tackle questions where good data is readily available. But taking this tack courts the danger of self-defeating method-drivenness, because there is no reason to suppose that the phenomena about which uncontroversial data are available are those about which valid generalizations are possible. My point here is not one about curve-fitting—running regression after regression on the same data-set until one finds the mix of explanatory variables that passes most closely through all the points to be explained. Leaving the well-known difficulties with this kind of data-mining to one side, my worry is that working with uncontroversial data because of the ease of getting it can lead to endless quests for a holy grail that may be nowhere to be found.

The difficulty here is related to my earlier discussion of contingency, to wit, that many phenomena political scientists try to generalize about may exhibit secular changes that will always defy their explanatory theories. For instance, trying to predict election outcomes from various mixes of macro political and economic variables has been a growth industry in political science for more than a generation. But perhaps the factors that caused people to vote as they did in the 1950s differ from those forty or fifty years later. After all, this is not an activity with much of a track record of success in political science. We saw this dramatically in the 2000 election where all of the standard models predicted a decisive Gore victory.[23] Despite endless post-hoc tinkering with the models after elections in which they fare poorly, this is not an enterprise that appears to be advancing. They will never get it right if my conjecture about secular change is correct.

It might be replied that if that is really so, either they will come up with historically nuanced models that do a better job or universities and funding agencies will pull the plug on them. But this ignores an occupational factor that might be dubbed the Morton Thiokol phenomenon. When the *Challenger* blew up in 1986 there was much blame to go around, but it became clear that Morton Thiokol, manufacturer of the faulty O-ring seals, shouldered a huge part of the responsibility. A naïve observer might have thought that this would mean the end of their contract with NASA, but, of course, this was not so. The combination of high entry costs to others, the dependence of the space program on Morton Thiokol, and their access to those who control resources meant that they continued to make O-ring seals for the space shuttle. Likewise with those who work on general models of election-forecasting. Established scholars with an investment in the activity have the protections of tenure and legitimacy, as well as privileged access to those who control research resources. Moreover, high methodological entry costs are likely to self-select new generations of researchers who are predisposed to believe that the grail is waiting out there to be found. Even if their space shuttles will never fly, it is far from clear that they will ever have the incentive to stop building them.

To this it might be objected that it is not as if others are building successful shuttles in this area. Perhaps so, but this observations misses my point here: that the main impetus for the exercise appears to be the

---

[23] See the various postmortem papers in the March 2001 issue of *PS: Political Science and Politics*, Vol. 34, No. 1, pp. 9–58.

ready availability of data which sustains a coterie of scholars who are likely to continue to try to generalize on the basis of it until the end of time. Unless one provides an account, that, like the others on offer, purports to retrodict past elections and predict the next one, one cannot aspire be a player in this game at which everyone is failing. If there is no such account to be found, however, then perhaps some other game should be being played. For instance, we might learn more about why people vote in the ways that they do by asking them. Proceeding instead with the macro models risks becoming a matter of endlessly refining the predictive instrument as an end in itself—even in the face of continual failure and the absence of an argument about why we should expect it to be successful. Discovering where generalization is possible is a taxing empirical task. Perhaps it should proceed on the basis of trial and error, perhaps on the basis of theoretical argument, perhaps some combination. What should *not* drive it, however, is the ready availability of data and technique.

A perhaps more promising response to the difficulties of bad data and of disentangling complex causal process in the "open systems" of the actual world is to undertake experimental work where parameters can be controlled and key variables more easily isolated.[24] There is some history of this in political science and political psychology, but the main problem has been that of external validity. Even when subjects are randomly selected and control groups are included in the experiments (which often is not done), it is far from clear that results produced under lab conditions will replicate themselves outside the lab.

To deal with these difficulties Donald Green and Alan Gerber have revived the practice of field-experiments, where subjects can be randomized, experimental controls can be introduced, and questions about external validity disappear.[25] Prediction can operate once more, and when it is successful there are good reasons for supposing that the researcher has taken the right cut at the problem. It yields decisive answers to questions such as which forms of mobilizing voters are most effective in increasing turnout, or what the best ways are for partisans to get their grassroots supporters to the polls without also mobilizing their opponents.

---

[24] For discussion of the difficulties with prediction in open systems, see Roy Bhaskar, *A Realist Theory of Science* (Sussex: Harvester Wheatsheaf, 1975), pp. 63–142, and *The Possibility of Naturalism* (Sussex: Harvester Wheatsheaf, 1979), pp. 158–69.

[25] Alan Gerber and Donald Green, "Do Phone Calls Increase Voter Turnout? A Field Experiment," *Public Opinion Quarterly*, Vol. 65, No. 1 (Spring 2001), and "Reclaiming the Experimental

Granting that this is an enterprise that leads to increments in knowledge, I want nonetheless to suggest that it carries risks of falling into a kind of method-drivenness that threatens to diminish the field-experiment research program unless they are confronted. The potential difficulties arise from the fact that field experiments are limited to studying comparatively small questions in well-defined settings, where it is possible to intervene in ways that allow for experimental controls. Usually this means designing or piggybacking on interventions in the world such as get-out-the-vote efforts or attempts at partisan mobilization. Green and Gerber have shown that such efforts can be adapted to incorporate field experiments.

To be sure, the relative smallness of questions is to some extent in the eye of the beholder. But consider a list of phenomena that political scientists have sought to study, and those drawn to political science often want to understand, that are not likely to lend themselves to field experiments:

- The effects of regime type on the economy, and vice versa
- The determinants of peace, war, and revolution
- The causes and consequences of the trend toward creating independent central banks
- The causes and consequences of the growth in transnational political and economic institutions
- The relative merits of alternative policies for achieving racial integration, such as mandatory bussing, magnet schools, and voluntary desegregation plans
- The importance of constitutional courts in protecting civil liberties, property rights, and limiting the power of legislatures
- The effects of institutional choices such as parliamentarism versus presidentialism, unicameralism versus bicameralism, federalism versus centralism on such things as the distribution of income and wealth, the effectiveness of macroeconomic policies, and the types of social policies that are enacted
- The dynamics of political negotiations to institute democracy

I could go on, but you get the point.

This is not to denigrate field experiments. One of the worst features of methodological disagreement in political science is the propensity

Tradition in Political Science," in Ira Katznelson and Helen Milner, eds., *Political Science: The State of the Discipline*, 3rd ed. (Washington, DC: American Political Science Association, 2002).

for protagonists to compare the inadequacies of one method with the adequacies of a second, and then declare the first to be wanting.[26] Since all methods have limitations and none should be expected to be service-able for all purposes, this is little more than a shell game. If a method can do some things well that are worth doing, that is a sufficient justifi-cation for investing some research resources in it. With methods, as with people: if you focus only on their limitations you will always be disappointed.

Field experiments lend themselves to the study of behavioral varia-tion in settings where the institutional context is relatively fixed and where the stakes are comparatively low, so that the kinds of interven-tions required do not violate accepted ethical criteria for experimenta-tion on human subjects. They do not obviously lend themselves to the study of life-or-death and other high stakes politics, war and civil war, institutional variation, the macro-political economy or the deter-minants of regime stability and change. This still leaves a great deal to study that is worth studying, and creative use of the method might render it deployable in a wider array of areas than I have noted here. But it must be conceded that it also leaves out a great deal that draws people to political science, so that if susceptibility to study via field experiment becomes the criterion for problem-selection then it risks degenerating into method-drivenness.

This is an important caution. Part of the disaffection with 1960s behaviorism in the study of American politics that spawned the model-mania of the 1990s was that the behaviorists became so mind-lessly preoccupied with demonstrating propositions of the order that "Catholics in Detroit vote Democrat."[27] As a result, the mainstream of political science that they came to define seemed to others to be both utterly devoid of theoretical ambition and detached from conse-quential questions of politics; frankly, boring. To paraphrase Kant, theoretical ambition without empirical research may well be empty, but empirical research without theoretical ambition will be blind.

---

[26] For discussion of an analogous phenomenon that plagues normative debates in political theory, see chapter 4 in this volume.

[27] Charles Taylor, "Neutrality in Political Science," in *Philosophical Papers II: Philosophy and the Human Sciences* (Cambridge, UK: Cambridge University Press, 1985), p. 90.

UNDERVALUING CRITICAL REAPPRAISAL OF
WHAT IS TO BE EXPLAINED

The emphasis on prediction can lead to method-drivenness in another way: it can lead us to undervalue critical reappraisals of accepted descriptions of reality. To see why this is so, one must realize that much commentary on politics, both lay and professional, takes depictions of political reality for granted that closer critical scrutiny would reveal as problematic. Particularly, though not only, when prediction is not going to supply the sorting device to get us the right cut, political theorists have an important role to play in exhibiting what is at stake in taking one cut rather than another, and in proposing alternatives. Consider some examples.

For more than a generation in debates about American exceptionalism, the United States was contrasted with Europe as a world of relative social and legal equality deriving from the lack of a feudal past. This began with de Tocqueville, but it has been endlessly repeated and became conventional wisdom, if not a mantra, when restated by Louis Hartz in *The Liberal Tradition in America*. But as Rogers Smith showed decisively in *Civic Ideals*, it is highly misleading as a descriptive matter.[28] Throughout American history the law has recognized explicit hierarchies based on race and gender whose effects are still very much with us. Smith's book advances no well-specified predictive model, let alone tests one, but it displaces a highly influential orthodoxy that has long been taken for granted in debates about pluralism and cross-cutting cleavages, the absence of socialism in America, arguments about the so-called end of ideology, and the ideological neutrality of the liberal tradition.[29] Important causal questions are to be asked and answered about these matters, but my point here is that what was thought to stand in need of explanation was so mis-specified that the right causal questions were not even on the table.

[28] See Louis Hartz, *The Liberal Tradition in America* (New York: Harcourt Brace, 1955); and Rogers Smith, *Civic Ideals: Changing Conceptions of Citizenship in U.S. Law* (New Haven: Yale University Press, 1995).

[29] Indeed, Smith's argument turns out to be the tip of an iceberg in debunking misleading orthodoxy about American exceptionalism. Eric Foner has shown that its assumptions about Europe are no less questionable than its assumptions about the United States. See Foner, "Why Is There No Socialism in the United States?" *History Workshop Journal*, Vol. 17 (1984), pp. 57–80.

Likewise with the debate about the determinants of industrial policy in capitalist democracies. In the 1970s it occurred to students of this subject to focus less on politicians' voting records and campaign statements and look at who actually writes the legislation. This led to the discovery that significant chunks of it were actually written by organized business and organized labor with government (usually in the form of the relevant minister or ministry) in a mediating role. The reality was more of a "liberal corporatist" one, and less of a pluralist one, than most commentators who had not focused on this had realized.[30] The questions that then motivated the next generation of research became: under what conditions do we get liberal corporatism, and what are its effects on industrial relations and industrial policy? As with the Tocqueville-Hartz orthodoxy, the causal questions had to be reframed because of the ascendancy of a different depiction of the reality.[31]

In one respect, the Tocqueville-Hartz and pluralist accounts debunked by Smith and the liberal corporatists are more like those of democratic transitions and the fertility rates of welfare mothers discussed earlier than the multiple descriptions problem. The difficulty is not how to choose one rather than another true description but, rather, that the Tocqueville-Hartz and pluralist descriptions fail on their own terms. By focusing so myopically on the absence of feudalism and the activities of politicians, their proponents ignored other sources of social hierarchy and decision-making that are undeniably relevant once they have been called to attention. The main difference is that the democratic transition and welfare mother examples are not as widely accepted as the Tocqueville-Hartz and pluralist orthodoxies were before the debunkers came along. This should serve as a salutary reminder that orthodox views can be highly misleading, and that an important ongoing task for political theorists is to subject them to critical scrutiny. Doing this involves exhibiting their presuppositions, assessing their

---

[30] Philippe Schmitter, "Still the Century of Corporatism?" *Review of Politics*, Vol. 36, No. 1 (1974), pp. 85–121; and Leo Panitch, "The Development of Corporatism in Liberal Democracies," *Comparative Political Studies*, Vol. 10, No. 1 (1977), pp. 61–90.

[31] It turns out that joint legislation-writing is a small part of the story. What often matters more is ongoing tri-partite consultation about public policy and mutual adjustment of macroeconomic policy and "private" but quasi-public policy (e.g., wage increases, or multi-employer pension and health plans). There is also the formalized inclusion of private interest representatives in the administration and implementation process where de facto legislation and common-law-like adjudication take place. The extent of their influence in the political process varies from country to country and even industry to industry, but the overall picture is a far cry from the standard pluralist account.

plausibility, and proposing alternatives when they are found wanting. This activity is particularly important when the defective account is widely accepted outside the academy. If political science has a constructive role to play outside the academy, it must surely include debunking myths and misunderstandings that shape political practice.[32]

Notice that descriptions are theory-laden not only in calling for a particular empirical story, but often also in implying a normative theory that may or may not be evident unless this is made explicit. Compare the following two descriptions:

- The Westphalian system is based on the norm of national sovereignty
- The Westphalian system is based on the norm of global apartheid

Both are arguably accurate descriptions, but, depending which of the two we adopt, we will be prompted to ask exceedingly different questions about justification as well as causation. Consider another instance:

- When substantial majorities in both parties support legislation, we have bipartisan agreement
- When substantial majorities in both parties support legislation, we have collusion in restraint of democracy

The first draws on a view of democracy in which deliberation and agreement are assumed to be unproblematic, even desirable goals in a democracy. The second, antitrust-framed, formulation calls to mind Mill's emphasis on the centrality of argument and contestation, and the Schumpeterian impulse to think of well-functioning democracy as requiring competition for power.[33]

Both *global apartheid* and *collusion in restraint of democracy* here are instances of problematizing redescriptions. Just as Smith's depiction of American public law called the Tocqueville-Hartz consensus into question, and the liberal corporatist description of industrial legislation called then conventional assumptions about pluralist decision-making into question, so do these. But they do it not so much by questioning the veracity of the accepted descriptions as by throwing their undernoticed benign normative assumptions into sharp relief. Redescribing the Westphalian system as based on a norm of global Apartheid, or political

---

[32] For a discussion of the dangers of convergent thinking, see Charles E. Lindblom, *Inquiry and Change: The Troubled Attempt to Understand and Shape Society* (New Haven: Yale University Press, 1990), pp. 118–32.

[33] For discussion of differences between these models, see my *The State of Democratic Theory* (Princeton: Princeton University Press, 2003), pp. 59–62, 108–9, 112–49.

agreement among the major players in a democracy as collusion in restraint of democracy, shifts the focus to underattended features of reality, placing different empirical and justificatory questions on the table.

But are they the right questions?

To answer this by saying that one needs a theory of politics would be to turn once more to theory-drivenness. I want to suggest a more complex answer, one that sustains problematizing redescription as a problem-driven enterprise. It is a two-step venture that starts when one shows that the accepted way of characterizing a piece of political reality fails to capture an important feature of what stands in need of explanation or justification. One then offers a recharacterization that speaks to the inadequacies in the prior account.

When convincingly done, prior adherents to the old view will be unable to ignore it and remain plausible. This is vital, because it will, of course, be true that the problematizing redescription is itself usually a theory-influenced, if not a theory-laden endeavor. But if the problematizing redescription assumes a theory that seems convincing only to partisans of her priors, or is validated only by reference to evidence that is projected from her alternative theory, then it will be judged tendentious to the rest of the scholarly community for the reasons I set out at the start of this chapter. It is important, therefore, to devote considerable effort to making the case that will persuade a skeptic of the superiority of the proffered redescription over the accepted one. One of the significant failings of many of the rational choice theories that Green and I discussed is that their proponents failed to do this. They offered problematizing redescriptions that were sometimes arrestingly radical, but their reluctance or inability to take the second step made them unconvincing to all except those who agreed with them in advance. This is in notable contrast to Gaventa's redescription of apparently consensual behavior among his Appalachian mineworkers as quiescence discussed in chapter 1. Much of the credibility of Gaventa's account can be traced to his efforts plausibly to link his redescription to the commonsense understandings of the participants, as well as to previous characterizations of such behavior in the power literature.

Concluding Comments

The recent emphases in political science on modeling for its own sake and on decisive predictive tests both give short shrift to the value of problematizing redescription in the study of politics. It is intrinsically worthwhile to unmask an accepted depiction as inadequate, and to make a convincing case for an alternative as more apt. Just because observation is inescapably theory-laden for the reasons explored in this chapter, political theorists have an ongoing role to play in exhibiting what is at stake in accepted depictions of reality, and reinterpreting what is known so as to put new problems onto the research agenda. This is important for scientific reasons when accepted descriptions are both faulty and influential in the conduct of social science. It is important for political reasons when the faulty understandings shape politics outside the academy.

If the problems thus placed on the agenda are difficult to study by means of theories and methods that are currently in vogue, an additional task arises that is no less important: to keep them there and challenge the ingenuity of scholars who are sufficiently open-minded to devise creative ways of grappling with them. It is important for political theorists to throw their weight against the powerful forces that entice scholars to embroider fashionable theories and massage methods in which they are professionally invested while failing to illuminate the world of politics. They should remind each generation of scholars that unless problems are identified in ways that are both theoretically illuminating and convincingly intelligible to outsiders, nothing that they say about them is likely to persuade anyone who stands in need of persuasion. Perhaps they will enjoy professional success of a sort, but at the price of trivializing their discipline and what one hopes is their vocation.

CHAPTER SIX

The Political Science Discipline:

A Comment on David Laitin

IN "The Political Science Discipline," David Laitin argues that there is an intellectual order to political science, but he laments that it is not reflected in the way in which we teach the discipline to undergraduates.[1] He proposes to remedy this state of affairs by designing an introductory political science course that mirrors standard introductory courses in economics. For reasons that are explained below, I believe that his perception of disciplinary order is illusory and that his prescriptions are pernicious.

Laitin makes a number of valid points and proposes a creditable introductory political science course. We should not favor its becoming *the* introductory course in the discipline any more than we should favor instituting the French system of secondary education in American high schools. Whatever benefits might be derived from the Minister of Education's knowing that the same chapter from the same text is being taught at the same time of day to children from Dieppe to Marseilles come at a considerable cost in terms of diversity and intellectual competition, investment by teachers in what they teach, and other well-known advantages of local knowledge. What holds for secondary education holds more obviously, to my mind, with the teaching of political science to undergraduates. In this field, however much Laitin might wish it were otherwise, there is little agreement about what to study and how to study it—let alone agreement on a body of established

---

[1] David D. Laitin, "The Political Science Discipline," in Edward D. Mansfield and Richard Sisson, ed., *The Evolution of Political Knowledge: Theory and Inquiry in American Politics* (Columbus: Ohio State University Press, 2004), pp. 11–40.

findings that can canned into an introductory course for all. All methods of studying politics have limitations; we should be forthright about this in our teaching as well as in our research.

Laitin's approach is wrongheaded for two sets of reasons. The first have to do with his taking the economics profession as a model for what should be done in political science, and his related aspiration to see done for Political Science what Samuelson did for Economics. This strikes me as resting on an erroneous conception of the role of introductory economics courses in the economics discipline. The second failing of Laitin's approach concerns his menu for the division of the discipline into political theory, political institutions, comparative politics, and international relations. This is a plausible way to organize a course, but it is also challengeable—as is every possible way of doing so—for reasons that can be found in Laitin's essay. I conclude with some additional remarks on why fostering a plurality of introductory courses makes better sense for political science than does Laitin's proposal.

Economics: A Model of What Not to Do

Political scientists are sometimes criticized for breathlessly chasing after ideas that economists are about to abandon. I think there is merit to this critique, but it is not my central point here. Rather, it is that an important difference between the way in which political science and economics are taught to undergraduates is that political scientists generally try to link introductory teaching to the debates at the frontiers of the discipline (as Laitin's model syllabus reflects), whereas economists do not. The introductory economics course seems to me to be a kind of LSAT for aspiring economists: a device to create barriers to entry that will filter out students who do not have mathematical minds and to teach a few elementary ideas about price theory. It has virtually nothing to do with what is going on at the frontiers of the economics discipline.

If one looks through journals such as the *American Economic Review* and the others I receive regularly as a paid-up member of the American Economics Association, perhaps the most striking fact is that the frontiers of economics research, while perhaps not quite as anarchic as the frontiers of political science research, are a lot more similar than political science stereotypes of economists (whether or not envy-based) would lead you to imagine. The merits of rational choice models are argued over at foundational levels, developments in psychology are having a large and unsettling impact on neoclassical orthodoxy, there is renewed interest in the effects of institutions on economic behavior and preference formation, and there has been a resurgence of interest in applied and empirical work under the label "behavioral economics" of the kind that a decade ago was pooh-poohed as the sort of thing you did if you weren't quite up to high theory.[2] Even among theorists, developments in game theory and the study of auctions take it a massive distance from what is done in introductory economics courses.

One symptom of the gap between research frontiers and introductory —and indeed much other—undergraduate teaching in economics is that those doing the cutting-edge research have no interest in doing the undergraduate teaching. They regard it as a waste of their time, and, at least in the elite departments of which I am aware, they hire one-year visitors and adjuncts to do the great bulk of it—often to the chagrin of university administrators, not to mention the undergraduates themselves. Just because the introductory economics course is tedious analytical hoop-jumping that bears scant, if any, relationship to what really interests them, they have no interest in doing it.

My view is that this is not a healthy state of affairs in economics— that a discipline in which there is so vast a disjunction between what goes on at the research frontiers and what is taught to undergraduates is a discipline in trouble. Political Science is so often portrayed as the scruffy wannabe cousin of Economics (this certainly seems to be Laitin's image), but what we do is arguably better. The reason our introductory courses differ so much from one another is that we do try to link them to our own research interests—inevitably reflecting the anarchy at the frontiers of the discipline, where people have competing perceptions of what the basic problems are and how to study them.

---

[2] This is an impressionistic claim, to be sure, based on browsing and conversations with economists. For three anecdotal illustrations of high powered technical economists who are moving away from orthodox economic models of human behavior, see Daniel McFadden's Nobel lecture, "Economic Choices," *American Economic Review*, Vol. 91, No. 3 (June 2001), pp. 351–78, on the empirical validity of rational actor models and alternatives to them; Truman Bewley's *Why Wages Don't Fall During a Recession* (Cambridge, MA: Harvard University Press, 1999), whose analysis of labor markets eschews conventional rational actor models in favor behavioral analysis and field research; and Robert Shiller's reliance on psychological theories of herd behavior, among other theories, to explain buying and selling in U.S. equities markets in his widely acclaimed *Irrational Exuberance* (Princeton: Princeton University Press, 2000), pp. 135–202.

This is evident in many parts of Laitin's model syllabus, but nowhere more dramatically than in his eight challenges to democracy.[3] There Laitin clearly wants to get the students up to speed in a set of current debates about democracy. His challenges concern (i) the difficulties that can arise in translating voters' preferences into government policies without falling prey to the cycles identified by Condorcet in the eighteenth century and formalized in Arrow's theorem in 1951; (ii) the limits to voter choice if parties converge, as Anthony Downs postulated, on the median voter, and the concomitant pointlessness of voting; (iii) the imperfect information available to most voters; (iv) the trade-offs between electoral systems that encourage and discourage strategic voting, and those that encourage and discourage party proliferation; (v) the overrepresentation of intense minorities and the undersupply of public goods if Mancur Olson is correct that small groups face fewer obstacles to collective action than do large ones; (vi) the monitoring problems that can arise between voters and politicians, legislators and the bureaucrats, and executives and judges; (vii) the tensions, for legislators, between acting as transmissions belts for their constituents' preferences and responding to the lobbying, logrolling, and deliberation that occur in the legislative arena; and (viii) the commitment problems that arise when the executive, who also controls the military, must be counted on to relinquish power voluntarily on losing an election.

I have no objection to an introductory course organizing its treatment of democracy around these themes, even though Laitin includes much that I would not and leaves several things out that strike me as important. One reason is that he has a view of democracy in which "rationally" aggregating voter preferences is important. On my view, by contrast, preference-aggregation is a comparatively unimportant feature of democracy. Features that are unaffected by the Arrow problem—such as fostering political competition and opposition—seem to me to matter more. This disagreement exemplifies the reality that there is little consensus in the field about what democracy is and why it is desirable. Indeed, many people who write and teach about democracy in American universities probably disagree with one another more than Laitin and I do. In this type of context, trying to suggest that there is an agreed-on view of the matter involves kidding ourselves or kidding

[3] Laitin, "The Political Science Discipline," pp. 23–26.

our students. I guess the latter is worse, but the former has little to commend it either. Kidding the outside world that we agree in order to do better at extracting funds from the foundations and federal government scarcely seems much better.[4]

Recently I completed an introductory book based on the survey course I have been teaching over the past two decades and I found myself grappling with this reality.[5] On the one hand, it is intended to give students a grounding in a variety of normative debates that concern political theorists, getting them to understand what the various protagonists think is at stake and why they proceed as they do. On the other hand, it is written from a distinctive point of view in which I frame the issues as they seem most important to me. So I found myself writing in the preface that although the book is aimed at introductory classes it is not a textbook, and I will regard myself as having succeeded if others find it a useful teaching tool yet feel that they must argue with it at the same time. A similar acknowledgement of the inherently controversial character of political science scholarship was implicit in what struck me as the wise instruction Ira Katznelson and Helen Milner gave those who were asked to contribute to the 2002 *State of the Discipline* volume when they asked that we survey a piece of the political science terrain, but to do it in a distinctive voice and from a distinctive point of view.[6]

VARIABLES VERSUS PROBLEMS

A second objection has to do with Laitin's remarks about the advisability of organizing teaching and research around dependent rather than independent variables. I fully agree with Laitin's preference for avoiding the choice of independent variables as the basis for disciplinary organization and training. Aside from the sheer silliness of trying to develop tools and equip a toolkit before one knows what one is going to measure, repair, or construct, there is no faster way to lose the interest of

---

[4] Laitin comes close to suggesting this when he says "There are other reasons to support a coherent discipline. Political scientists do themselves a disservice when they represent their field as a 'blob' or a 'big umbrella.' Funders take us less seriously. The National Science Foundation a few years ago increased funding for Psychology and Economics at the expense of Political Science." *Ibid.*, p. 37.

[5] Ian Shapiro, *The Moral Foundations of Politics* (New Haven: Yale University Press, 2003).

[6] Ira Katznelson and Helen Milner, ed., *Political Science: The State of the Discipline*, 3rd ed. (Washington, DC: American Political Science Association, 2002).

undergraduates. Unlike graduate students and junior faculty, many of whom understandably, if sadly, believe their careers depend on investing in the theories and methods favored by those who they expect to decide their professional fates, bright undergraduates have a nose for what is important and demand to know the implications of academic research for some discernible bottom line.[7]

Yet Laitin's instinct to avoid organization of teaching and research around independent variables is at odds with his recommendations for dividing up the discipline as he does. He does not go far enough in his discussion of what is wrong with the independent variable focus for teaching (as distinct from researching a problem once it has been specified, where we all know that the pitfalls of selecting cases on the dependent variable). Something can only be a dependent or an independent variable in relation to a problem for which one is trying to account. Whether or not it is important to study political institutions, for instance, depends on how important they are hypothesized to be for what one is seeking to understand. It is not clear to me whether Laitin thinks we should study institutions because they are they are deemed an important independent variable or an important dependent variable. In order to clarify this he would have to give an account of what he takes the important questions of politics to be which, surprisingly, is nowhere supplied in his account.

If, for the sake of discussion, politics is considered to be the study of who gets what, when, where, and how, then institutions might be important, but they might not. In the early part of the twentieth century institutions were thought to be exceedingly important, but then they fell out of favor as independent variables. Marxists, elite theorists, behaviorists, and early rational choice theorists all deemed such factors as class position, path-dependent access to the instruments of power, political behavior, and individual self-interest to be more consequential in determining political outcomes. In recent years institutions have come back into favor among political scientists as potentially important explanatory variables. This is partly because of the failure of these various other approaches to deliver much substantive knowledge and partly because historians have stopped studying institutions as a by-product of their increased interest in social history.

---

[7] In this connection it may be of interest that a few years ago one of my colleagues in the Yale Economics department taught *Pathologies of Rational Choice Theory* to a joint seminar of economics seniors and graduate students. He reported the seniors to be fully engaged with our argument, whereas the graduate students dismissed it as irrelevant to their concerns.

Whatever the reason, political science has once again been bitten by the institutions bug, with different methodological camps squabbling over who are the "real" new institutionalists.

Without seeking to takes sides in these debates here, it seems to me unwise to reorganize the discipline around whether or not a particular theory or hypothesis will turn out to be true. Perhaps the next generation of scholars will discover that institutions matter less than is presently thought. Current scholarship on the subject of democratic stability suggests, for example, that Linz and others were partly mistaken in thinking parliamentary institutional forms contribute as much as they believed was the case to the apparently greater stability of parliamentary than presidential systems. Other factors, such as the structure of coalition politics and the representation of the president's party in the legislature, may well account for more of the variation.[8] In the study of regime stability generally, it now seems that economic variables are probably more important than institutional ones.[9] Again, without wishing to take sides in these controversies here, surely they are the meat and potatoes of ongoing research rather than the basis for organizing and reorganizing the discipline every time a theory falls in or out of favor.

Comparable points can be made about Laitin's treatments of international relations and comparative politics. Much innovation in these areas over the past decade has revolved around breaking down the obviously artificial barriers between these fields due to the abandonment of the "black box" view of national polities among international relations scholars. This resulted from their recognition of what most people would have said all along is obvious: that domestic politics has a large impact on the international behavior of countries. In many circumstances there is, in any event, a degree of arbitrariness to declaring an aspect of politics to be part of international relations rather than domestic politics. Civil wars, for example, are part of domestic politics, whereas inter-country wars belong to the realm of international relations. But in much of Africa national boundaries were drawn on maps

[8] See Joe Foweraker, "Institutional Design, Party Systems and Governability—Differentiating the Presidential Regimes of Latin America," *British Journal of Political Science,* Vol. 28, No. 4 (October 1998), pp. 651–76; and José Cheibub and Fernando Limongi, "Parliamentarism, Presidentialism, Is There a Difference?" Unpublished, Yale University, 2000.

[9] Adam Przeworski, Michael Alvarez, José Cheibub, and Fernando Limongi, *Democracy and Development: Political Institutions and Well-Being in the World, 1950–1990* (Cambridge, UK: Cambridge University Press, 2000), chapter 2.

by nineteenth- and early-twentieth-century colonial administrators, often with no regard to the politics of identification within and among the countries that were thus minted. The result is that what might appear to outsiders, and coded by international relations scholars, as inter-country wars might be understood by the protagonists as civil wars, and vice versa. Then the political scientist's disciplinary grid will not correspond to the phenomena under study.

With respect to comparative politics, it again seems odd to assume, as Laitin's discussion does, that variation among national polities should be the basic unit of analysis in advance of the specification of a problem. Obviously if one wants to understand the consequences of different national electoral systems such an assumption makes sense, but there are many political questions that call for comparative investigation where it is logical to look at sub-national or other forms of intra-polity variation. This is most obvious in federal systems, but urban politics is another area in which intra-polity comparative politics might be more illuminating than national comparisons—depending on the question one is trying to answer. Or one might become persuaded that it is important to study intra-polity regional variation, as Robert Putnam in his study of the determinants of institutional performance in Italy.[10] Then again, there might be good reasons for comparative study of transnational regionalisms when we reflect on the kinds of questions that may work their way onto the political science research agenda due to the creation of regional political-economic entities such as the North American Free Trade Agreement (NAFTA) and the European Union.

Concluding Remarks

As should by now be evident, my view is that the best way to organize both teaching and research is by reference to problems or questions, not variables. Particularly if the goal is to interest bright undergraduates in political science (though I would make this case regardless of that consideration), step one is to articulate a problem and make the case for its importance. This is appropriately followed by moving to more rigorous specification of it, which involves sorting out what the dependent and independent variables might be. Then hypotheses are spelled

---

[10] Robert Putnam, *Making Democracy Work: Civic Traditions in Modern Italy* (Princeton: Princeton University Press, 1993).

out and the most appropriate tools for evaluating them are selected, and so the endeavor proceeds. Contrary to the current practice in economics, the shape of undergraduate teaching in political science should embody this research structure. For the most part I think it does. The real reason for the multiplicity of introductory courses in political science is that political scientists differ over what they think politics is and what questions they deem worthy of study. As a result, they naturally reach for different specifications of problems and different ways of studying them.

This strikes me as a healthy state of affairs. A significant danger for political scientists to guard against seems to me to be their penchant for confusing their discipline with their object of study. Most people are attracted to political science because they want to understand more about, and perhaps some because they want to influence, politics—not the political science discipline. It is easy to lose sight of this fact, and there are many professional incentives pushing political scientists to do so. But the incentives should be resisted in favor of the problem-driven approach proposed here, where the tools of the discipline are brought to bear on problems that have been independently identified rather than being artifacts of those tools. If the cost of this is a plethora of curricula that embodies the conflicting views of political problems in the discipline, so be it. These are better costs to pay than those of mimicking the last generation of economists. We are less likely to produce an inward-looking discipline designed primarily for the benefit of its practitioners and more likely to say things that are worthwhile. In any case, there are signs that economists have begun to realize the limitations of their disciplinary orthodoxy—in their research if not their introductory teaching.